Architectural Tiles: Conservation and Restoration

Butterworth-Heinemann Series in Conservation and Museology

Architectural Tiles: Conservation and Restoration

From the Medieval Period to the Twentieth Century

Lesley Durbin BA(Hons) Dip Eur Hum. PACR

ELSEVIER
BUTTERWORTH
HEINEMANN

AMSTERDAM • BOSTON • HEIDELBERG • LONDON • NEW YORK • OXFORD
PARIS • SAN DIEGO • SAN FRANCISCO • SINGAPORE • SYDNEY • TOKYO

Butterworth-Heinemann
An imprint of Elsevier
Linacre House, Jordan Hill, Oxford OX2 8DP
30 Corporate Drive, Burlington, MA 01803

First published 2005

British Library Cataloguing in Publication Data
A catalogue record for this book is available from the British Library

ISBN 0 7506 58320

For information on all Butterworth-Heinemann publications visit our website at: www.bh.com

Composition by Newgen Imaging Systems (P) Ltd, Chennai, India.

Working together to grow
libraries in developing countries

www.elsevier.com | www.bookaid.org | www.sabre.org

ELSEVIER   BOOK AID International   Sabre Foundation

Front cover (clockwise from top left): Detail from the 'Maypole' pancel, 1930s tiles made by Carter's of Poole, Middlesex Children's hospital; 13th century tiles, Guy's Tower, Warwick Castle; Interior of the Pearl Assurance Building designed by Alfred Waterhouse, Liverpool; Geometric tile floor, The Atrium, Osgoode Hall, Toronto

Contents

Acknowledgments and thanks

I wish to express my most grateful thanks to all those who have helped me in the preparation of this book by allowing me to make positive use of their time, knowledge, experience and expertise. They are many and some remain unacknowledged by name but those which are forefront in my mind are: Michael Durbin; Chris Cox; Michelle Cox; Diana Hall; Pieter Jan Tichelaar; Faith Graham; the production and office staff at Craven Dunnill, Jackfield Ltd; Joseph Taylor, President and Co-Founder of the Tile Heritage Foundation; Jonathon Taylor; MSc IHBC; Jill Taylor of Taylor Hazell Architects, Toronto; Michael Kay; Chris Blanchett of Buckland Books, Little Hampton, West Sussex; Dr Sara Lunt, Senior Curator, English Heritage; Parker H. Jackson; Lisa Dorithy; library staff at Ironbridge Gorge Museum Trust; the St Stephens Preservation and Restoration Trust; Mr D. Longman, BAL Technical Advice Service.

Disclaimer

While every effort has been made to present accurate information designed to offer guidance in the restoration and conservation of architectural tiles schemes neither the author nor the publishers can be responsible for the accuracy of that information or for the results of any actions following the advice offered in the text.

Acknowledgements for photographs

Photograph numbers 1.11, 1.16, 1.17 and 4.2 are by courtesy of the Ironbridge Gorge Museum Trust.

Photograph numbers 1.8, 2.8, 2.9, 2.10, 2.11, 2.12, 2.13, 2.14, 2.15, 2.16, 2.17, 2.18, 2.19 and 2.20 are by kind permission of Pieter Jan Tichelaar.

Photograph numbers 2.5, 2.6 and 2.7 are by kind permission of Diana Hall.

Photograph numbers 2.33, 2.34, 2.35, 2.36, 2.37, 2.38, 2.39, 2.40, 2.41 2.42 and 2.43 are by kind permission of Craven Dunnill Jackfield Ltd.

Photograph number 7.2 is by kind permission of Michael Kay.

Photograph numbers 7.21, 7.22 and 7.23 are by kind permission of Robert Nachtreib.

Photograph numbers 7.23, 7.24 and 7.25 are by kind permission of Jon Old, Head of Conservation, Tyne and Wear Museums, Newcastle on Tyne.

All other photographs belong to the author.

List of illustrations

Chapter 2

Chapter 3

Chapter 4

Chapter 5

Chapter 7

List of colour plates

Introduction

The term 'architectural tile scheme' covers a very broad church of ceramic decoration found usually on the inside but also frequently on the outside of buildings. Tiles are superficial to the structure of the building, being used to cover walls, floors and sometimes ceilings for both functional and decorative reasons. Neither roof tiles nor faience and terracotta are included under my heading 'architectural tile scheme' because even though they may also be functional, decorative and worthy of conservation they are mostly used structurally and therefore in need of additional considerations in conservation to that of non-structural ceramic. For the purposes of what I hope will be a better understanding of conservation ethics and treatments I have sub-divided this discussion of 'architectural tile schemes' into distinctive groups of tiles, not as you may imagine along the lines of function, i.e wall, floors or ceilings, but into groups defined by age, technology in manufacture, and provenance.

A tile scheme may be highly valued by virtue of its age and historic or artistic importance. The technology used in manufacture is important because of the direct relationship between the type of clay body and glaze, the causes of degradation, and the methods of conservation. Finally provenance has a direct bearing on the balance between conservation and restoration techniques. I have divided all of my discussions in the following text into three groups of tiles which follow each other chronologically: medieval; seventeenth and eighteenth century tiles; and nineteenth and early twentieth century tiles, largely because those divisions reflect the distinct changes in the technology used to manufacture and install tiles, which directly affects conservation practices. In the main my discussions relate to tiles found outside of the museum environment which do not necessarily have the benefit of a secure and protected location.

Medieval tiles form part of the group of tiles which we may still find outside the museum environment in churches and a small number of secular buildings. Archaeologists from the mid-nineteenth century onwards have taken an interest in the international heritage of ancient and medieval tiles. It is largely due to their interest in recording and

methods of preservation rooted in archaeology that we have a significant insight into the artistic and cultural development of tile making in its many forms, and have subsequently enhanced our ability to
conserve these important historic artefacts.

The peak of manufacturing of the Dutch and Flemish tin glazed tile
industry during the seventeenth and eighteenth centuries produced
tiles in enormous quantities for widespread domestic use across northern Europe. An appreciable heritage has survived, particularly in
Holland, mainly because there has remained in place a constant, if
small, manufacturing base which has kept the tradition alive. The conservation and restoration of this significant heritage was considered in
the past to be unproblematic because the clays and glazes used in
early manufacturing remained available. In Great Britain, however, no
such tradition survived in the face of the burgeoning nineteenth century tile industry, consequently we seek to conserve the heritage
which remains without recourse to replacement.

Similarly the traditional methods of tile making still thrive in southern
Spain, Portugal, and across the Islamic world. The continuing tradition
of tile making using much the same skills, materials, and decorative
styles makes the conservation of historic tiles in southern Europe, outside of the museum environment, a less than viable economic option.
A product indistinguishable from the original has always been cheaply
and readily available making replacement the preferred option.
Additionally the absence of a damp cold climate, which is so detrimental to the survival of architectural ceramics, considerably reduces the
instance of many of the problems found in tiles further north. It is for
these reasons that we have not specifically included the tiles of southern Europe in this study, they are, however, so similar in terms of clay
body and glaze types to those of the delft tradition that the techniques
for conservation of the latter can apply without apprehension.

At the very end of the 1970s it became apparent among a small and
scattered group of enthusiasts in the UK that there was a significant
part of the built environment, not only in the UK but also across those
parts of the developed world that had formerly been the trading
empire of Great Britain, which was artistically and culturally important
but which was being largely ignored; decorative tiles of the nineteenth
and early twentieth century. There are many reasons to preserve, conserve and restore this important part of our architectural heritage; it
represents an impressive leap forward in technological development
coupled with the real desire of our Victorian forefathers to improve
not just the surroundings but also the artistic sensibilities of society at
large. It is also important to preserve the finished product of the industrial skills and techniques of mass production and the variety of raw
materials which have been lost to today's world of economic competition and improved working conditions.

The aim of this book is not to dictate absolutely the precise methods, technology and uses of materials which combine to encompass all aspects of conservation, but to advise and encourage on appropriate means towards preservation of this valuable heritage. The text is arranged to begin at the start of the process of conservation and each group of tiles is dealt with chronologically within that process. All of the projects used as source material, except where stated, are taken directly from the portfolio of the Jackfield Conservation Studio covering 20 years of experience in the field of architectural ceramics conservation.

The causes of degradation in ceramics and related building materials are well documented, namely:

- Water, movement of moisture
- External stress
- Deterioration by salt crystallisation
- Use, abrasion, impact damage
- Dirt and staining
- Climate and weathering
- Unsuitable treatments and materials

Detailed analysis of the causes can be found in recognised research on the deterioration of ceramic, glaze and similar siliceous materials carried out by Buys and Oakley (1993), Warren (1999), Fielden (1992) and Ashurst (1988). Research into deterioration is beyond the scope of this book; however, the results of deterioration are identified throughout. The text deals with the responses to deterioration in terms of prevention and treatment and the materials and techniques required in those treatments. The materials and methods chosen for architectural tile conservation and restoration in this text are not necessarily those which come most highly recommended for use in the controlled environments found in museums and conservation laboratory studios, but are those which have been selected by experience to perform best in the environmental and economic conditions which tend to prevail at the site of most building refurbishment programmes.

The historian and scholar Hugh Trevor-Roper commented, 'fertile error is to be preferred to a sterile accuracy' (Sharpe, 2003). Conservators, a professional group which encompasses backgrounds from the arts, engineering and science, have a history of fertile and imaginative solutions for seemingly insurmountable problems of resisting the decay and loss of valuable heritage, solutions which eventually become accepted as standard practice. If there is any axiom which describes the daily working routine for conservators it must surely be 'nothing ventured nothing gained'. It was in this same spirit, which we must applaud, that much of the early work towards the conservation of nineteenth century architectural tiles was carried out under the auspices of the Jackfield Tile Museum and the Tiles and Architectural Ceramics Society almost 25 years ago.

1

Looking at tile schemes

Introduction

Though the material condition of the tile scheme is the primary concern of the conservator, attribution is another area of interest which is of great value. The conservator need not be a tile historian, the subject is vast and can range worldwide, but to have a working knowledge of the history of tiles, and the capacity to identify the status of a scheme and to place it in the correct historical context is a worthwhile tool. The use of tiles ranges from the purely utilitarian, for example the interior of a stable block or water pumping station (Figure 1.1), to high status art decoration. The ability to identify the origin of a scheme and disseminate the information if it might otherwise be overlooked will support the move towards conservation for the future. The aim of this chapter is to give a broad overview of the different ways in which tiles have been used in the past to create recognisable styles within the history of decorative architectural design of northern Europe.

The use of design in tile schemes falls into two main categories: decoration on individual tiles, and the juxtaposition of plain and decorated tiles to create a larger design plan. The use and variety of decoration and methods of decoration on individual tiles is too large a subject to be discussed in great detail here, suffice to say that from the earliest efforts in manufacture, artists and artisans have used their skills and inspiration to decorate tiles in countless different ways. The decoration found on tiles reflects not only the skills and fashions of the times but also the dominant religious and secular themes in society.

The conjunction of plain and decorated tiles, or permutations and arrangements of individually decorated tiles, to create a larger design has been part of the development of the history of the tile scheme from the beginning of manufacture. Distinctive arrangements of tiles or distinctive colour combinations can sometimes give an indication as to geographical origin or school of tile making in the case of pre-industrial age tiles, or in nineteenth century or later tiles the identity of the manufacturing company. Deviations within the design or colour

Figure 1.1
A utility tile scheme in an old stable block.

1

scheme can indicate that a scheme may have been altered or undergone a change of location in its lifetime.

At the beginning of the twenty-first century, while there is still a place for artful tile decoration on a small scale, the main function of mass produced tiles in architecture is utilitarian. The use of tiles as a design statement is falling out of favour as mass producers place cheapness of raw materials and ease and consistency of production above design aesthetic. Tiles are no longer the chosen medium for designed decoration of high status interiors.

Medieval pavements

In the UK there are few medieval pavements that have lain undisturbed or unchanged in their original design format. Two exceptions are the pavements at Bylands Abbey in Yorkshire dating from the thirteenth century, and Cleeve Abbey in Somerset, also thirteenth century. It is fair to say that there are probably none remaining which have not received the benefit of scholarly attention to investigate their origin, format and later history.

A summary of studies of medieval pavement design, particularly the work carried out by Elizabeth Eames at the British Museum in the 1950s and 1960s, shows that large tile pavements were often laid in diagonal fashion, while smaller pavement areas were laid square on. Both the pavement in the small refectory at Cleeve Abbey, and the Canynges pavement (fifteenth century) found in Bristol, but now in the British Museum, demonstrate this format. Two lesser known pavements – the refectory pavement at Denny Abbey (thirteenth century) (Figure 1.2)

Figure 1.2
Part of the thirteenth century refectory floor at Denny Abbey, Cambridgeshire, showing the diagonal format with single lines of tiles inserted.

Figure 1.3
Part of the thirteenth century floor in the suite of guest chambers in Guy's Tower, Warwick Castle, showing the diagonal format with double tramlines of inserted tiles.

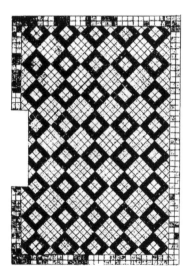

Figure 1.4
Diagram of the Canynges pavement, British Museum, a diagonal format of groups of 16 and four decorated tiles surrounded by plain dark tiles.

and the guest room floor in Guy's Tower, Warwick Castle (early fourteenth century) (Figure 1.3) – also demonstrate the same format with the addition of tramlines of tiles at intervals laid square on. Diagonal configurations are often arrangements of 16, nine, or four individually patterned tiles which make up a complete design surrounded with single rows of plain dark glazed tiles (Figure 1.4).

Plain tiles set in square-on fashion were often in chequerboard configuration of dark green or black and plain yellow (Figure 1.5). Small pavements of square-on tiles are found arranged in panels of decorated tiles, sometimes of random design, sometimes of repeating pattern. The small pavement located in the south transept chapel at Bylands Abbey is a square-on format with a central roundel, though this form of configuration was probably reserved for important areas.

Armorial designs of royal, noble or ecclesiastical origin found on individual tiles usually signify a particular patron or significant family in the locale of the original site. Some armorial designs can date a pavement quite accurately. However, it was general practice for tile makers to sell on surplus tiles for use in other pavements to anyone who wished to buy. It was also common practice to continue to use designs which had been specially commissioned for one location in other subsequent locations.

The majority of pavement designs are unattributable. According to Eames (1992) the pavier is likely to have worked from a design sheet drawn up by a monk who was resident in the abbey or priory, but they may equally have been designed by the master tile maker himself or by the master builder in charge of construction.

Figure 1.5
Chequerboard format found at
Thetford Abbey, Norfolk.

Some pavements have no recognisable design features and display random placement of tiles, usually indicating that the floor has been moved, altered or reset from the original design, though there are other reasons why a floor might not display a regular discernible design; the tiles may be excess material from a large important pavement which have found their way onto a lower status floor or possibly they may be part of a purchase of stock material bought for use in a secular or domestic building. During the later phase of medieval tile making in the mid- to late fifteenth century, tileries tended to be in fixed locations and wealthy merchants provided a ready market for excess material.

Delftware interiors

Dutch tin glazed delftware tiles have been liberally used to cover and decorate utility surfaces in northern Europe from the late seventeenth century onwards. The fashion for using tiles to cover not just floors but walls also can be traced to the Islamic influenced tiles of southern Spain. Dutch made delftware tiles continue to be manufactured for the same decorative purposes today. Utility uses include fireplaces, stoves, kitchens, wash-houses or bathrooms and dairies (Figure 1.6). In England tin glazed tiles became popular from more or less the beginning of the eighteenth century and were for the most part, other than occasional notable exceptions, used without any particular architectural design format other than decorative arrangements, including

Figure 1.6
English delftware tiles found in a dairy of a private residence in Shropshire, England.

Figure 1.7
Delftware tiles found in a wash-house behind modern tiling in a private residence in Oxfordshire.

grouping of flower patterns, biblical stories, landscapes, ships or other social narrative themes, perhaps interspersed with plain tiles (Figure 1.7). Repeating corner motifs sometimes forms a strong alternative decorative diagonal feature to the overall composition. The English delftware tile manufactured in Liverpool for the same utilitarian purposes and featuring many of the same designs as the Dutch tile was, in part, intended for export to New Englanders on the eastern seaboard of America.

On the northern European mainland, from the late seventeenth and throughout the eighteenth centuries, alongside the continuing utilitarian

Figure 1.8
Seventeenth century Dutch tiles in
Makkum, Northern Holland, with
elaborately painted frame.

use, there flowered an extravagant but considered use of delft tiles in an
architectural sense in some of the wealthiest interiors. Tile painters
began to copy illustrious and fashionable Dutch seascape and flower
paintings over large expanses of tiles, to the extent that tile panels
became a substitute for paintings, complete with elaborate frames
painted onto surrounding two or three courses of tiles. Architectural features such as columns, swags and entablatures, all painted on flat tile
surfaces, also became characteristic of wealthy interiors, particularly in
northern Holland (Figure 1.8).

Early in the eighteenth century, large tile picture panels began to be
exported from Holland to wealthy houses and palaces throughout
Europe. Sizes of such panels varied enormously, some were very large
indeed and often depicted the leisurely pursuits of the wealthy
classes. Two large panels dating from 1707 were among many painted
by Willem van der Kloet of Amsterdam as a royal commission for a
palace in Lisbon: 'A Meal on the Terrace' in the collection of the
Rijksmuseum in Amsterdam, and 'Couple Dancing on a Terrace' in
the collection of the Museuo Nacional de Azulego in Lisbon. Speke
House near Liverpool, itself a major delft tile producing centre from
the 1730s, holds a sizable tile panel featuring a large house set in a
prosperous landscape, after the fashion of English eighteenth century
society painting (Figure 1.9).

There is also another strand of architectural use of delftware tiling
fashionable from the late seventeenth and early eighteenth centuries.
William of Orange and Queen Mary engaged the influential French
architect Daniel Marot to collaborate on the design of their hunting

Figure 1.9
Detail of an eighteenth century panel at Speke House, Liverpool.

Figure 1.10
Detail of the panel format in the bath house at Carshalton, Surrey.

lodge at Het Loo in Appeldorn, Netherlands. The decoration of the tiled cellar is attributed to Marot. It is much more restrained in its use of pattern, with repeating panels of decorated tiles being restricted to below dado height, above is all plain tiling with the architectural form of the vaulted ceiling being picked out with single rows of flower and vase patterned tiles. Daniel Marot was brought to England by William and Mary on their accession to the throne in 1689 to design and decorate various parts of the new palace and garden at Hampton Court. He decorated the new dairy with delft tiles. It no longer survives, but the remarkably similarly decorated bath house at nearby Carshalton, Surrey, displays the same restrained and elegant use of plain tiles with single rows of 'flower and vase' decorated tiles to pick out the architectural features of tall slender windows and curve headed niches (Figure 1.10).

Nineteenth and early twentieth century interior schemes

One of the purposes of the nineteenth century floor tile was to provide a cheap but elegant substitute for polished stone or marble flooring aimed at the middle classes. It was marketed in America expressly as such. Eventually tiles were produced for wall, floor and ceiling as a colourful, hygienic, and cheap covering for almost any interior. Manufacturers were not shy of educating their clients in the best ways to use this most practical and decorative of materials. Most manufacturers employed both in-house and freelance designers and

Figure 1.11
Wall tile schemes displayed in the
nineteenth century Craven Dunnill
catalogue.

published their catalogue of suggested designs for interior tile
schemes for domestic or less prestigious interiors. Builders, sometimes
with the help of their clients, would simply choose a design from the
catalogue and reproduce it (Figure 1.11).

For prestigious municipal, civic or commercial buildings manufacturers would produce designs in-house specific to that interior, usually recommending and providing designs which would cover every
possible surface and function. The Victoria Baths in Manchester are

Figure 1.12
The Burmantofts ceiling in the former ballroom of the County Hotel, Carlisle.

Figure 1.13
The chancel floor at St Mary Magdalen, Battlefield, Shrewsbury, by Minton's of Stoke on Trent.

adorned with ceramic balustrade the entire height of the stairwell and Burmantofts of Leeds designed and built several complete ceramic interiors, including extravagant tiled ceilings (Figure 1.12).

Manufacturers also found a ready ecclesiastical market during the flurry of church building and restoration in the nineteenth century. Floor patterns, both on individual tiles and as design configurations, were actively modelled on actual or perceived medieval designs and many churches large and small were the willing recipients of gifts of tiles from pious manufacturers, notably Herbert Minton (Figure 1.13).

Unfortunately the gifts were sometimes made up of excess stock causing an often haphazard result in the overall design of the church floor.

Thus the manufacturers themselves were more often than not the source of the flagrant use of flamboyant colour and pattern which typifies much of Victorian tile design and use.

The advent of the mass production tile industry in the mid-nineteenth century also saw the emergence of the architect designed tile interior.

Probably the first Victorian to initiate and put into practice the idea of a complete design concept was Augustus Welby Northmore Pugin. Pugin was not only influential in his advocacy of medieval gothic style and architecture, he also advanced the idea applying a high standard of design (preferably medieval gothic of course) to modern, mass produced materials in order to build complete interiors. The Palace of Westminster was completed in 1860 and although its architect was Sir Charles Barry, he gave the interior decoration over to Pugin who we know was responsible for designing every facet of the interior down to the very smallest details. He engaged Henry Minton expressly to make wall and floor tiles to his own design at great expense and much trial and error. Minton's continued to advertise for sale Pugin's House of Commons designs for at least another 20 years after completion. It was Pugin who encouraged Minton's to develop the technique for mass producing block printed wall tiles, the forerunners of our modern tile, for the Strangers' Smoking Room.

During the 1994–96 restoration programme of the Smoking Room the team from Jackfield who carried out the conservation work on the tiles discovered that the design on basic green and white ground tile had been cleverly stretched or squeezed to fit differing sizes of tile required for different parts of the detailed architectural form of the room. This is an unusual detail which is generally not found in later schemes, the conventional practice for finishing oddly sized areas was to cut standard size tiles to fit, irrespective of how the reduced tiles would sit visually within a scheme. The likelihood is that this fine tuning was demanded by Pugin, the designer of the interior.

Other architects followed the precedent set by Pugin of using tiles as an integral part of the interior design of their buildings. George Edmund Street (1824–81) architect to the Royal Courts of Justice on the Strand, London, had complete involvement with every detailed aspect of his buildings. He favoured Godwin's of Hereford as manufacturers for his tiles. Drawings of his kept at the library of the Royal Institute of British Architects indicate that his concern was with the position of panels, runners and borders or the graphic expression the tiles created and was less interested in which particular encaustic design would be used to fill in the decorative element (Figures 1.14 and 1.15).

Figure 1.14
Godwin's tiles used in the Royal
Courts of Justice, The Strand, London.

Figure 1.15
Diagram of the floor tile design by
G.E. Street at the Royal Courts of
Justice.

William Butterfield was another architect of the Victorian gothic
school who used tiles as a material which contributed to the whole
ethic of the design. Tiles provided a robust surface which could also
supply the range of colour to which Butterfield was particularly
attracted. All Saint's Church, Margaret Street, London (1849), is a good
example of Minton's early use of coloured enamel glazes. The upper
wall and ceiling colour in the church is achieved with the use of paint.

Whereas below dado level and on the floor lively contrast of colour is achieved using tile and stone (Plate 1).

Samuel Teulon (1812–73), architect of St Stephen's Church, Hampstead, was more eclectic in his style and chose Moorish influences, among others, for his designs. At St Stephen's (1869) he chose the colour of his simple and elegant tiled floor designs to echo the unusual red, purple and cream colour combination of his brick and stonework. Several important architects such as Mackay Ballie-Scott and Norman Shaw used the tiles of William de Morgan to great advantage. Although de Morgan tiles were hand crafted and very expensive consequently they were more often used to decorate fireplaces or on a small scale rather than as large-scale architectural design features. Ballie-Scott's use of de Morgan tiles for the first floor fireplaces at Blackwell Hall in Cumbria, built in 1898, moved away from the Arts and Crafts Movement's taste for mock medieval towards a more simple modern style which prefigured the art deco movement of the 1930s.

Towards the close of the nineteenth century many architects readily used tiles to perform a particular role to enhance the colour or graphic form of their interior designs. Alfred Waterhouse used Burmantoft's of Leeds to provide a glazed interior for his Pearl Assurance Building, St John's Lane, Liverpool, which contains remarkably similar elements to his design for the Natural History Museum, London. William J. Neatby began his working life as an architect but soon began to use his design skills with architectural ceramics; his move from Burmantoft's in 1890 to join Doulton's of Lambeth also signalled a move towards the art nouveau style. His best known work is the interior of Harrod's meat hall, London, completed in 1902 (Plate 2).

As the late Victorian and art nouveau styles gave way to the art deco style of the 1930s tile manufacturers still had a ready market for instant catalogue design particularly for bathrooms, kitchens and fireplaces (Figures 1.16 and 1.17). Many architects were also still favouring tiles as a medium to express the simplicity of geometrical form and function. Carter's of Poole took a leading role in the market providing tiles for architect designed art deco inspired interiors. Sir Owen William was architect and engineer of some of the most celebrated art deco buildings in England, his tiled interior of Boots' D6 Building in Beeston, Nottinghamshire (1930–32), manufactured by Carters, still retains a modern elegance today (Figure 1.18).

The interiors which most typify the move from architectural use of tiles as a design form in their own right to a merely functional use to provide cleanliness and durability are the below ground tiled interiors of London Underground. In 1905 Leslie Green was one of the first designers to create a complete architectural design statement for

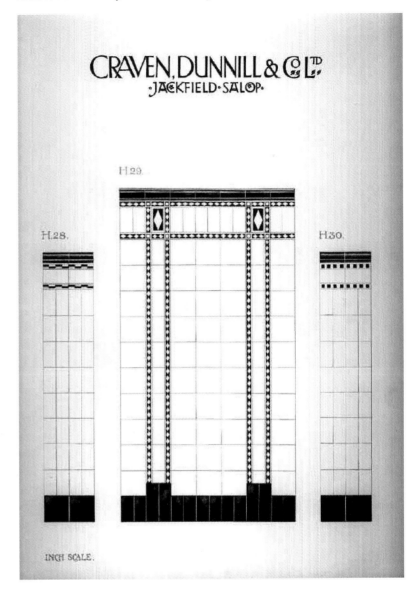

Figure 1.16
Catalogue example of art deco tiles
made by Craven Dunnill in the 1930s.

London Underground using tiles as the medium. Many of his stations
still exist and are listed interiors. Covent Garden on the Piccadilly Line
was tiled using material from Maw & Co. but many other manufacturers
were engaged for the project including Carters of Poole and
W.B. Simpsons, London. The existing schemes were added to in the
1930s to create the largest complete design concept using tiles ever
constructed. Some stations were refurbished with new tiling in the
1960s and 1970s still using tiles as design statements. Refurbishment

CRAVEN, DUNNILL & C⁰ L^{TD}.
JACKFIELD, SALOP.

No. 109.

Figure 1.17
An elaborate bathroom scheme from
the Craven Dunnill catalogue of the
1930s.

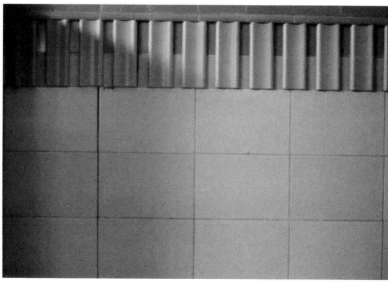

Figure 1.18
A detail of the architectural scheme
designed by Sir Owen Williams in the
Boots' D6 Building in
Nottinghamshire.

works in 2003, however, while taking care to correctly restore the listed designs of the 1905 and 1930s phases, have nevertheless used tile for utilitarian reasons rather than as an expression of art or design to complete the larger part of the London Underground renovation programme.

2 Tile making – past and present

Introduction

Nearly all conservators and restorers, whether of buildings or objects, recognise that a good working knowledge of past techniques of manufacture or construction is essential in order to arrive at the best and most sensitive approaches to the conservation of the original material. Equally recognised is that conservation can also include restoration techniques. These two approaches to historical material are not mutually exclusive. Buildings in particular are complex and continuously evolving structures, and their conservation inevitably requires the introduction of newly sourced material into the structure. The new material must be judged against the original and not be found wanting in terms of composition, integrity and visual appearance.

Integrating new ceramics alongside historic ceramic presents different problems to those of naturally sourced materials such as stone, slate or timber. Ceramic is not a material in itself but the end result of a production process. A good conservation carpenter while in the process of restoring a timber-framed building can return to the use of hand tools to work similarly aged timber in order to produce a new component part indistinguishable from the original; a ceramicist cannot sensibly return to the techniques and materials used in former times to recreate a tile of the same exactitude. The same raw materials used to produce tiles are not always available, sometimes for commercial reasons, sometimes to protect the health and safety of the ceramicist and sometimes because we cannot identify the exact source of the raw materials. The use of electric or gas fired kilns had to take over from the use of medieval wood fired or Victorian bottle kilns for reasons of time and accuracy in predicting the results of the firings. Consequently there are sometimes limitations in what can be achieved in terms of precise reproduction; however, it is the imprecise nature of the process and the challenges that it presents which underpin the labours of ceramicists working in restoration who produce some truly wonderful work in the sphere of reproduction of valuable historic tiles. If we are to keep our remaining historic architectural tile schemes in place in a functional as well as decorative role for the future, we rely on the resource of reproduction tiles in order to complete and enhance the original schemes.

Understanding and recognising the detail and distinctions within the original manufacturing processes is also an aid towards building a case or qualifying a decision to retain, conserve or restore historic material or to allow the introduction of replacement material into tile schemes. This chapter examines past methods of tile making along with some of the conservation implications of those methods. Some tiles have in-built destruction mechanisms resulting directly from the circumstances of manufacture, which may be recognisable and possibly dealt with in the conservation process. Likewise certain manufacturing processes produced effects which could easily be mistaken for flaws and removed when they should be conserved. This chapter also looks at methods of restoration tile making used today, its achievements in replicating the past and its limitations.

I have chosen to discuss three types of tiles: medieval floor tiles, tin glazed wall tiles from the seventeenth and eighteenth centuries, and nineteenth and early twentieth century mass produced tiles for both wall and floors, because they represent the three basic changes in the history of tile making technology and mass production. The first two groups – medieval floor tiles and tin glazed wall tiles – fall into the category generally referred to by ceramicists as 'soft bodied', indicating a fairly low firing temperature, and relatively porous clay body, while mass produced tiles from the nineteenth century and later fall under the heading 'hard bodied' indicating a high fired semi-vitrified clay body with a lowered tendency towards porosity.

Medieval tiles

Early tile making

Floor tile manufacture in England began around the second half of the tenth century, specifically to serve the most important ecclesiastical sites such as York, Winchester and St Albans, but it took until the middle of the thirteenth century before a commercial tile industry began to be established in a widespread form. The industry thrived until the onset of the black plague in the mid-fourteenth century when it fell into decline; there was a re-emergence towards the end of the century until the sixteenth century before virtual disappearance as a result of the Dissolution. During that time, it would be safe to say that most of England's many priories, abbeys, monasteries and cathedrals had some part of their floor areas tiled in decorative fashion, quite often it was the most important areas of the altar, chancel and nave. By the later fifteenth century there were, additionally, many wealthy secular buildings decorated in the same fashion, though few survive now. The recently discovered medieval floor of Guy's Tower, Warwick Castle, is a secular floor which could be contemporary, or only slightly later, with the building of the Tower in 1392, although the archive is inconclusive. The location which was originally used as a suite of rooms in which to accommodate important guests is an indication of the high status in which decorated tiled floors were perceived. Most commonly after the Dissolution, decorated tile floors were salvaged from ecclesiastical sources to be resited in wealthy homes, still an indication of their high merit.

The body of medieval tiles is usually made up of a fairly course red clay. The degree of redness of the body is dependent on the amount of iron in the clay and the amount of oxygen in the kiln. Kilns were usually built close to sources of locally dug clay, thus, fired body clay can vary in colour from quite light rose pinks, through orange red to dark red with very often quite striking regional differences which can help to identify the source of manufacture. Before the manufacturing process could begin the freshly dug clay was left outside to 'weather' during the winter months to allow the frost to break down the structure of the clay and the rain to wash away impurities. After weathering the clay was brought undercover where it was repeatedly kneaded, rolled out and folded in a process known as 'pugging' or 'wedging' to remove pockets of air. The wet clay was then ready for use in manufacture.

Research by Habberly in the 1930s showed that the likely method of tile making in the medieval period was still being used in England in the 1930s. Tile makers used simple equipment, a wooden square former without top or bottom, oversized to allow for shrinkage when the clay dried, placed on a sanded board or table. Wet clay was pushed into the moulds until it was over full, excess clay was stripped away from the top in one move using a small bow-like implement, semicircular strung with a taut wire. The surface was smoothed using a wet straight edged piece of wood slightly bigger than the mould. The wood former was then lifted with the clay inside and turned out onto a sanded board to dry; it is likely that the tiles were stacked in open air sheds or lean-tos, certainly there was ready access by small cats and dogs, footprints are often found on tiles. Fifteenth century Walcot Hall in Shropshire has a small collection of unglazed medieval floor tiles, found in-situ, which show evidence of the original unworn surface, apparently having been smoothed using a piece of wetted leather.

At some stage in the making process, probably when the clay was 'leather' hard, the edges of the tiles were chamfered so that the face of the tile was larger than the underside. This allowed a space for mortar

Figure 2.1
Showing a distorted tile in the centre
of the picture.

to push in between the tiles when laid, giving greater adhesion and allowing tiles to be set close together.

Examination of the edges of apparently unglazed red body tiles will often indicate whether they were originally glazed and, if so, with what colour. Glaze may have run down the sides of the tile during the making process and remain there unscathed. We can be relatively certain from examination of tile 'wasters' found at kiln sites that English medieval tiles were fired once only. Tile 'wasters' are the unusable tiles from unsuccessful firings that are always discarded in the nearby area of a kiln. It has been quite common to find glazed tiles that have bulged severely in the middle of the face (Figure 2.1), to an extent which today we would regard as unusable, though we have found such tiles in reset pavements. The bulging is caused by trapped, expanded air in the middle of the clay body, and it is safe to assume that no tile maker would bother to glaze such distorted ware if it had been previously biscuit fired. Glazing directly onto unfired clay resulted in a certain amount of absorption of the liquid glaze into the clay body allowing the colour to remain on the surface of the tile long after the glass-like shine of the glaze has worn away.

The basic glaze was a colourless lead glaze, which was rarely pure enough to remain colourless, traces of iron usually found its way into the glaze giving the clear glaze a yellow taint of varying depth. Copper was added to the mix to produce green glazes, with higher concentrations of copper producing a near black glaze, and sometimes extra amounts of iron were added to make a dark purple or black glaze. High temperature firings of this last mix are responsible for the metallic quality sometimes seen on dark glazes.

Tile kilns were rectangular in shape and, for the most part, fuelled by wood fires. The furnaces were divided into two equal sized chambers spanned by a series of arches which sprang from piers on the dividing or edge wall. The arches were built up into solid straight walls with flat tops to accommodate the specially made roof tiles which were used to bridge the gaps between the arches and form the roof of the kiln. Spaces were left between the roof tiles to allow the heat of the fire to rise into the oven above. Gaps were left at the back wall of the furnace to act as a flue to draw the heat to the farther end of the oven. The oven was a single chamber over the double chamber of the furnace. The walls of the ovens were usually about 1.5 m high from the oven floor and contained no door, meaning that the tile maker must climb into the kiln in order to stack it.

There is evidence that tiles were stacked vertically on edge, in rows, with the glaze face of one tile placed towards the underside of the next with a space between. The tiles were placed obliquely so that another row of tiles would be placed on top of the first row at the opposite angle, covering the oven floor this way and building up to the necessary height. Many tiles show the marks on their opposite edges of the tiles fired above or below them in the kiln, the British Museum also holds samples of tiles fused together in such a way, found at various kiln sites including Bawsey in Norfolk. However, it is quite difficult to reconcile this method of kiln stacking and firing with the fact that, in general, most tiles, as has been previously noted, have bevelled edges. Indeed recently excavated tiles at the site of Coventry Cathedral Priory, founded in 1043, which are in fine condition, have quite definitely oblique edges, making it quite difficult to see how they could stand vertically on edge individually, as well as support subsequent upper rows of tiles.

The Coventry tiles have circular indents on the reverse side, the usual and most obvious explanation for these indents is that they are keying marks associated with a particular maker, but they may also be a clue pointing to an early use of a horizontal stacking method rather than the most commonly excavated vertical stacking method. Keyholes have also been found on the reverse of tiles from Winchester Cathedral, and Cleeve Abbey, Somerset.

A further difficulty created by vertical stacking was the problem of glaze running down the surface and fusing tiles together in the kiln, the effect of which would be to cause a considerable amount of waste material; however, the lack of evidence for kiln furniture leaves the vertical method described as the best option. Makers of delftware tiles in the seventeenth and eighteenth centuries also stacked their kilns vertically but used additional strips of rolled clay to fix the tiles in position.

Once the tiers of tiles had reached the top of the oven walls then a temporary roof made up of roofing tiles was put in position, again with gaps to allow a good circulation of heat around the oven. The two furnace chambers were usually sited in a dug-out pit, to give greater insulation, while the oven walls were above ground. There are a number of variations on this general plan, but most excavated sites conform to the rule.

Before firing tiles would have been dried for about 48 hours at a temperature close to 250 degrees centigrade, rising to a full firing temperature which would need to reach 950 degrees centigrade, but go no higher than 1200 degrees centigrade for complete success. Firing the kiln took about one week, with the firing season always being in the summer months. The result was a tile with a relatively soft body and high degree of porosity.

The extreme haphazardness of medieval glaze mixes and enormous variations in kiln temperatures, not least due to the positioning of the tile inside the kiln, resulted in a wide variety of shades and tones within the basic palette of colours, giving medieval tiles a subtle beauty not present in the later Victorian attempts to mass produce the medieval gothic style.

Tiles were decorated in a variety of different techniques. Familiarity with the various processes is a helpful tool during conservation as many medieval tiles can be worn to such an extent that the pattern is barely discernible, indents or faint remains of glaze colours can easily be missed resulting in the tiles being wrongly documented. The many hundreds of designs found on medieval tiles are outside the remit of this book, but it is useful for the conservator to become familiar with typical forms in order to recognise possible design work on particularly worn examples.

Glazes were applied directly to the unfired clay body to produce brown, olive, dark green or black. Light shades of yellow, orange, and light green were produced by applying a coating of light coloured clay slip to the tile before glazing (Plate 3). There are polychrome effect tiles which are likely to be early in date, with separate glaze colours painted into simple indented designs. Sgraffiato was used as a method of decoration on tiles as it was used on most other ceramic wares; white clay was coated onto the surface of the tile and the design was tooled on, removing the white surface to reveal the red clay underneath forming a design or pattern. The design was then coated in a clear lead glaze. This method was not suitable for mass production so is not frequently found.

More common is line impressed decoration where the linear design is pressed into the tile body with a stamp before glazing. Research carried out by Elizabeth Eames at the British Museum suggests that the stamps were made of metal, most likely lead, and fixed to a wooden block. The most common form of decoration was the two colour decoration, this was sometimes applied as a white clay slip painted, printed or stencilled onto the surface of the tile; often crude and unsatisfactory as a decoration method it can usually be identified by rough edges around simple motifs. This type of decoration can be fragile as it is applied to the surface of the tile, and can be prone to fragmentation. Inlaid two colour decoration eventually provided the most satisfactory results for mass production of decorated tiles, it is therefore the decoration most commonly found. The wet clay tiles were stamped with an impressed design probably to a depth of between 2 and 3 mm. The indents were filled with light coloured clay, which may have been in slip form or may have been soft clay depending on the individual tile maker. The surface was then pared down, as described previously, to reveal the sharp edges of the design and also provide a flat surface on which to apply a coating of glaze. The glaze was not always clear, greens or yellows were often used to give a variety of colour to the coated light clays. This was the method which was later taken up by Herbert Minton in the early stages of Victorian mass production.

Degradation associated with manufacturing techniques

The clay used in the manufacture of medieval tiles received very little in the way of preparation compared with modern techniques; we know from medieval illustrations that it was dug and left to weather in the open air during the winter months. Weathering allows the frost to break up lumps in the clay and the rain to wash away some of the impurities. Larger pieces of stone were removed by hand but smaller stones and pebbles were often left in the body clay. With the passage of time the fired clay body around the stone can wear away, the stone can become dislodged leaving behind a round hole or depression which weakens the surface of the tile. If the surface of the tile is subject to continuing wear from footfall, or other agents like the build up of dirt and waxes, the edges of the hole will in turn break down causing further destruction and loss of tile body or surface decoration.

The skill and competence of the tile maker have a direct bearing on the structure of completed tiles. Medieval tiles vary greatly in body structure. Clay which has been more consistently pugged and wedged, will have a finer, denser, body because more of the air present in the clay has been removed, as a consequence it will be much more robust. Lamination fractures found in tiles will sometimes correspond with, and will have been caused by, weaknesses in the body where the clay has been folded incompletely.

Kiln temperature is also very important to the final quality of the tile, an underfired body will tend to be soft and friable, while tiles subjected to too high a heat will be darkened and brittle. The position of an individual tile in the kiln will have a bearing on its finished state. Medieval tile makers and setters seemed not to be too conscious of product quality control, and in any group of tiles examined today examples of tiles erring to either end of the temperature spectrum will be found, and consequently have a bearing on the wear pattern of a medieval floor. Soft friable bodies of underfired tiles will wear quickly and quite severely, whereas overfired tiles are more likely to suffer fracturing. Differences in quality can be seen quite clearly when comparing, say, fourteenth century tiles from the commercial kilns at Bawsey in Norfolk (Figure 2.2) and tiles produced in roughly the same era found at Stokesay Castle and Buildwas Abbey in Shropshire (Figure 2.3). The Shropshire tiles are larger, thicker and have a much denser body clay giving them a more robust quality than the smaller

Figure 2.2
Fourteenth century tiles made at the Bawsey kiln in Norfolk.

Figure 2.3
Tiles at Buildwas Abbey, probably made at Malvern.

tiles from Norfolk which have a more aerated, porous and friable body clay; as a consequence the stronger, better quality tiles in Shropshire have survived the rigours of exposure on their original sites much better. It is not known exactly where the Shropshire tiles were manufactured, there is evidence of a local kiln at Much Wenlock, but they may have been made as far afield as Malvern.

As previously described, keying holes were cut into the reverse of some early tiles. Tiles found at Winchester Cathedral include examples where spalling (i.e. flaking and loss of clay body) on the face exactly corresponds with the indents on the reverse. Tile maker Diana Hall demonstrated that tiles can be significantly weakened on the surface by the use of a knife rather than a scoop to cut the keying marks into the wet clay, and by the relative depth to which the indents are cut.

Contemporary tile making techniques in the medieval style

Discussions with Diana Hall, tile maker, at her studio in Dorset made it possible to compare the findings of the accepted research into techniques in tile making of the thirteenth and fourteenth centuries, with the technical process of remanufacturing medieval tiles at the beginning of the twenty-first century. The two processes must include similarities in order to produce a tile which will have the feel and authenticity of a medieval tile, but they will also have substantial dissimilarities. The 300 year period, roughly speaking, which saw the manufacture of medieval tiles in large quantities in the British Isles also produced, not surprisingly, individual tile making craftsmen whose skills and techniques varied enormously from place to place, leaving a legacy of tiles varied in detail of glaze, body and design beyond calculation. Good manufacture of medieval style tiles today uses authenticity of technique and materials as its touchstone, rather than slavish duplication of an aged or distressed tile, to produce the best tiles for use as additional material to complete important original pavements in a meaningful way. New material produced using the authentic techniques creates a continuing legacy of tile making within our cathedrals in the same spirit of restoration in which new stone is sculpted and added to the fabric. However, as with all original fabric, medieval tiles should never be discarded in favour of new if remedial or preventive conservation will preserve early tiles in the location for which they were intended.

Tiles remanufactured in the medieval style have recently been added to the retro choir pavement at Winchester Cathedral to good effect. During the 1970s parts of the pavement had been removed, in order to install underfloor pipe work, and replaced by modern plain red mass produced floor tiles; the overall effect of such unsympathetic tiles cutting through the collection of original medieval tiles was aesthetically poor. Whereas the introduction of new sympathetically fashioned 'medieval' tiles had several positive effects, it continued the tradition of craftsmanship within our cathedrals. It gives a valuable insight into the visual lavishness of the original fabric and gives meaning to the pavement which the addition of mass produced material did not (Plate 4).

Diana Hall described her methods for remanufacture at Winchester and other locations. As has been previously noted, medieval tiles differ greatly in colour and texture depending on the source of the clay from which they were manufactured, it is therefore fundamentally important to the production of good new tiles that the source of the clay should be as near to or as similar in geological structure as possible to the original. An exact replication of the source is never possible because the depth from which the clay was dug originally is indeterminable. The impurities present in the clay, which may affect its colour or structure, will vary depending on the depth from which it is dug even if the location is the same. Once one or a range of suitable clays has been obtained they are weathered in the open air and cleaned of pebbles and other debris by hand in much the same way as in medieval times.

Extensive testing to evaluate shrinkage rate, colour change and texture after firing of a variety of different clays, or clay mixes, is required until the correct combination of clay, firing time and temperature is arrived at to produce a tile comparable with the original medieval tile. The process is lengthy and subject to accurate record keeping. Gas fired kilns are the preferred choice over electric, because they more closely replicate the effect of a wood fired kiln in aiding the production of the colour variation across a batch of tiles, which is typical of medieval manufacture. Heat is driven in circular movement around the oven of a gas kiln by the force of the gas jets positioned at the base, whereas the heat in an electric kiln radiates from the elements positioned each side of the oven; the difference in the way the heat is distributed within the kiln can greatly affect the variety of colour across a batch of fired tiles.

In addition to the research to find the most appropriate body clay, inlay tiles also require the use of white or cream coloured slip clay as infill for the design. To date no medieval recipes for slip clay have been discovered, though it is thought that some medieval tile makers may have mixed a small amount of white clay with their body clay to effect a better bonding between the two colours. It is known that white clay was expensive and the bulk of clay used in medieval manufacture probably came from china clay pits in Cornwall, though there will have been many scattered local small-scale sources of white clay available. Present day tile makers must rely on their own research and experience in order to find a good slip which will have an equivalent shrinkage rate to match whichever body clay has been chosen, and also produce the desired shade of white or cream colour when fired.

Figure 2.4
Stamps used for replica tiles. Left to right, lead stamp used for impressed tile, Prior Crauden's Chapel, Ely Cathedral. Brass stamp used for inlay tiles at Chertsey Abbey, Surrey. Holly wood tile for inlay tiles at the Chertsey Museum.

Equal in importance to finding the correct clay source is the detailed examination of the style and form of the decoration which is to be emulated. Stamps, which were used to impress the design into the body clay, were made from both wood and metal. Close examination can work out from which material the original stamp was made, further detailed study can deduce which type of wood or metal was used. There is some evidence from the style of the fine inlay on the very early tiles found at Chertsey Abbey, Surrey, that they may have been produced using finely cast and chased metal stamps possibly bronze or iron; some of the later, more mass produced impressed tiles used cruder lead stamps. Similarly wood stamps could be finely carved and made from holly or fruit wood or more simply cut motifs made from courser grained beech, ash or elm wood. Using the correct material to make the stamp as well as replicating the form and style of the decoration exactly has a direct bearing on the finished product and its ability to sit comfortably alongside an original tile (Figure 2.4).

Modern tile makers differ in opinion as to whether the body of the medieval tile was rolled and cut to shape or whether it was pressed into a wooden frame in order to form the actual tile slab; either way, the tools employed by a twenty-first century maker of medieval style tiles are in most respects the same as their counterparts in the past and are used to perform the same functions. The tiles, once formed, are allowed to dry slowly before glazing (Figure 2.5).

It is in the glazing that a good tile maker will allow a measure of artistic licence and creativity in order to produce a finished effect which will be in sympathy with original tiles and all their variations in

Figure 2.5
Tools used for tile making.

depth and colour of glaze. Glazes are made from 100 per cent refined lead sulphide, or galena, mixed with natural additives such as ale, wine or soured milk. Although the glazes are clear, orange staining from the iron content of the body clay will permeate through the liquid glaze to produce variation of colour across the tile, sometimes a little copper is added to give the familiar green glaze. The method of glazing has an unpredictable quality which echoes medieval tiles and the success of each batch of tiles is determined by the way in which that quality has been reproduced.

The use of reproduction medieval tiles should never take the place of conservation of original tiles, but there are many instances either where original pavements have already been lost, or valuable and fragile medieval tiles are being irretrievably damaged through the tramp of feet encouraged by tourism, where replication could provide a useful and proper addition to the continuing life of our built ecclesiastical and secular heritage.

Delftware tiles

Early tile making in the Netherlands

The dissolution of the monasteries during the sixteenth century saw the virtual end of floor tile making on a large scale in England. The decorative tile making industry did not revive again until after the arrival at Lambeth, London, of the first wave of Antwerp potters fleeing religious persecution in northern Europe in the late sixteenth century. With them they brought an entirely different style of tile making which used tin glaze rather than the lead glazes previously used by tile makers in the medieval period. Tin glazed tile making was well established in Mesopotamia and Persia by the ninth century AD, from there it travelled to Spain with the Moslem conquest, and on up through the low countries, establishing itself first at Antwerp and then in Meddelberg by the sixteenth century. Tile making as a particular industry, rather than as an extension of pottery manufacture, centred on Rotterdam, Haarlem, Gouda, Amsterdam, Utrecht, and Harlingen in the seventeenth century and Makkum in the eighteenth century; sizable factories with prolific outputs exported tiles all over northern Europe and beyond. Pottery marks were not in use on tiles but small differences in design and quality were notable in the product from different regions and factories. The hotter countries of southern Europe continued to use their own locally produced tin glazed tiles to provide cool decorative interior surfaces; the style of decoration was far more elaborate, flamboyant and highly developed than in the north, echoing the Moorish and Islamic influence. The use of tiles as wall coverings to provide cool interiors originated with the development of the tile in Persia.

While it is common enough to find examples of seventeenth century tin glazed tiles in English locations, the majority of delftware tiles (as they have become known) found in the UK date from the eighteenth century, when the Dutch potters had fully established their tile making centres at Liverpool, Bristol, London and Glasgow, and the tile makers in Holland were at the height of their export trade.

Initially, as one would expect, the later part of the seventeenth and early part of the eighteenth centuries saw the use of tiles in interiors built and decorated by the wealthy, but in Europe at least, as output and manufacturing locations increased, the widespread use of tiles in the homes of the merely moderately wealthy was commonplace. The primary use for delftware tiles was as wall coverings. Though highly decorative, their use was mostly functional, adorning the walls of dairies and bath houses, and in surrounding fireplaces and cooking stoves, they were chosen for their ability to be heat resistant and easily cleaned (Figure 2.6). Dutch homes used tiles liberally to adorn the walls of hallways (Figure 2.7) and frequently as skirting around rooms in order to prevent dirt and moisture creeping up the walls (Figure 2.8).

Traditional Dutch tiles measured approximately 130 mm² and their English counterparts measured much the same, though in the nineteenth century some Dutch factories produced and exported larger tiles measuring 152 mm × 152 mm specifically for the English market. As a consequence of their use as a wall covering they were constructed to be light in weight and relatively thin. Early tiles were about 18 mm thick, but the thickness became reduced to approximate 6 to 7 mm thick in the eighteenth century.

Figure 2.6
Dutch kitchen interior, the panel over the fireplace was painted by Willem ten Zweege in 1867.

Figure 2.7
Hallway tiles in a Dutch interior
dating from 1731.

Figure 2.8
Skirting tiles in a Dutch interior
dating from 1669.

The body clay of delftware tiles was usually dug locally to the site
of manufacture; it is rich in calcium carbonate and fine sand deposited
as silt from waterways, the addition of marl clay from different locations was sometimes included in a carefully balanced mix which
slightly from place to place. Marl is defined as a natural deposit mix of

clay, calcium carbonate and sand in varying proportions. Once mixed and pugged the clay was rolled onto a flat, sanded board and cut into rough squares, the squares were pushed into frames where the surface of the clay was rolled or scraped flat within the frame, it was then left to dry and partially shrink. After rolling for a second time the tiles were trimmed to size with a square wooden template. The style of trimming was mainly a matter of individual technique, but most factories, particularly in Holland, trimmed the tiles with a slight inward chamfer which was an advantage when setting the tile. The sizing process was aided with the addition of small copper nails fixed to the corners of the template which prevented the clay from moving or slipping. The nails left behind small holes in the corners of the tiles which often remained visible in the finished product.

Some of the English factories, with the exception of those in Liverpool, seemed to have some difficultly producing a perfectly flat tile. No doubt it was this ability to produce a flat tile that encouraged the development of the transfer printing technique of decorating tiles introduced by Sadler and Green in Liverpool in the latter part of the eighteenth century.

After the drying period tiles were carefully stacked into wood fired kilns. Unfired blanks, plain glazed and decorated tiles were all fired at the same time, with the blanks for biscuit firing being placed at the lower, hottest part of the kiln. Glazed tiles were stacked vertically in pairs with a small space between each pair, and a space of a few centimetres between each stack to allow the heat from the flames to spread evenly. The tiles for biscuit firing were laid horizontally with fragments of fired broken tiles used to separate the bodies from each other. Glazed tiles were positioned with glaze face to glaze face in the upper part of the kiln, plain tiles were fired with decorated tiles (Figure 2.9). The tiles were held in their vertical position both underneath and above by strips of rolled clay, which were removed after firing. Marks left on the sides of tiles as a result of the stacking technique should not be thought of as damage when tiles are examined in preparation for the conservation process. Occasionally a plain tile can be found where the colour and design from its neighbouring decorated tile have migrated onto the plain surface. The firing temperature reached about 1000 degrees centigrade over a period of about 36 hours and produced a soft bodied, porous, yellow biscuit clay which was suitable for applying white tin glaze both in terms of colour and ability to fuse. Large kilns could hold up to 30 000 decorated tiles plus twice as many biscuit ones. Tiles dating from the late sixteenth and early seventeenth centuries have a clay body which tends towards pink rather than yellow, indicating that a different clay source was used in the earlier period of production than during the era of the highest output a century later.

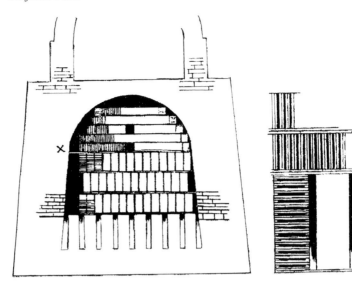

Figure 2.9
Diagram showing kiln ready for firing, packed with three tiers of unfired blanks, each tier formed by 12 pairs of tiles, each pair separated by fragments of broken biscuit tiles. Detail at X showing the top tier of unfired blanks and the bottom row of decorated tiles arranged vertically in pairs, back to back (permission P.J. Tichelaar).

Tin glaze is a clear lead glaze to which tin oxide, sand and an alkali are added to give a white opaque colour to the glaze. The amount of tin oxide can vary to produce different shades of white, and the English tile makers tended to use a glaze with more lead and less tin oxide than the Dutch, which produced a glaze more blue in colour and less likely to craze. Impurities also produced variations in the shades of white in both Dutch and English tiles.

The white tin glaze was dipped onto the biscuit tile. Once all of the moisture had been absorbed the decoration was applied directly onto the unfired glaze, using a pouncing as the means for transferring the design onto the face of the tile. A pouncing is a design on thin paper which has small holes the size of pinpricks along all of the main outlines, the paper is placed over the tile and charcoal is dusted through the holes to leave the imprint of the design on the tile which is then followed by hand painting. The decoration was usually applied using cobalt blue or manganese purple paint (pigment suspended in a medium), and great skill and quickness of hand were required to apply the pigment in this manner. This method of applying the decoration allows the cobalt or manganese to spread or migrate slightly into the background glaze during the second or glaze firing, giving the unique soft quality to delftware design which is its trade mark. Early tiles made before 1650 were given a final coating of clear lead glaze, which was applied with a drizzling or flicking action from a brush, to give the deep glassy effect also notable on delftware pottery. The practice ceased after that date and from 1650, probably for reasons of economy, tiles were given only one glaze firing. All colours, blue, manganese, green or yellow, were applied before the single glost (glaze) firing.

The glaze firing was controlled by the use of spy holes or small vents in the kiln to detect whether the glaze had reached the correct colour change, consequently cool air rushed into the open gap damaging those tiles nearest the vent. The firing process carried with it numerous hazards, such as sudden changes of wind direction and force, causing ovens to change temperature, resulting in slightly cracked tiles and glazes that spread or ran further than predicted. This sort of firing damage is generally recognisable and as such should not be included or 'corrected' in the conservation process as it is unlikely to be the cause of further deterioration of the tile. However, if kiln temperatures fell slightly too low this resulted in a less than adequate fusion between the glaze and the clay body. Often as little as only 25 per cent of tiles would be of the first quality from a firing.

Degradation associated with manufacturing techniques

The structure of the clay body used for delftware tiles can itself be the direct cause of conservation problems. Poor mixing results in fault lines and structural weakness in the tile after firing; weaknesses can turn into fractures if the tile is subject to movement or thermal stresses. The body clay is highly porous, making it prone to being friable when exposed to sudden changes in temperature, and at risk from the growth of salt crystals after changes in moisture levels. It also has an increased capacity to absorb soot and tar substances from around fireplaces (Figure 2.10).

The formation of salt crystals within the tile body can be a particular problem. If tiles are subject to changes in the absorption of moisture salt will readily migrate from the mortar, and form salt crystals inside the clay, which expand and push their way to the surface of the tiles causing devastating damage to the glaze by forcing it to separate from the clay body; tiles used in kitchens and dairies are prone to this type of damage. It is advisable to desalinate tiles in preparation to conservation work if the tiles are not in a fixed position. If tiles are unfixed this is achieved by soaking tiles in distilled water for as long as possible, six to 12 weeks with daily water changes is a rule of thumb which will remove most salts.

The consequence of acute difference between the shrinkage rates of the body and the glaze in the cooling process after firing manifests in crazing across the surface of the glaze. A too low firing temperature will prevent the glaze from bonding properly to the clay body. Both sets of circumstances lead to the possibility of shedding fragments of glaze from the body of the tile, particularly around the edges, thus leading to severe disfigurement and further fragility of the glaze decoration. Further degradation, although stemming from the manufacturing process, can be held in check as part of the conservation treatment.

Figure 2.10
Showing loss of glaze fragments from the edges of the tile, also the extent of soot absorption from use in a fireplace.

Current tile making techniques

The pottery company Royal Tichelaar, Makkum, is the oldest commercial business in the Netherlands. It has been making delft tiles and pottery at Makkum since 1594 and has been under the direction of ten generations of the Tichelaar family since 1674 (Figures 2.11 and 2.12). We spoke to Pieter Jan Tichelaar, historian and head of the company from 1964 until 1991, about current production techniques at Makkum and how the process has been adapted to encompass the many nationally important restoration projects carried out at the factory in recent years.

Uniquely, the clay used at the factory today is taken from the same source that the family has had rights to since 1674. It is dug from the same location and from the same level. It derives from North Sea silt laid down in 2000 BC and has a 20 per cent content of lime but no salt content. The clay is weathered for six years in the open air and marl is added to bring the lime content up to 28 per cent in order to bring about the correct thermal expansion rate to correspond with the thermal expansion rate of the tin glaze. In 1965 the company reduced the size of their clay mixing, or blunging machines from large machines which were capable of water washing and mixing the clay once a year, to smaller machines which allowed the clay to be processed every few weeks. This was one of the modernisations which enabled better quality control and avoided the problem of poor mixing which produces faults in the clay body leading to cracks, fissures and air pockets after firing; it was also a time span more in line with current production demands.

Figure 2.11
Flamboyant domestic fireplace made by Royal Tichelaar, Makkum, painted by Adam Sigbel in 1803.

Figure 2.12
Large panel situated above a fireplace
made by Royal Tichelaar, Makkum,
painted by Gatse Sytses in 1772.

The company make their own tin glazes, mixing together powdered
lead sulphide, tin oxide, silica sand, sodium or potassium carbonate
and feldspar. The mixed powders are melted together, the heating
process forms hard blocks of melded glaze. The blocks are broken up
and wet ground in the same pebble mill which was introduced into
the factory in 1906 (Figure 2.13).

After a period of drying, the clay which is to be turned into tiles is
rolled and cut to size in the traditional way, but without the use of the
positioning nails which made pinholes in the corners of earlier tiles
(though these can be reintroduced if required for special restoration
projects).

Gas fired kilns are used for biscuit firing because they are faster and
give good temperature distribution from the circulation of heat caused
by the gas jets, resulting in a more homogenised product (Figure 2.14).
Electric kilns are used for glost firing because they give a slow, constantly radiating heat which allows slower evaporation producing a
glaze finish with a high shine. During his time at the factory, Pieter
Tichelaar introduced only those modernisations which gave better
quality control to the traditional methods.

The glaze technicians at Royal Tichelaar have developed in excess
of 150 different shades of blue, 100 shades of manganese pinks and
250 shades of white, many of which have been developed specifically
for restoration projects. The task of the glaze laboratory staff is to test
glazes for shrinkage against biscuit clay, colour consistency, and thickness and fluidity (an important factor in delft decoration which gives
the 'water colour' effect of the hand painted line).

The glaze mixes are suspended in water and when applied to the
dry biscuit tile, water is quickly absorbed by the body leaving the

Figure 2.13
Glaze process showing melded glaze
in block form.

glaze adhered to the surface in a dry powdery consistency. The background or field glaze is applied to mass produced lines by a mechanised technique which spreads the glaze over the surface of the tile, but tiles are hand dipped for special runs destined for restoration projects. Designs are applied using the traditional pouncing method; however, the black dust used at Royal Tichelaar to penetrate the pinholes is not charcoal but burnt bones, charcoal is considered to be too sticky (Figure 2.15). The decoration is hand painted straight onto the

Figure 2.14
Gas fired kiln for biscuit tiles.

Figure 2.15
Pouncing, showing pattern and pouncing bag.

unfired background glaze, which is highly absorbent, using the traditional mix of pigments suspended in medium. The painter needs to be extremely dexterous and fast to avoid the decoration paint spreading too far into the background resulting in indistinct lines, and to attain the boldness and vigour of the delft style. The finished design is fired once only to give the distinguishing quality of delft tiles. When compared directly with seventeenth and eighteenth century tiles, the modern equivalent has a slightly higher gloss finish, whether this is due to abrasion of the surface over the passage of time on the historic tiles or the consequence of less refinement during the manufacture of the glazes prior to 1900 has not been established.

During the 1960s Royal Tichelaar introduced a back stamp onto their tiles as a recognition mark for quality work from their factory, in the past makers did not use pottery marks and work from different factories was recognised by small differences in design and quality.

Factory restoration techniques

Restoration techniques used at Royal Makkum differ somewhat from those used by ceramic restorers in the UK. Essentially they have at their disposal the unique capability of being able to reproduce exactly the missing or damaged parts of historic tile schemes using the same source materials as their forbears who originally created the work. Consequently it requires a keen eye to distinguish the old from the new. Because the clay body is relatively easy to cut and shape even after firing, small pieces of new biscuit can be shaped to a close fit against a fragment edge of a broken original tile (Figure 2.16).

Figure 2.16
A restoration project carried out at Royal Tichelaar, Makkum. The tile on the bottom left is a new tile, painted before firing. The adjoining tile shows how a new fragment is cut to fit and glaze painted to match.

The new fragment can be glazed and decorated to match in with the colour and design of the original. After firing the fragment can then be fixed in place with adhesive and the joint filled and painted over in the usual way of ceramic restorers. Royal Tichelaar are able to manufacture missing areas or whole tiles without recourse to making up large areas with alien materials such as plaster or resins. Original historic material is never refired and although new material is virtually indistinguishable from the original on the decorated face, examination of the back of the tile instantly reveals newly inserted modern tile material thus ensuring the historical integrity of the object as a whole (Figure 2.17 and Plate 5).

Nineteenth century tiles

Industrial mass production of nineteenth century floor tiles

In 1904 William J. Furnival published what has become the definitive text describing nineteenth century tile making, *Leadless Decorative Tiles Faience and Mosaic*. At the time of its publication it's aim was to present a manual of best practice for the industry. It was dedicated to

> Manufacturers of Decorative Tiles and Faience throughout the world who desire to protect their operatives from Lead Poisoning, and to all who are interested in the highest welfare of the Ceramic Industry.

We can deduce from this statement that the author, at least, considered that there was room for improvement within the industry, particularly

Figure 2.17
Shows the reverse of the tile.

in the realm of safety for workers in respect of the use of poisonous ingredients in the manufacture of body clay and glazes. It is largely in respect of improvement of safety within the industry that the difference between manufacturing techniques in the past and modern techniques for reproducing tiles lies.

The British tile making industry reached its peak of production between 1870 and 1900. During those years tiles and the grandiose architectural style to which they were suited were exported to all major cities throughout the then British Empire and beyond. Additionally many entrepreneurial and skilled tile makers moved away from companies in the Potteries of Stoke on Trent to America to found their own successful companies.

It is clear from the outset that once Samuel Wright of Shelton, Stoke on Trent, had taken out a patent for making inlaid tiles in 1830 and established a method for mass production of tiles, that the leading lights of the tile industry, Herbert Minton, George and Arthur Maw, Henry Godwin and Jesse Carter, were equal and serious in their intent to use science as a basis for manufacturing a product which was materially consistent and quick to produce for an affordable cost. They eschewed the haphazard nature of previous technologies which were based on hand crafting rather than machine production. Furnival lists the desirable qualities to be provided as elements in the manufacture of good geometric tiled floors as follows:

> uniform durability, evenness of colour, distinctness of colour, regularity of size, good foothold, level surface, tolerable fineness of grain, insusceptibility to permanent discolouration, facility in cleansing, frost resistance, strength, adhesion to cements.

Most of these qualities could be said to be demonstrably lacking in medieval tile production values (Figure 2.18).

Samuel Wright's patent for inlaid tiles included the method for impressing tiles by means of a plaster of Paris mould, which had been previously cut with a pattern, set in a metal frame with screw studs attached to two sides. The mould was filled with clay and the metal die, which configured the maker's mark and aerating holes in the reverse of the tile, was placed on top and secured to the screw studs, the whole thing was then pressed, giving an exact same depth and position for the imprint on every tile (Figure 2.19).

Herbert Minton bought Wright's patent in 1835, but it took a further five years of experimentation in clay mixes, firing temperatures and shrinkage rates before he or his former partner Walter Chamberlain could confidently market a product which could be relied upon to be consistent in production, indeed all of the main manufacturers gave up their early production years to the development of clay sources,

Figure 2.18
The old Maw & Co. tile factory at Jackfield, Shropshire.

Figure 2.19
Above is a plaster mould for an encaustic tile fixed into a former, below is a hand operated backstamp used for wet clay tilemaking, the two wooden handles are missing. The stamp, reading Maw & Co., was simply pushed into the wet clay.

mixes and colours, the recipes of which mostly remained secrets within the companies.

Up until the development of Richard Prosser's patent for 'dust pressed tiles' in 1840, which by 1860 was in widespread use, all floor tiles were made with wet or 'plastic' clay. Early efforts made by Chamberlain's and Godwin's dating between 1830 to 1850 using plastic clay resulted in tiles up to 3 cm thick in an effort to prevent warping. Both Minton's and Maw's used Wright's patent to develop a method of sandwiching the plastic clay which improved stability. A layer of course, cheap clay about 1 cm thick was sandwiched between two layers of matching fine clay, each about 3 mm thick, the top layer containing the imprinted, or 'encaustic', as they became known, design. The two layers of fine clay encouraged an equal amount of shrinkage to prevent warping, and the course clay middle section provided a cheaper bulk of clay (Figure 2.20). Encaustic pattern making remained essentially a hand crafted operation. Patterns were impressed into the wet clay with the use of machine presses, but pouring the colour 'slip' (slip is the term given to wet clay mixed to the consistency of cream) into the impressions was a hand skilled job, which after two or three days' drying, would be scraped flat by hand, revealing the pattern with sharp clear edges. The tile was then left to continue to dry slowly, as speeding up the drying time too much could also result in warping. Drying time for plastic clay was up to three weeks before firing, resulting in a slow production time.

After the drying period, tiles were fired once only to fuse the clays together and produce a good standard of vitrification. Temperatures

Figure 2.20
The edges and reverse of these tiles
indicate if a tile was wet clay pressed,
as the Minton tile in the bottom left,
or dust pressed, as the Craven
Dunnill tile on the bottom right. The
other two tiles are examples of the
sandwich method of wet clay
pressing.

had to reach 900 to 1000 degrees centigrade or above, but the exact
temperatures needed to produce a floor tile hard enough and of consistent colour to be a good product were a matter of much trial and
error, and personal judgement, by the fireman. Two and three colour
tiles needed the correct combination of clays and temperatures in
order to fuse the inlays, but not burn the colours or cause them to
shrink away from the imprint. In the early years of production,
Minton's, Chamberlain's and Godwin's all favoured glazing their tiles,
with either clear glazes, yellow enamels or green glazes in an attempt
to replicate the medieval style, but those finishes fell out of favour
fairly quickly, and encaustics were marketed unglazed but with a hard
vitrified surface.

Production times, however, were revolutionised by the introduction
of Prosser's dust pressing technique. Prepared clay was dried and
ground up to a fine powder, retaining a small moisture content of
between 5 and 8 per cent, which, when subjected to extreme pressure
between steel dies, forced the clay into a compressed state forming a
slab or tile about 1 cm thick, the design could also be imprinted at the
same time using a patterned die stamp. In this way not only was
pressing time cut down, but the all important drying stages were
reduced to days instead of weeks. In addition to those advantages tiles
could be made thinner with a reduced shrinkage rate and less propensity to warping. Dust pressing, as a technique, created the opportunity
for floor tile production on a huge scale. Coloured geometric and
encaustic floor tile designs were part of every tile manufacturer's
mainstay of production. Each company had their own range of

colours and designs in a variety of geometric sizes and shapes. Many of the ranges were so similar that it is difficult to identify a specific company's wares without detailed knowledge of company catalogues, back stamps or sales archive.

Choosing, preparing and mixing the clays were the most important preliminary exercises in nineteenth century tile production. The quality of the tile depended directly on the quality of the clay and method of preparation. Cheap tiles were made from local clays, sometimes a mix of more than one. Each component clay and ingredient was pulverised, measured, and mixed. The mix was 'pugged' (i.e. continuously turned and folded in a wet state), then dried; it was passed through a series of sieves and left to mellow in bins before use. More expensive tiles had more complex ingredients sometimes including colour stains, which were mixed, put into tanks with double their volume of water and left in order to fatten, after several hours the mix was 'blunged' (i.e. mixed with a paddle-like action to a slip clay of creamy consistency). The slip was past through a series of sieves and then poured onto drying floors, where it remained until the clay was completely dry. The dry clay was stored in bins where it was allowed to mellow before use. A typical recipe for a red floor tile was:

10 cwt of mixed red marls or clays, carefully selected and weathered
12 lb of finely levigated common ironstone
14 lb of Cornish china clay

The final colour of the tile also dictated its position in the oven, which was subject to considerable variation in temperature at the bottom, middle and top, for example black tiles were best placed in the middle of the kiln at the hottest part. Different positions in the kiln could produce different variations within a single colour according to temperature, and much was left to the fine judgement of the fireman. However, the Victorian bottle kiln was much more efficient in reaching sustained high temperatures than any which preceded it and the result was a much harder semi-vitrified tile with low porosity.

Degradation of floor tiles associated with production techniques

The production techniques we have seen so far impact on the conservation and restoration of Victorian floors in a number of ways. The early plastic clay produced tiles are generally a more robust object than the thinner dust pressed tiles. They are more likely to have been set in lime mortar because they were already in production just prior to the beginnings of widespread use of Portland cement, therefore they are prone towards shifting with building stresses and becoming unseated, whereas the later dust pressed tiles, set in Portland cement,

Figure 2.21
An example of clay slip inlay shrinkage. The blue clay around the white flower motif has shrunk considerably.

are more apt to fracture under movement stress. Plastic clay tiles are more likely to suffer damage to the encaustic pattern in terms of flaking away of parts of the design, the marrying up of the different colours of clay is more difficult to achieve in the wet state, and the technology being in its infancy produced many tiles which were less than perfectly fused. Tiles were frequently used in elaborate floors which are obvious examples of the clay inlay slip shrinking during firing (Figure 2.21).

Floors dating prior to the 1860s generally show a much greater variance in colour shade within each colour produced, for example a shade of dark chocolate brown that Maw's produced in the 1850s was subject to such an inconsistency of tone that almost no two tiles were exactly alike, the colour presumably proved too unreliable to continue in production and is not found in Maw's later floors (Plate 6). We also find that different colours produced from different clays and fired at different temperatures will be harder or softer accordingly. Colours with a slightly lower firing temperature, therefore softer, will be more susceptible to shelling of the fire skin around the edges of the tile not only in the course of normal wear but especially as a result of intrusive works. The Architectural Pottery Company was founded in Poole, Dorset, in 1854 and their encaustic tiles exhibit all of the problems inherent in early manufacturing techniques, namely the soft body resulting in excessive wear and delamination, extensive colour variation and shrinkage of clay inlay; however, their tiles are beautifully designed with more delicate colour combinations than their Midland rivals (Figure 2.22). Jesse Carter bought the company in 1895 and abandoned the production of encaustic tiles, preferring to concentrate on building the successful Carter's of Poole, manufacturers of wall tiles.

Figure 2.22
A small part of the Ninevah Chapel floor, Wimbourne, Dorset.

Figure 2.23
Surface wear to a group of encaustic tiles.

Dust pressed tiles form the bulk of tiles in place on floors in nineteenth century buildings, the vast majority have been installed post 1870 and will have been fixed with the system favoured by the tile producers themselves using Portland cement. In most cases, where there has been no extraneous forces to create fracturing, the most visible damage will be that of surface wear (Figure 2.23). The encaustic inlay on dust pressed tiles was not usually more than 2 mm deep at the outset, and as a result of over 100 years of wear, we find that, in some of our busiest public buildings, the encaustic patterns on the floor tiles will simply have worn away. There is no remedy for this condition and tiles must be replaced with matching material. Understanding and recognising the distinctions between the early and later processes, and the differences between the individual manufacturer's techniques, is also an aid to qualifying the decision whether to retain, conserve or restore original material or to allow the introduction of replica material into tile schemes.

Industrial mass production of nineteenth century glazed wall tiles

Glazed wall tiles with white dust pressed bodies began to be developed alongside the floor tile industry, though in general they took a longer time to gain in popularity. In 1850 Minton produced a range of wall tiles decorated with enamel glazes and designed by Augustus W. N. Pugin (Figure 2.24). Examples are to be found in the Strangers' Smoking Room at the Palace of Westminster; these were probably among the first to be used. They also produced a range of embossed tiles glazed with a range of opaque glazes derived from lead and tin

Figure 2.24
Three tile designs by AWN Pugin for Herbert Minton.

oxides; these were first shown at the 1851 Great Exhibition and then later installed in Refreshment Room of the South Kensington Museum. Opaque tin glazes gave way to translucent colour glazes or art enamels, though the major developmental problem to be solved was the correct marrying up of the body clay and the glaze mix, without which the finished tile would quickly have a propensity to surface crazing with possible loss of glaze. Given the limitless combinations of clay body mixes, glaze mixes and firing temperatures, the producers of glazed wall tiles often failed to prevent crazing, which they considered to be a fault, not only disfiguring but also negating the hygienic qualities of the glazed tile.

The best manufacturers each developed their own sound clay tile body in the first instance, and thereafter developed their dies, glazes and firing temperatures to suit shrinkage rates and adhesion respectively. Body clay recipes were complex, stains or additives were introduced to offer alternatives to the white body. Some nineteenth century tiles achieve very beautiful hues by combining a coloured clay body overlaid with a different colour glaze, for example a yellow body coated with a blue glaze. A typical recipe for a white dust pressed tile body was:

5 cwt best ball clay, dry
6 cwt best china clay, dry
8 ½ cwt ground calcined flint
2 ½ cwt ground Cornish china stone

In developing new lines for mass production it was not uncommon for manufacturers to alter body formula, vary the ingredients, alter the size of dies or moulds, burn the tiles in a different part of the oven, or even burn the whole oven differently. However, despite the incalculable opportunity for variation, most manufacturers developed their own distinctive ranges of colours and designs which are very often identifiable as a house style.

The vast majority of both plain and embossed tiles were dust pressed, though 'specials' and larger faience pieces were cast in plastic clay. Tiles were decorated in many different ways, the most common forms being embossed, impressed, transfer printed, and tube lined (Figures 2.25–2.27). Heavily embossed tiles allowed the glaze to run and form deep pools in the recesses of the embossing, creating a two tone effect from one glaze colour. Tube lining was a method of separating different glaze colours using trails of clay slip applied directly onto the biscuit tile. The slip was applied by hand, following a predetermined design, forming the separating barrier. Tiles were also hand painted with under-glaze colours straight onto the biscuit,

Figure 2.25
Part of a tube lined panel.

Figure 2.26
An embossed ceramic pillar.

then coated with a clear glaze to protect the colours during firing. Under-glaze colours were made from a variety of metal oxides with mineral additives. The Ironbridge Gorge Museum Trust houses at Jackfield Tile Museum, Shropshire, the national collection of plaster moulds and patterns, originating from one company, Maw and Co., spanning the decades from the 1850s to the 1920s, alongside which is also the largest single collection of decorated tiles representing all of the major companies.

By the turn of the century the tile industry was moving away from lead glazes in response to the unacceptable levels of lead poisoning cases among pottery workers. The industry, admitting the poisonous nature of lead glazes for both worker and consumer, turned to the use of alkali-lime glazes, though at the same time bemoaning the loss of the deep gloss finish peculiar to lead, along with the deep ruby reds and French pinks which were impossible to replicate without its inclusion. Glazes composed with a high proportion of oxide of lead produced easily managed glazes which gave darker, richer hues with a glassy quality, their failing was that they were prone to crazing. Alkaline glazes were difficult to manage, arguably lacking in gloss, but they were thinner, less likely to craze and their colours had a brilliance not present in lead glazes. Their non-poisonous base made them the way forward.

Degradation of glazed wall tiles associated with production techniques

Removing damaged tiles from nineteenth century glazed wall tile schemes is subject to health and safety precautions. Cutting or drilling into lead glazes produces harmful dust which should not be inhaled. In conservation terms we now accept crazing in glazed wall tiles as part

Figure 2.27
Transfer printed fireplace tiles.

and parcel of the ageing process, even though it originally represented a loss of integrity within the material. In most instances it is acceptable to retain heavily crazed tiles where the crazing has become visually distinct due to high absorption levels of organic staining into the tile body. However, certain situations, such as food service areas or bathing pools, demand that tiles with a deteriorated surface glaze quality, allowing a high rate of absorption, should be replaced for the sake of good public health.

In some instances, the yellow enamel and the green glaze, which Minton's used to give their early floor tiles a gloss finish, has not lasted well. Church floors subjected to heavy tread may have entirely lost the glaze from their encaustic tiles. There is some evidence to show that all of the encaustic pattern tiles at St Albans Cathedral, which are now red clay with a yellow inlay, were once coated with a green glaze (Plate 7). A scheme which contains tiles in areas away from traffic routes with varying degrees of colour left on the surface, whether the colour remains glossy or not, is a good indicator of previous glazing. Many high quality geometric floors also contained glaze tile elements in their design. Again in areas of heavy tread this glazing has often worn thin or completely away, so changing the original intention in the dynamics of the colour scheme.

Current tile manufacturing techniques for restoration projects

Tile production techniques did not substantially change through the beginning part of the twentieth century, but the interruption of two world wars, combined with changing fashions and the introduction of new materials into interior decorative schemes, for example vinyl floor coverings, began to signal the need for modernisation or closure for many companies. The post war years of the 1950s and early 1960s saw the industry regroup to form two major producers H. & R. Johnsons in Stoke-on-Trent and Pilkington's in Salford, at the same time changing and modernising its production technology in response to competition in the global market. Both Minton's and Maw & Co. became part of the H. & R. Johnsons group, while Craven Dunnill ceased manufacturing and moved into distribution. Carters of Poole, major manufacturers during the 1930s, became Poole Pottery concentrating on tableware and art pottery.

Aside from a brief period between the late 1960s and the early 1980s, tile making at Jackfield, near Ironbridge in Shropshire, has been part of the Severn Gorge economy since the late eighteenth century. Initially the reason for this lay with the local geology which contained both clay and coal deposits in good supply and in close proximity to the River Severn. In the nineteenth century the network of canals and waterways gave way to the railways which allowed the Jackfield clay deposits to be exploited to their best potential. After one or two false starts in the 1980s, the 1990s saw the return of tile making to Jackfield on an enthusiastic and technically sound basis. The year 2000 brought Craven Dunnill & Co. Ltd back to their original factory site, now owned by Ironbridge Gorge Museum Trust as the Jackfield Tile Museum, to take up production again using the same technical and production staff who had initiated full-scale production ten years earlier. It is no longer the local clay deposits or transport links that drives tile production at Jackfield but the steadily rising demand for tiles commissioned for specific conservation and restoration projects, large and small. The production staff at Craven Dunnill Jackfield Ltd have generously supplied the information for the reproduction of historic manufactured tiles.

The fundamental importance in the replication of medieval and delftware tiles of using a clay source which matches the material structure of the original tile has already been noted. What has not been noted, however, is that although there is very wide variation of colour, texture and design within the limited bounds of both medieval and Dutch and English delft tiles, the variations are subtle and slight when compared with the mass of variety of colour, design, size, decoration and function, into which the humble tile was pressed, moulded, decorated and utilised in the nineteenth and early twentieth centuries and continues to be so today.

We should remind ourselves that during the nineteenth century each manufacturer, and there were many, sourced and managed their own clay pits from which they developed their basic body clays, from there they developed the glazes which matched their own particular clay mixes. If, as they expanded their range and productivity, a particular clay they required was not available locally they brought it in by rail from anywhere that could supply at the right price. All companies had their own basic white, yellow, black and red clay. Reds and yellows particularly, in the early period, were the product of locally found natural clays, but in addition to the use of a basic naturally occurring clay, the manufacturers mixed clays and minerals in an infinite variety of ways to produce the many different clay body types they required, and continued to pursue changes as and when required right through the period to which we are referring. There were literally tens of thousands of clay sources and recipes available to the tile maker, some recipes were recorded, most were not. As a result, visual or laboratory examination of a nineteenth century tile cannot reveal the location of the clay source or the exact recipe which was used to produce it, thereby facilitating easy reproduction. Additionally, if an original clay source could be pinpointed, the likelihood is that it will have closed down as a source many years ago.

Traditional clay pits are no longer commercially viable in such a way as would support the variety of clays which were available in the past. Reopening a nineteenth century source on anything like a large scale would also bring health and safety issues into the economic picture, though small amounts from known sources can be dug without complication or risk, and in some limited cases these can be utilised by the restoration market. The unarguable fact is that there are little or no nineteenth century sources of floor tile clay available today.

Tile makers in today's restoration market are confined to sourcing all of their raw materials from a handful of companies which supply the ceramic industry nationwide, or they must extend their search abroad. The raw materials industry is vast and global, suppliers are, as a rule, secretive as to the location of their sources, and because the industry is so vast the turnover of source locations for the right price is quick, leading to the additional complication of batch variation at source. Consequently, it is possible for a restoration project involving colour matching geometric floor tiles to be successful at the development and testing stage, but to encounter difficulties at a later stage if production is not followed up immediately, owing to a change in the raw material. Any change in a raw material can be significant or slight and it will still affect the outcome of a colour recipe.

Today's raw materials, both clays and oxides, are also significantly more refined than raw materials of the past, which can prove problematical when replicating the surface texture of a historic tile, both on glazed wall tiles and geometric floor tiles. Further complications arise connected to examining health and safety issues – cadmium, arsenic, uranium and vanadium are all substances widely used to produce yellows, reds and oranges in glaze mixes during the Victorian era, but which are not available, for good reason, today.

That said, the research and development technicians at Craven Dunnill Jackfield have shown great skill, ingenuity and patience over the past ten years developing manufacturing techniques which can overcome many, albeit not all, of the difficulties in producing thoroughly convincing replacement tiles for restoration projects.

The process for geometric floor tile colour development starts with a standard white base clay with a known stable behaviour at a standard firing temperature, to this is added the desired colourants which are sometimes oxides, sometimes stains. A series of mixes are made in small amounts, or 'buttons' which are all fired at a standard temperature, the results are assessed and a selection of mixes are put forward for firing at slightly higher or lower temperatures until the correct colour match is achieved.

All of the data at this testing stage is meticulously recorded and standardised wherever possible to enable the building of a good reliable archive of recipes. It is important for test buttons to be fired during normal production runs, because the capacity of the kiln, whether it is full or half empty, as well as the position of the button in the kiln, can significantly affect the final colour, i.e. at the higher or lower positions the kiln temperature is cooler or hotter. Some colours, reds in particular, are very temperature sensitive and any one kiln batch will produce a considerable variation in colour shade simply due to the position of the tiles in the kiln; this is completely acceptable and was part and parcel of Victorian production for exactly the same reason.

Once approved, multiples of the test mix are weighed for a production batch of clay. The dry ingredients are mixed thoroughly with water in a blunger, the mix is sieved to remove impurities and then pumped through a filter press to take out excess water. The clay is allowed to rest for a period of about one week and when it has reached the correct plasticity it is extruded into slabs to whatever the depth of the tile should be, usually 1 cm. The slabs are rough cut into squares approximately 160 mm^2 and allowed to dry for a further period before firing. After firing the squares are cut to the required geometric size. The process is largely carried out by hand, necessarily so because a production run can be any number of tiles from one to several thousand.

Patterned encaustic tiles are completely hand made. The process begins with an accurate tracing of an original tile, the design is hand tooled into a plaster block (Figure 2.28). which is oversized to allow

Figure 2.29
Tiles and mould together showing
allowance for shrinkage.

Figure 2.28
Plaster moulds for encaustic tiles.

for clay shrinkage (Figure 2.29). The plaster block is cast to fit inside a wooden former. The former is sturdily made with handles either side, somewhat like a frame for the plaster.

The moist coloured clay which forms the design is pushed into the mould to cover the whole surface of the design. Very quickly the body clay, which is usually of a somewhat courser texture, is pounded onto the soft clay causing them to bind together. The excess body clay which is up to the level of the former is struck off, the back stamp and date are pressed into the wet clay and the mould with clay still attached is pushed out of the former and left to dry for about half an hour.

Both clays are initially quite soft but moisture is immediately pulled from the clay into the plaster causing it to harden enough to be able to strip the clay tile away from the mould. The clay tile is now placed face up on the bench, the design motif is raised up above the surface and the area that will be the ground colour is recessed. A liquid clay slip of the ground colour is poured into the recesses taking care to avoid air bubbles. The clay tile is left to dry at workshop temperature for two to three days (Figure 2.30), when 'leather' hard the surface is scraped flat to reveal the design in sharply contrasting colours. After a further drying period of two weeks the tile is fired at the standard temperature. The use of soft clays or slip clays for the design or the ground colour can be interchanged, and as many as four different clay colours can be used in either slip or soft form.

The process for wet clay manufacture of encaustic tiles is little different from the Victorian method. Encaustic tile making was always labour intensive and costly, particularly when the design called for the

Figure 2.30
Slip coated encaustic tiles left to dry.

Figure 2.31
The semi-automated fly press in use.

use of blues or greens. The Victorian palette of colours used in encaustic tile making was considerably more limited than can be found in the plain geometric range, the reasons being primarily economy, and the limitations imposed by the technical problems of clay compatibility.

Glazed wall tiles are also produced at Jackfield in as many varied methods as were commonly manufactured in the nineteenth and early twentieth centuries. The standard body is white base clay, though frequently a yellow body is substituted in order to enhance the translucent glaze with the correct hue. The clay tiles are usually dust pressed using probably the same fly presses as were used at Maw & Co. since the 1860s, although they have been modified to be semi-automated and conform to health and safety standards (Figure 2.31). Elaborate embossed or profile tiles are slip cast in plaster moulds, made from casts taken from original samples (Figure 2.32). After a drying period the tiles are biscuit fired in electric kilns to the standard firing temperature.

A good basic colour palette of lead-based oxide glazes is available to the glaze technician from which to mix and test at various temperatures until the exact colour and luminosity are achieved. It is important in order to retain the same quality of luminescence that lead-based glazes are still used; however, the lead is now encapsulated in a frit in order to comply with modern health and safety standards. Lead glazes are very soft and fluid when hot and will contract significantly on cooling. The clay body used here has been developed to avoid damaging problems of shrinkage, but to allow a measured amount of crazing to take place over a two year period, finishing with a surface texture identical to the crazing found on old tiles. All tiles at Craven Dunnill Jackfield are hand dipped in order to replicate the surface texture and depth of colour found in Victorian tiles.

Oxides are, by their nature, extremely temperature sensitive, and it is the firing temperature combined with the glaze mix that produces the desired colour in the final glaze firing. The capacity of the kiln has a direct bearing on the variation of tone in a colour batch. The kiln, whatever its size, has hotter and cooler positions which can be utilised to advantage and while there is an expected colour variation to be found in fairly small batches of restoration tiles, the range of variation is not as wide as was created in the large mass production kilns in the past. To overcome this, glaze technicians at Jackfield will often develop two or three shades of a colour to compensate for natural variation when tiles are placed within an original scheme. Meticulous records are kept of all glaze and body developments which are stored on computer to provide an extensive archive for future reference (Figure 2.33).

The different methods of decoration – embossed, impressed, hand painting or tube lining (Figures 2.34 and 2.35) – are carried out in largely the same way as in the nineteenth or early twentieth century, with the exception of printed tiles which are now screen printed rather than block or transfer printed. Transfer printing was used for large runs of cheaply reproduced patterns, but because the process requires the initial costly production of an etched or engraved copper plate to manufacture the paper transfers in enormous numbers, the restoration market is best served by the use of more cheaply produced silk screens for the often small numbers of matching tiles required to extend or repair existing schemes.

Patterns are printed onto standard white biscuit tiles, each colour in the design requires an individual screen (Figure 2.36). Glaze colours are mixed and matched from an extensive palette of colours and with reference to a large back catalogue of previous projects, all meticulously recorded. Painterly effects can be obtained by adapting artwork and glazes accordingly, and glaze colour testing will often run to 15 or more tests until an accurate combination of colours within the design is reached.

The glazes can be applied as under- or on-glaze techniques, the difference being whether the colour is applied under a final clear glaze coating or printed over, or on, an initial plain colour glaze coating. Under-glaze patterns require a drying time before firing, whereas on-glaze colours need a drying period between each colour. On-glaze

Figure 2.32
A large slip cast embossed tile with glaze tests applied.

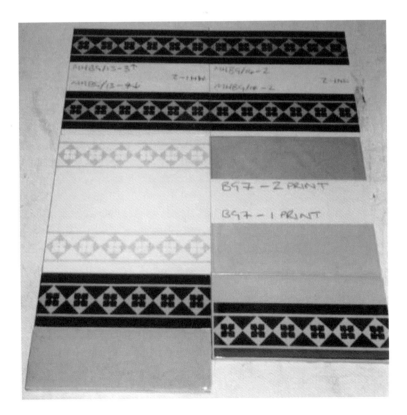

Figure 2.33
Body and glaze colour tests for printed tiles.

Figure 2.34
Unglazed tube lined tile showing the pouncing marks.

Figure 2.35
Tube lining onto a decorative panel.

patterns are fired at about 820 degrees centigrade while under-glaze colours are fired at a higher standard firing temperature (Figure 2.37).

Conclusion

It seems that since medieval times tile makers have extended their skills to produce both elaborate and expensively made tiles alongside affordable mass produced tiles. The Victorians took mass production to new heights, using the development of new machinery and the factory environment to manufacture tiles destined for the farthest flung places on the globe. What also seems clear is that they were aware

Figure 2.36
Four separate screens made for replicating a Minton block printed tile.

Figure 2.37
On-glaze printed tiles, the original Pugin designed tile is on the left of the picture.

that their product was often far from perfect and continuous changes were made in order to improve the final product as well as changes to enhance and extend the product range.

The practice of selling on, or locating in lower status environs a less than perfect product, or 'second', seems to have always been with us, and because we value historic tiling for a variety of different reasons and seek to preserve it, reproduction tile makers often find themselves required to produce tiles which were once thought of as flawed. Tile makers find themselves consciously repeating the mistakes of the past.

Finally the practice and skills involved in restoration tile making differ significantly from the skill and practice of production tile making in one obvious way, tile makers in the past were concerned with producing a tile with a look and feel of quality at the right price. The aim of the restoration tile maker is to produce a tile which matches those early production tiles still in existence as exactly as possible, whatever the quality of the original and almost whatever the cost.

3

Mortar and construction methods used in historic tile schemes

Introduction

The technology of both tile manufacture and the corresponding materials used for the purpose of adhesion has evolved and changed in northern Europe into three recognisable phases during the history of the built environment. Along with the changes in tile manufacturing technologies which have been outlined in Chapter 2 there were also changes in the techniques used for tile setting. An understanding of the different methods and materials used historically for construction and fixing is important when embarking on the conservation of a historic tile scheme because it will underpin choices for reconstruction and consolidation. The aim of this chapter is to identify both mortar types and construction methods which are most commonly found in conjunction with the three different phases of tile manufacturing technology: medieval, seventeenth and eighteenth century tin glazed tiles, and nineteenth and early twentieth century mass produced tiles.

The general principle when choosing a mortar or construction method for resetting historic tiles is to apply a 'like for like' replacement policy. This chapter includes suggested mortars and setting techniques which may be used in the reconstruction or resetting process for each group of tiles.

Laboratory analysis of mortar and adhesives is a useful and sometimes necessary tool in the conservation process, it can provide important archive information which may prove useful in the decision making process for reconstruction. In many instances, however, the resources needed to carry out laboratory analysis are not available and a visual analysis based on familiarity with typical mortars and construction methods must suffice. Whichever method is used to analyse the mortar and construction method it is important to retain samples of mortar for future reference and record the original method or phases of construction as part of the conservation process.

Tile setting was initially a craft skill which usually employed the use of locally available materials and was carried out to each craftsman's own level of skill or precision. Skills were adapted to the style and form of the tile and the location. As a result no two tile schemes are exactly alike, but broadly speaking there is a correlation between the age of the tile, the method of construction and the type of mortar most commonly found as an adhesive. This correlation is useful because it is often a good indicator as to whether the tiles under scrutiny have a history of relocation.

Finally, while the 'like for like' principle of replacement is, in most instances, the preferred option for resetting tile schemes it is evident that if the historic mortar or substrate has been under-, over-, or poorly specified initially, causing failure or damage, it will not serve the cause of conservation well to reinstate the same defective system when there may be opportunity to make changes which will improve the prospect of longevity and not jeopardise the integrity of the scheme. In some circumstances, particularly in relation to the use of Portland cement, modern adhesives may give increased flexibility, enough porosity and better reversibility than traditional materials.

Construction methods in the medieval period

Medieval floors in their original setting are not common in the UK, the first wave of disruption was during the dissolution of the monasteries, when many floors were removed and found their way into secular buildings, such as guildhalls or the homes of the wealthy. The second wave of destruction to medieval tile floors came during the late Victorian period, when many small churches were 'modernised' and many of our large cathedrals were 'restored' by Sir George Gilbert Scott (1811–78), St Alban's Cathedral being a case in point where many medieval tiles were removed to the British Museum to be replaced by tiles of the same design made by Herbert Minton.

Those high status pavements which remain in our cathedrals and abbeys are now treated with respect and are usually placed under the care of specialist buildings conservators. Intervention into the substrate is not usually undertaken without thorough analysis of all the factors surrounding the condition of the floor and the circumstances of proposed treatments. Treatment and care of one important medieval floor will not necessarily relate or have a bearing on the care of another because the circumstances of their history and location will not be the same.

Fortunately, however, the tiled refectory floor at Denny Abbey in Cambridge was excavated by archaeologists in the 1980s after remaining largely undisturbed for many generations. This lead to a set of

Figure 3.1
Tiles with footprint in the mortar, the
Refectory floor, Denny Abbey,
Cambridgeshire.

circumstances which permitted visual analysis of the original medieval
construction method. There are areas where tiles are lost but the
footprint of the tile remains in the mortar (Figure 3.1) and areas where
the whole substrate has fallen away or has been dug for drains in the
recent past revealing a cross-section of the mortar layers. The floor is
made up of four layers; the base is a beaten earth floor containing
stones and rubble in colour and texture closely resembling the surrounding landscape, indicating that no special material was brought in
as a subfloor. The first mortar layer is laid directly on to the earth floor
and is between 50 and 60 mm deep, it is a mix of lime and sand which
contains small stones and aggregate to about 50 per cent of its make-up.
The final layer of mortar into which the tiles are set is a fine sand and
lime mix with no aggregate and is between 5 and 10 mm deep. The
final layer is made up of the tiles which were pushed into the mortar
setting bed while still in a wet state. The visual evidence on this
particular floor suggests that the substrate layer was allowed to harden
before the setting bed layer was added (Figure 3.2).

The dimensions of medieval tiles suggest that they were never
intended to be grouted in their original setting. The surface face is
slightly larger in area than that of the underside. This enables the tiles
to be laid butted up closely together onto a bed of soft wet mortar.
Wet mortar can push up the side of the tile to hold it firm but not
appear on the surface area between tiles, providing extra adhesion
surfaces around all four sides of the tile as well as underneath.
However, because of the nature of the manufacturing process during
the medieval period, tiles were made only an approximation of a standard size and depth, thus occasionally creating spaces between tiles
when possibly it was intended that there should be none (Figure 3.3).

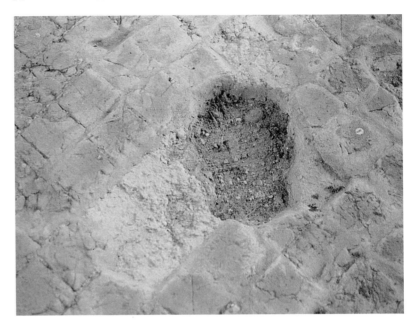

Figure 3.2
Tiles with mortar substrate and beaten earth floor, the Refectory floor, Denny Abbey, Cambridgeshire.

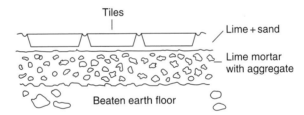

Figure 3.3
Diagram showing tile setting method.

Medieval tile floors are often laid with a diagonal format as the strongest feature. A diagonal format will more easily allow disparities in size to be absorbed successfully into the whole scheme than a square or offset format. Although borders and steps were tiled using a standard horizontal format. Medieval tilers also knew the value of combining single or double tramlines of straight rows at regular intervals in the diagonal pattern, such a format helps to tighten the scheme and prevent a spreading movement of the tiles (Figures 3.4 and 3.5).

Early lime mortar

Medieval tiles, whether in their original location or resited in post reformation Tudor buildings, are typically found set into lime mortar, if any other type of mortar is evident the implication would be that the tiles have been relocated or reset in the relatively recent past.

Figure 3.4
Diagonal formation with tramlines,
Guy's Tower, Warwick Castle.

Figure 3.5
Steps and border formation, the Lady
Chapel, Thetford Priory, Norfolk.

An indication of whether the tiles are contemporary or later additions to the fabric of the building can be determined by examination of the mortar used as tile adhesive and comparing it to the mortar used in the surrounding building. Laboratory analysis of ostensibly similar mortars could have an impact in correctly dating the constructional phases of a building. However, in the main, the reason for careful examination of the existing early mortar is to form a basis for replication in terms of strength, texture and colour.

Lime used for mortar was traditionally obtained by burning limestone (calcium carbonate $CaCO_3$) in kilns to produce pure or burnt lime (calcium oxide CaO); when submerged in quantities of water burnt lime liberates large amounts of heat and forms calcium hydroxide $(Ca(OH)_2)$ which is referred to as slaked lime. Slaked lime, also called lime putty, when mixed with sand (usually by volume, one part slaked lime to three or four parts sand) and water to make a paste becomes lime mortar and is used to bond brick, stone and tile in the construction of buildings. As a result of absorption of carbon dioxide and evaporation of water when exposed to the atmosphere the wet mix sets hard, initially over a period of seven to ten days and continues to harden further for up to two years.

The source of the sand used in the mix has tremendous importance for the resulting mortar; sand provides the structure to the mortar. The granular size of the sand will affect not only the texture of the mortar but also its setting capabilities. Granules should be angular or sharp and well mixed in size to give more surface area with which to react with the lime; however, if the sand is too course with smooth round granules the mortar becomes difficult to work, loses setting capability and cannot be used for finely bonded joints or detailed work. Sand inevitably contains impurities which greatly affect the natural ability of the mortar to set and its resulting strength and permeability. The source of the sand will also determine the natural colour of the finished mortar. Building techniques before the industrial revolution invariably included the use of sands which were locally obtained, therefore early lime mortars varied hugely from place to place or even within the same building at different phases. Historic mortars often contain traces of ash, coal or charcoal which may affect setting and permeability.

In some locations the locally available sand would not produce a set when added to lime; however, the practice of adding a pozzolan to the mix to induce a chemical reaction set has been used since Roman times. A pozzolan is an extra ingredient added to the mix in a variable and suitable ratio, typically 10 per cent to the volume of the mixed mortar, which is reactive with calcium hydroxide to induce a set. Pozzolan is a generic term used for a naturally occurring but added extra setting agent, it can be ground brick dust (course or fine), volcanic ash, or granulated blast furnace slag and various types of fuel ash among many other agents. Early building mortars are likely to contain pozzolans which are either no longer used, are specific to the geology of the area or are possibly unidentifiable because they are naturally occurring within the course aggregate added to the mix along with the sand.

Slaked lime putty mixed with sand with an added pozzolan may have been used for tile setting but because it has a very slow set that requires proximity to air it has disadvantages for tile use that could have made it less than satisfactory. It is more likely that early tile setters used a naturally occurring hydraulic lime mortar.

Natural hydraulic lime (NHL) is burnt lime with a naturally occurring high clay (or other form of reactive silicate) content which is activated in the burning process to produce a lime which has setting properties brought on by chemical reaction when mixed with water, similar to that of Portland cement. It does not rely on contact with the atmosphere to set hard as does lime putty. It also typically has a much faster setting time, usually between 24 and 48 hours but with a continuous hardening process for up to two years in some instances. Both necessary qualities required for setting tiles, the tile layer itself preventing contact with the air and the faster setting time providing confidence in the mortar to withstand the stresses of footfall. However, all burnt limes have varying degrees of natural hydraulicity, depending on source, which can only be determined with use.

As described above early tile setters used two types of lime mortar in conjunction to construct solidly built tile pavements. One is a course mix made of lime, course sand, and aggregate which was used as a bed (or substrate) onto which to set the tiles. The purpose of the bed was to level the floor and provide a hard foundation for the tiles. The second type was made of lime mixed with fine sand to provide a less hard but finer mortar (adhesive layer) with which to fix the tiles onto the substrate layer and enable detailed grouting where necessary.

Mortar mixes for resetting

Lime mortar is the recommended mortar for resetting medieval tiles. Lime mortar is relatively soft and if the correct ratio of lime to sand is observed the finished setting strength of the mortar will be less hard than the body of the tile. This will allow reversibility, permeability of moisture and air, and will accommodate minor structural movements. A mortar made with natural hydraulic lime (NHL) is more suitable for use with tile pavements than lime putty because it gives a chemical set in a faster time.

Natural hydraulic lime produced by modern, strictly controlled production methods is classified by European and British Standard BS EN 459 into three strength classifications determined by the optimum strength achieved in controlled conditions after 28 days. They are NHL2.0, NHL3.5 and NHL5.0, traditionally classified as 'feebly hydraulic', 'moderately hydraulic' and 'eminently hydraulic'. It should be noted that these classifications have been arrived at by mixing one part hydraulic lime with three parts sand (1:3) by weight rather than volume, the same mix by volume would approximately be one to one (1:1).

Ideally all mortar mixes used with medieval tiles should be tested for use first to make sure that the resulting set will be hard enough to withstand footfall but not too hard as to be irreversible without causing damage to the valuable tile. Two samples each of identical mixes should be prepared. Pieces of cut brick or earthenware tile of similar clay body density as the medieval tile may be substituted as test pieces. After 28 days the first sample should be tested. The tile substitute must be firmly adhered to the substrate but the mortar should give way easily from the edges of the substitute tile, using a small half inch chisel and hammer, without damage to the clay body of the tester piece. The second sample should be tested at 91 days to identify any changes that may have taken place.

Test mixes can begin with the following ratios which may be adjusted after testing, if necessary:

For the substrate bed, two parts by volume NHL3.5 to five parts well-graded course sand.

For the adhesive layer, two parts by volume NHL2 to five parts well-graded fine sand.

The mortar for the substrate bed can be harder than the mortar used as the adhesive layer.

The granule size, texture and colour of the sand is important. The granule size can be measured in simple fashion by using sieve mesh sizes 0.075 mm to 2.5 mm for fine graded sand. Course grade sand is measured with sieve mesh sizes 2.5 mm to 5 mm and above. Whether the sand is classified as course or fine it should be well graded, that is it should contain a varied mix of granule sizes within the parameters of its grade. The granules should be sharp rather than rounded, as sharp sand bonds better with the lime. The sand should be clean, free from salt, silt or clay content and other impurities. The colour of the sand should be compatible with the surrounding mortar. Traditionally the sand used for lime mortar will be a mix of 60 per cent well-graded sharp sand and 40 per cent local sand (if available to give a comparable colour match to the surrounding mortar). NHL2 may be mixed with all fine silver sand to make a fine mortar for grouting.

To achieve a good mix the dry ingredients should be thoroughly mixed together using a reliable set of volume gauges in order to achieve an even dispersion of lime and sand. The sand must not be too wet as this will affect the even dispersion of the added water. Water is then added while continuing to mix the ingredients until a suitable workability is achieved. The mix must not be too dry as this may prevent a good set, nor must it be too wet as this will result in shrinkage and cracking. The wet mortar should sit well on the trowel without slumping.

The adhesive layer for medieval tile pavements is usually relatively thick, anywhere between 5 and 15 mm, depending on the substrate. The substrate should be pre-wetted first with a fine mist spray, excess water should not pool on the surface. The mortar should be workable enough to push the tiles down into, allowing the wet mortar to be forced up the sides of the tiles forming a joint between tiles. Excess mortar on the surface of the tile must be wiped away immediately using a damp cloth. Once the tiles have been laid, the area should be kept slightly damp for about a week, usually by covering with damp cloths which allow the mortar to dry out fairly slowly. However, it should be noted that too much moisture introduced within the body of a medieval tile can precipitate the growth of salt crystals which is to be avoided; overwetting an area is undesirable.

Construction methods in the seventeenth and eighteenth centuries

In England the occurrence of Dutch or English delft tiles in their original location is fairly uncommon. Delft tiling, which had largely been utilitarian in nature, fell out of favour in the nineteenth century under the impact of mass produced tiles from the centres of manufacturing

Figure 3.6
Eighteenth century fireplace tiles, flower motifs, Drapers Hall, Shrewsbury.

Figure 3.7
Carshalton Water Tower, Surrey.

in Stoke on Trent and Jackfield which used new mechanised techniques to produce considerably more choice of style and design for the consumer. Delft tiles in the kitchens and dairies of large houses were mostly stripped away and replaced with the new, stronger, more robust and more uniform tiles pouring out of the factories. The ubiquitous nineteenth century cast iron fireplace or cooking range took the place of less efficient open fires with built-in cooking paraphernalia which may also have included delft tiles as part of their scheme. Consequently only a few of those places which resisted or were overlooked by the march of industrialisation retained their delft tiling in its original location.

Nevertheless there are many good examples of delft tiles used as decoration for fireplaces in eighteenth century houses, more often in the large entrance halls, anti-rooms, or servants rooms rather than main drawing or dining room fireplaces. Often set as vertical runs of two or three tiles immediately either side of the fireplace surrounded by a decorative mantlepiece. The popular choice of decoration was individual tile designs following a theme such as ships, birds, flowers or religious themes. (Figure 3.6).

However, one of the most stunning uses of interior delft tile decoration in the UK is to be found at Carshalton Water Tower in Surrey; the 'bagnio' or bathroom is part of a suite of entertainment rooms built by Sir John Fellowes in his garden in the early eighteenth century. Fellowes, a member of the 'nouveau riche' society whose wealth came from trade and investment in the City of London, built the water tower, which was designed by Charles Bridgeman, as a focal point in his garden, primarily for entertainment, although the water pump also provided water for nearby Carshalton village. The bath itself is fairly large even by modern standards at 328 cm by 258 cm and 137 cm deep, and is lined around all sides with plain tin glazed tiles. Each wall of the bathroom is lined from floor to ceiling with an elegant scheme of tall, narrow panels of plain tiles surrounded by tiles decorated with blue flower vases in a manganese 'powder ground' frame (Figure 3.7). The flower vase designs are arranged schematically, according to type, around the panels indicating that pre-established quantities were ordered from the factory. The tile setting is of extraordinarily high quality, showing off the three niches in the east wall to their best effect (Figure 3.8). Every decorated tile which forms the curved surround at the niche heads is perfectly cut to size, while the covering of the inner curves comprises perfectly cut and tightly placed plain tiles (Figure 3.9). Each tile has been rubbed to size, probably on a stone, in much the same way soft brick was rubbed to form decorative elements of eighteenth century brickwork (Figure 3.10). Dutch made tiles were favoured over English made tiles for their ability to be shaped more accurately due to the softer body. The indication is that the work was carried out by a master

Figure 3.8
The niches, Carshalton Water Tower, Surrey.

Figure 3.9
Rubbed tiles, the niches, Carshalton Water Tower, Surrey.

Figure 3.10
Rubbed tiles, the niches, Carshalton Water Tower, Surrey.

craftsman, not necessarily a tile setter but possibly one of the celebrated Flemish craftsmen bricklayers who were popularly brought over by the very wealthy to carry out the fashionable and finest brickwork of the time, under the direction of an architect or designer.

The whole effect is one of superior quality and echoes Queen Mary's Candied Fruit Cellar at Hett Loo Palace, Appeldorn in Holland. However, Sir John is more likely to have been familiar with the Queen's Dairy at nearby Hampton Court Palace designed by Daniel Morot for Queen Mary in similar style, which is no longer in existence.

Fixing methods and materials in the seventeenth and eighteenth centuries

The method of fixing used for late seventeenth and eighteenth century tiles was fairly unsophisticated and not particularly robust. Tiles from this era, which are the ones most commonly found in Britain, are made of a relatively soft body clay, and are consequently highly porous, light in weight and usually quite thin, 6 to 7 mm thick. The mortars historically used for fixing delft tiles are either fine lime plaster or gypsum plaster, usually between 1 and 2 cm thick and adhered onto brick or stone (Figure 3.11). The sand content of these plasters is very low and of very fine grain size, if used in the mix at all. It had a propensity towards shrinkage and cracking and will often be found to be very fragile or have failed.

Gypsum is a naturally occurring mineral, widely used in plaster and cement in the construction industry. When heat treated to 128 degrees centigrade it converts into plaster of Paris. Plaster of Paris reacts swiftly when mixed with water to form hard blocks of gypsum plaster.

Figure 3.11
Eighteenth century mortar substrate,
Carshalton Water Tower, Surrey.

The adhesion was made using the principle of moisture absorption. The brick or stone surface onto which the tiles were to be fixed may have been pre-wetted depending on the absorption rate of the material. The tiles were kept completely dry, the soft body clay having a very rapid absorption rate. The evidence suggests that wet lime plaster was applied to the wall in a fairly thick layer, about 15 mm, and the tile quickly pushed into place in the wet plaster. Water is immediately pulled from the wet plaster into the tile forming a bond.

Both Dutch and English tiles usually had an inward chamfered edge, if the chamfer was not built in during the manufacturing process then the tile setter would bevel the edges of the tiles with a stone before setting. The bevel allowed the wet plaster to push up the sides of the tiles to aid adhesion.

The method was haphazard and not especially robust. Frequently tiles were not flat, another reason for the overall haphazard effect often seen as part and parcel of delft tile schemes. Occasionally fireplace tiles were made up as panels. The tiles were probably placed face down adjacent to each other on a board or table with a roughly made timber frame surrounding the panel. The reverse of the tiles was coated in wet plaster, laid down fairly thickly, between 2 and 3 cm deep, and lengths of scrap wrought iron were pushed into the plaster to form strengthening bars. When set the panels were removed from their temporary timber frames, the panels turned and cleaned of any excess plaster, then fixed into place beside the fire in wrought iron frames. Ironwork used as internal support is usually detectable by the presence of iron staining through the plaster.

Mortar and resetting for seventeenth and eighteenth century tiles

It may be necessary to remove tiles from their original setting. The grip formed by plaster made up of lime or gypsum used in the manner described is not usually tenacious, soaking the area with water will cause the plaster to swell and soften, facilitating removal.

The traditional method of fixing as described above can be easily replicated using plaster of Paris. The plaster of Paris provides a very fast chemical set which will provide additional bonding to that provided by absorption. However, there are many different grades of density and setting times for casting plaster available, so again testing the materials beforehand is time well spent. Traditional, very low density, potters casting plaster has high porosity and low shrinkage which makes it suitable for use. Some modern casting plasters used in the dental profession and the modern pottery industry have been developed to be extremely hard with high density, but are best avoided as their relative strength and hardness compared with the tile will be too high, making the system irreversible. The plaster used as an adhesive for fixing delftware tiles must not be stronger or harder than the body of the tile itself.

We have seen that the traditional method was not an especially robust or long lived fixing method, it can also result in a somewhat haphazard overall finish, a suitable visual aesthetic in an historic setting, but not always acceptable in all situations. Collections of eighteenth century tiles are quite often relocated into new settings which require a much more reliable adhesive that will allow the tiles to perform the function intended and at the same time be reversible.

Modern ready-to-use pot tile adhesives used by professional tile fixers, but also found in do-it-yourself stores, make a useful alternative fixing system if carefully chosen and used sparingly. Non-water resistant acrylic-based adhesives may be used to fix historic tiles but should not to be confused with water resistant adhesives which should never be used on historic tiles.

Non-water resistant tile adhesives are, typically, viscous pastes based on an acrylic copolymer binder with organic rheology modifiers and inorganic fillers, the fillers providing the bulk and the structure to the mix. The mineral filler may be composed of a blend of different fillers chosen by the manufacturers for reasons of performance and cost. To ensure reversibility, the adhesive should be used sparingly onto demountable plasterboard panels. A small amount of adhesive on each corner of the tiles is enough to secure it to the plaster board. To reverse the system, thoroughly soak the area with water to soften and expand both the adhesive and the plasterboard substrate, carefully lifting the tiles only when there is no resistance. Product data sheets can be obtained from manufacturers which will identify the most suitable adhesives.

Short case study

During 2002 conservation and restoration works were carried out at the Carshalton bath house, the restoration consisted of rebuilding a number of fragmented tiles in order to reset them in their correct locations within the scheme. Alongside this work, one of the wall panels was recognised as being unstable, inasmuch as it was no longer securely fixed to its plaster bed resulting in a significant bulging out from the surface plane, though each tile remained adhered to its neighbour both by force of pressure and the plaster grout between each tile. In order to resecure the area, which was in imminent danger of collapse, the complete panel of tiles was first securely taped in position, in order to avoid a mass fall when the tension which held the tiles together was broken. The centre tile was carefully removed using an electrically operated oscillating diamond blade to cut the grout bond around the tile. The width of the blade was 1.3 mm, fine enough to avoid damage to the edges of the tile (Figure 3.12). Once the central tile had been removed, the remaining loose tiles were carefully lifted away until tiles which were fully adhered onto a sound substrate were reached.

Using the oscillating diamond blade the plaster substrate was cut through back to the brickwork around the inside edge of the area, in order to completely separate it from the rest of the structure, thus making it safe to knock away the old plaster. All of the loose substrate material was removed. The next stage was to consolidate the inside edges of the area. The edges of the tiles and plaster were first dampened to facilitate extra absorption and then painted using a 40 to 60 per cent solution of conservation grade poly (vinyl acetate) emulsion and water in order to bond loose or fragile pieces of the substrate to the edges of the remaining tiles. After cleaning the edges and backs of the lifted tiles by first softening the mortar in distilled water and then removing the

Figure 3.12
The central tile removed after taping the surrounding tiles safely in position.

mortar mechanically with a sharp blade, they were refixed using low density grade potter's casting plaster as described. Casting plaster has a fast setting time, so small amounts of fresh plaster were mixed for every one or two tiles fixed to avoid excessive wastage. The same plaster was used as a grouting material, but with added pigment to match the colour of the surrounding original grout.

Construction methods in the nineteenth and early twentieth centuries

The nineteenth century tile manufacturers possessed what was essentially a new, mass produced product which they wished to be used in the best possible ways both functionally and decoratively without failure. Tiles produced by different manufacturers could differ quite dramatically in terms of quality and precision, which in turn affected the quality and precision of the setting. Geometric floor tile setting was a new technology in the early years of mass production with no established conventions concerning joints or finishing. Forward thinking manufacturers published advice on the recommended methods for setting their tiles; however, much of the information given was fairly loosely specified and more open to interpretation than we have come to expect from manufacturer's technical advice services and product data information today, leaving much room for error or manoeuvre on the part of the tile setter, again to suit his skills, available materials and location. It is not far from the truth to say that no two schemes were fixed alike because the available skills and the conditions in which those skills were applied to a variety of materials and locations will rarely be replicated. It is not until after the late 1950s that we begin to see uniform and precise methods of tile setting which match, and are appropriate to, the uniformity in production quality which is the hallmark of modern tile manufacture.

The steady rise of Victorian tile manufacture began in 1840 and reached its zenith between 1880 and 1900. At the same time, though probably linked more closely to the expansion of the brick making industry than tile manufacture, the first modern Portland cement was manufactured in 1845 and was in widespread use by about 1880. Victorian buildings decorated with tiles prior to 1860 can be typically found to have either lime plaster or lime mortar used as the adhesive layer. Post 1870 the tile industry moved wholesale into the use of Portland cement as a medium for fixing and grouting tiles, and it is unusual to find any other medium used, but during the intervening decade either types of mortar can be found.

The tile manufacturers were not slow to recognise the positive attributes of Portland cement as a fixative. It did not stain as readily as traditional lime mortar, an advantage when setting polychromatic tile schemes, and was a hard, robust, durable adhesive which gave a faster, more reliable set than traditional lime mortars. The new geometric floor tiles were manufactured in much smaller size units than old style quarry tiles, making them more likely to become unseated easily if the adhesive mortar was insufficiently hard.

The 1870 recommendations from *Directions for Laying the Pavements*, Maw & Co. catalogue, include the use of lime in the cement which is to be used as the adhesive layer:

> A cement composed of a mixture of Lias and Portland is specially manufactured for our tile work, and can be supplied in casks or sacks, but either Lias, Portland or roman cement of good quality may be used. Either of the above cements may be mixed with about one third of its bulk of good sharp sand. No cement that is very quick setting is suitable, as it does not afford sufficient time for the proper adjustment of the tiles.
>
> Sand employed for the mixing of cement should be sharp and free from loam.

These somewhat ambiguous instructions seem to describe a strong mix of two parts of cement to one part of sand. Experience, for the most part, re-enforces this description as Victorian tile floors from that period are generally found to be laid on a hard cement subfloor. The depth of the cement adhesive required is set out specifically thus:

> Preparation of the Foundation. If the foundation is not sufficiently solid, lay, as evenly as possible, a bed of concrete, composed of one part finely riddled quick lime, and three of gravel, and bring it to a perfectly level surface with a thin coat of cement allowing three eighths of an inch more than the thickness of the tiles for the cement to be used for bedding them. In tiles of half an inch substance, the level surface of foundation should be brought to within three fourths to seven eights of an inch of the intended surface of the pavement, and for tiles of an inch substance to within one and a quarter inches of the intended surface.

Maw & Co. specified 'finely riddled quick lime' because lime was not always pre-slaked for long periods to form lime putty before use; a common technique was to place the amount of raw burnt lime, still in lump form, which was estimated for use the following day onto the ground and surround it with a ring of sand. A small amount of water was sprinkled onto the lime causing it to react, breaking down the lumps into powder form. While the reaction was still taking place the lime was covered with a layer of sand and left until the next day when further sand, aggregate and water would be added to the mix to make a wet mortar. This technique often resulted in lumps of inadequately slaked lime to be left within the mortar which could continue to react long after the mortar had been laid as substrate. It was this possibility which the tile manufacturers regarded as less than satisfactory.

By 1904, W.J. Furnival, taking direct advice from published material by the Tile Manufacturers of the United States of America, November 1900, completely rejects the use of lime in the cement used for floor tile setting:

> A good foundation is always necessary and should be both solid and perfectly level. Tiles should always be laid on a concrete foundation, prepared from the best quality Portland cement, clean sharp sand and gravel, or other hard material. Cinders should never be used as they destroy the quality of the cement. A foundation may be formed using brick or tile imbedded solidly in, and covered with cement mortar. Lime mortar should never be mixed with concreting. Concrete should be allowed to thoroughly harden before laying the floor, and should be well soaked with water before laying the tile. Concrete should consist of:
>
> 1 Portland cement
> 2 Clean sharp sand
> 3 Clean gravel
>
> thoroughly mixed with sufficient water to form a hard solid mass when well beaten down into a bed two and one half inches to three inches thick. The surface of the concrete must be level and finished to within one inch of the finished floor line, when tile one half inch thick is used, which will leave a space of one half inch for cement mortar, composed of equal parts of the very best quality Portland cement and clean sharp sand.

The formation of the substrate layers below tiles on upper floors or ground floors above basements will largely depend on the structure of the building itself. Steel joists and concrete floor structures were becoming more common at the end of the Victorian period, but most buildings that were tiled from the middle to the end of the nineteenth century have traditional timber joist structures for upper floors. The following extract, again from Furnival, usefully describes what we may be likely to find as substrate under tiles from that period:

> Wood floors in upper stories may be readily replaced with mosaic, the foundation being prepared by nailing fillets to the joists at three inches from the upper surface, and the floor boards sawn into short lengths and fitted in between the joists upon the fillets; concrete may then be filled in flush with the upper face of the joists and faced with the coat of cement before mentioned. (Figure 3.13)

Pure Portland cement, with no added sand, mixed with water to a creamy consistency was recommended as a grouting medium for both wall and floor tiles. Furnival also describes, courtesy of the Tile Manufacturers

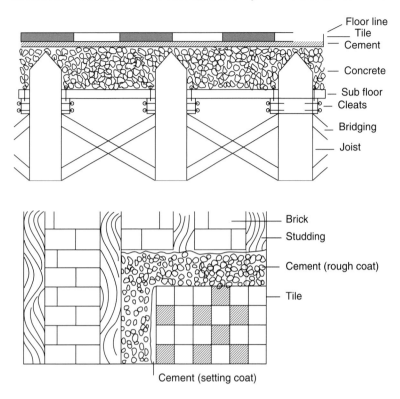

Figure 3.13
Diagram nineteenth century floor substrate, Furnival.

Figure 3.14
Diagram nineteenth century wall substrate, Furnival.

of the United States of America, detailed methods for wall tile fixing; there are some slight differences in the fixing methods and the ratios of the mortar mixes to those given for floor tiles. It is advised that new brickwork should not be pointed, or if the brickwork is old then the pointing should be removed in order to create a key into the brickwork. A rough coating of cement about one half inch thick, mixed from one part Portland cement to two parts of sand, should cover the bricks and be allowed to harden for at least one day (Figure 3.14).

Fixing the wall tiles comprised of three stages. First, to ensure a good bond, the rough foundation should be coated with a mix of pure cement and water. The setting coat or adhesive layer is added immediately to a further half inch depth, the ratio for the setting coat is one part Portland cement to two parts sand mixed to a stiff consistency. The advisers concede that if lime must be added to the mix it must be no more than 10 per cent, and point out emphatically that all tiles should be soaked in water prior to setting, to help the cement to unite with the tiles. Extra assistance towards fixing was provided by the manufacturers with the development of sometimes quite elaborate back stamps, which not only identified the manufacturer but also acted as a key into the wet cement.

The same mix of 2:1 of sand and Portland cement used for setting the tiles was also used as the grout, providing a seamless adhesive

Figure 3.15
Mid-nineteenth century tile scheme, Terrace Restaurant, House of Commons, London.

layer which not only coated the back of the tile fixing it to the floor or wall, but also fixed the edges of the tile to the edge of its neighbour, effectively bonding all surfaces except the face.

The fixing methods described seemed to have been used as standard practice by builders and tile setters from the mid-1870s up until the late 1950s, with very little deviation. In the 1950s new, more user friendly, adhesive preparations began to be developed. However, though the new style adhesives and grouts were user friendly many ready mixed pot adhesives were not necessarily beneficial for the longevity of tile schemes. Some adhesives were epoxy resin based and therefore impermeable to water and extremely hard resulting in many of the same problems associated with Portland cement.

Among Augustus Welby Northmore Pugin's (1812–52) many other achievements and influence was his role in encouraging Henry Minton to develop the first block printed tiles for use as interior wall decoration. One of their early collaborations is to be found in what was the Stranger's Smoking Room, which is now the Terrace Restaurant in the House of Commons, London. The scheme is colourful and has an energy and balance typical of Pugin's design work; however, it is comprised solely of flat, square or rectangular tiles used in a manner differing very little from the style in which tiling had been used over the previous two centuries in continental Europe. The tiles are fixed to dado height in simple fashion, the decorative effect being derived from the placing of the ground and border designs, while the edging and finishing is made up with simple half round plaster mouldings and a deep timber skirting board (Figure 3.15).

As the incongruity of any large expanse of wall tiling mixed with timber dado rails and skirting became apparent, an almost inevitable

Figure 3.16
Typical late nineteenth century tile
scheme, Church Tavern, Birmingham.

Figure 3.17
Typical late nineteenth century tile
scheme, Church Tavern, Birmingham.

consequence was the need to develop moulded ceramic tiles to form
a termination or framework for schemes. The development of semi-
constructional mouldings to form not only skirtings and dado rails
but corner beading, architrave, friezes, arches, columns and the like,
moved forward until any typical large interior scheme would include
a complete architectural framework for the main body of the tile wall
covering, built entirely from a range of different tile mouldings, shapes,
sizes and colours.

Many schemes follow a similar and recognisable format. Dados are
often made up of elaborately embossed tiles in panel format, the
panels being surrounded by combinations of different coloured, offset,
rectangular, slip tiles, topped by moulded capping tiles which form
the dado rail and are finished by deeply moulded skirtings at floor
level. The over-dado work is often to ceiling height, usually more simply constructed of 6 inch × 6 inch tiles set in diagonal fashion, and
more often than not finished with a flourish of deeply embossed and
elaborate friezes and entablatures (Figures 3.16–3.18).

Victorian floor tile designs tend to follow fairly strict ruling principles; diagonal central panels surrounded by deep borders of parallel

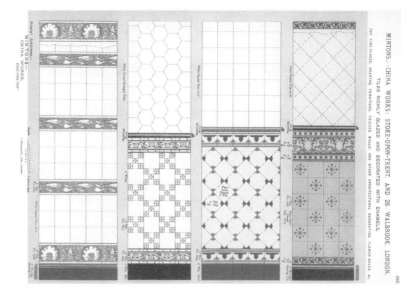

Figure 3.18
Minton's of Stoke on Trent tile
catalogue circa 1870.

offset tiles. Certain tile measurements lend themselves to use in diagonal format to create the base measurement of a 6 inch × 6 inch square, they are: 4½ inch, 3 inch, 2⅛ inch, 1½ inch, frequently the 4½ inch tile will be patterned encaustic, or a star motif made up of small tiles (Figure 3.19).

Hotels were often sumptuous in their decoration while the most flamboyant schemes found their natural homes in the richly decorated interiors of the ubiquitous 'gin palaces' (Figure 3.20). Design of interior tile work in national and urban municipal buildings was often the preserve of architects.

It sometimes seems as though the Victorian imagination for using tiles knew no limits, from the starkly utilitarian interiors of workhouses or pumping stations, through schools, hospitals, railway stations, and shops to some of the most magnificently decorated interiors of our most important national buildings. The nineteenth century tile heritage with its beginnings in the UK and spreading the world over is a tremendously rich one, and although a good deal of it has been lost in the latter part of the twentieth century, much of it still remains in place and in relatively good repair.

Problems connected with the early use of Portland cement

The use of Portland cement as a fixative for floor and wall tiles was eventually adopted wholesale by builders and tile setters, but even as early as 1891 at a meeting of the Royal Society of Arts a Mr H. Stannus remarked: 'The wall should be well settled before the work was begun, otherwise it would be almost certain to crack and spoil the design.' At the same meeting, discussion also centred around the

Figure 3.19
Geometric floor designs (Furnival).

necessity of walls being completely dry before the application of tiled decoration after a Mr C. Baskett related an experience of decoration to a damp church wall being destroyed within a few months. Both men's experiences highlight the most common problems, associated directly with the use of Portland cement as an adhesive for tiles, which the conservator will encounter.

Portland cement is a harder material than the ceramic tile body to which it is adhered. Also the determination, which the best tile fixers applied to obtaining a strong adhesion, ensures that the bond

Figure 3.20
Interior staircase, the Barton Arms,
Birmingham.

between tile and cement is very strong, therefore any shifting or
movement in the building, either sooner or later, will result in fracturing of the tile along the same fault lines and cracks in the Portland
cement. If the same problems of movement or shifting occur in walls
where lime mortar has been used as an adhesive, in many instances
the tile will be sufficiently hard and the mortar sufficiently weak to
withstand the shift. The bond between the tile and the mortar will be
the weakest point, and will mostly be the point at which the bond will
break, allowing the tiles to become loose. This scenario can have
problems of its own, of course, but if dealt with swiftly is far less damaging and difficult to rectify than severe fracturing of tiles and cement.

Portland cement is similarly unforgiving when it comes to water penetration. Flooding of tile surfaces, for whatever reasons, leaking roofs,
burst pipes etc. can result in water dispersion through and under the
tile; cement is a non-porous material so water is unable to get away,
forcing expansion between the tile and the cement. If tiles are under
tension, once the adhesion is broken the tiles can be forced upwards
ultimately causing volatile fracturing (Figure 3.21). Lime mortar, on the
other hand, is more able to absorb excessive amounts of water with
less likelihood of the adhesion suffering; if, however, the adhesion
does fail, then tensions are more easily taken up across the floor
or wall.

Tiles used externally, usually found on commercial retail premises,
have often suffered badly with the passage of time as a result of the

Figure 3.21
Damage caused to tiles under tension by floodwater, the Hallway, Osgoode Hall, Toronto.

use of Portland cement as an adhesive. Moisture is absorbed into the body of the tile and trapped by the Portland cement adhesive layer; the 'freeze thaw cycle' and the different thermal expansion rates of the glaze, clay body and cement cause a separation between two or all three of those elements resulting in delamination of the glaze surface, and fracturing and falling away of whole or part tiles from the cement layer (Figure 3.22). External tiles which have survived unscathed have done so only because their location is frost protected in some way.

Mortars and adhesives for resetting nineteenth and early twentieth century tiles

As we see nineteenth century sources recommended mixes for setting tiles with ratios of sand to cement which gave a particularly dense, non-porous, and hard final set. Nevertheless during the same period many technicians used an all-purpose building mortar mix, one part Portland cement, one part hydrated lime to six parts well-graded sharp sand, for general construction purposes other than tile setting; the cement to sand ratio recommended by the tile manufacturers was exceedingly hard by comparison. Hydrated lime is calcium hydroxide in powdered form and is produced by the controlled slaking of quick lime with steam or minimum amounts of water. It is generally much less reactive than lime putty and it is non-hydraulic.

The hardness, non-reversibility and sometimes damaging effects of historically correct cement and sand mixes as recommended by the nineteenth century tile manufacturers, and which found widespread use, present the conservator of Victorian floor and wall tiles with the dilemma of using the historically correct mix which will replace like with like, or changing the adhesive mix to ratios closer to those acknowledged in

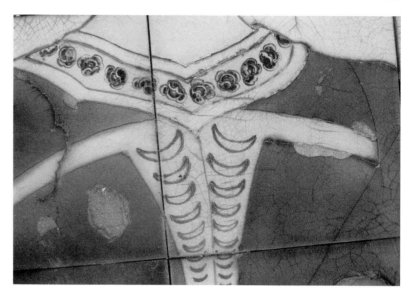

Figure 3.22
Delamination caused by frost
penetration.

conservation building practice as being more permeable and forgiving, or even introducing modern adhesives. Both of which would give greater effectiveness of flexibility and ability to 'breath', i.e the easier transference of moisture and air through the material, which Portland cement is notably lacking.

Prior to the introduction of Portland cement most tiles were set using lime mortars in some form. The main concern for the conservator when resetting early period tiles is to develop a lime mortar mix, whether it be hydraulic or lime putty with an added pozzolan, of a corresponding strength of adhesive bond and length of time in which the 'set' takes place which will match with the surrounding mortar – in other words to replace the original adhesive layers with ones which closely resemble and meld with the original mortar, as far as possible. NHL3.5 for walls and NHL5 for floors mixed with suitable sand ratios will generally give good results. When making patch repairs within an existing scheme this is particularly important because if the new mortar which has been introduced is significantly harder or softer than the surrounding mortar then any subsequent external movement stress will cause fracturing at the point where the two mortars join.

While the mortar must not be allowed to dry out too quickly, which would cause shrinkage and cracking, neither should it be too slow to dry out. An environment where humidity is too high will prolong the drying out stage and cause the lime to leach through the body of the tile and result in staining of the surface.

There are a number of reasons why the use of Portland cement in the ratios recommended and used by nineteenth century tile setters is not in line with current conservation practice, which stresses reversibility and the use of non-damaging materials in association with historic fabric. The hardness of Portland cement renders it unforgiving and therefore subject to fracturing under stress. It is irreversible – historic tiles cannot be successfully removed from Portland cement without a high risk of damage to the ceramic material. Some of the problems which can be caused by the relative inability of Portland cement to absorb and disperse water have also been previously noted. The use of Portland cement, in the ratios used in the past, will effectively store up problems, leaving the ceramic threatened in the future.

When resetting nineteenth and early twentieth century tiles it is necessary to avoid adhesives which could, because of their inherent properties, directly threaten the future of the ceramic. The threats are identified as fracturing, delamination, and irreversibility. However, new mortar or adhesive must have enough qualities of adhesion to be relevant in a working building. New mortar should have some flexibility, to allow for thermal expansion and natural movement, for example traffic vibration or constant footfall. Nineteenth and early twentieth century tiles are almost always close set, sometimes referred to as 'butt jointed', with no allowance for expansion; a flexible mortar will help to overcome the lack of expansion joints in extensive schemes. It must allow a degree of moisture absorption, and should also be weaker than the ceramic body, in order to avoid severe damage if subjected to flooding, frost or movement stresses caused by subsidence or settling. Finally it should have a provision for reversibility which would safeguard the tiles during future relocation. There is no single adhesive which has all of these qualities and can be applied to any environment and location.

Considered use of modern materials can overcome some of these problems. Many good quality tile adhesives now contain a mixture of Portland cement (usually 30 per cent), sand (usually 50 per cent) with the addition of 20 per cent of other non-organic or organic additives which give greater workability and plasticity. Rubber or latex granules are also added in some instances to give flexibility. Provided water resistant epoxy resin-based mixtures are avoided, most are moisture permeable; however, they are not weak enough to be easily reversible. Product data sheets will usually indicate if an adhesive is a Portland cement and sand mix with additives, and most reliable manufacturers will have technical advice departments with whom to discuss whether it is possible to weaken the adhesive properties of a standard product with the addition of a little extra fine sand, thereby bringing it more into line with the reversible conservation materials ethic. While product manufacturers will never directly advocate the adulteration of their product, some advisers are sympathetic to the needs of conservation and will co-operate with advice on running your own tests for adhesion and strength.

An element of reversibility can be introduced into the substrate layer by, in the case of wall schemes, setting the tiles onto either a plaster or plasterboard substrate at least 10 mm in depth, thereby introducing a sacrificial layer in between the tile and the structural wall. The same system will reduce problems caused by building subsidence or movement because the plaster will provide the weakest layer of substrate material which will take up any stresses.

Similarly floor tiles can be reset using the same principle; a standard manufactured Portland cement and sand floor tile adhesive with additives to give flexibility set onto a substrate made up with a weak mix of low cement to high sand ratio. Tests for strength and adhesion using various mixes and products are very important prior to resetting floor tiles. A balance needs to be found between reversibility and flexibility, and a robust fixative to hold the tiles in place under the strain of continuous footfall.

When making patch repairs into original tile and Portland cement floors, compatibility with the original mortar is an important factor, otherwise the eventual likely result is a failed bond between the repair work and the surrounding floor. The Portland cement element of the original mortar cannot be ignored in favour of traditional lime mortar because the difference in structure and strength between the two is too great. The traditional, all-purpose mix as used in much nineteenth century construction work is a good compromise. A good starting ratio for testing a mortar mix for use as both an adhesive and substrate is one part Portland cement, one part hydrated lime, and six parts well-graded sand mixed with a little water. The addition of a hydrated lime into the mix along with a reduction in the amount of Portland cement and an increase in the amount of sand used will give a degree of flexibility and porosity which is absent in late Victorian and early twentieth century tile setting mortars.

The area into which the tiles are to be fixed must be clean and free from loose debris, dust and grease, and should be pre-wetted with a fine spray mist of clean water. To test the ratio prior to general use, fix two or three substitute, but of the same quality, tiles into the edge of your repair area, and allow 24 hours for the mortar to set. If the mix is successful, the tiles should be adequately fixed to the substrate and the adjacent tiles, but at the same time they should be removable without damage using a hammer and chisel. If the tiles come away too easily, reduce the amount of sand in the mix. Mixes for the substrate can be tested in much the same way. Many Victorian floor tile schemes will include very small geometric components which are particularly susceptible to loosening if the adhesive mix is too weak simply because their surface area for adhesion is small.

It is important to remember that lime was not a favoured material for tile setting from the 1870s onwards. It had a tendency to stain the coloured clays used in geometric floor tiles and the alkaline properties of lime were not compatible with and could adversely affect some glaze colours, particularly those in the red range, so its use as mortar for late Victorian tiles is limited.

There are one or two other important points to make concerning resetting Victorian floor tiles. If a sand and cement mix is chosen as a fixing medium, floor tiles should be soaked in water and the substrate kept damp just prior to laying. If a manufactured adhesive is used then soaking the tiles and substrate may not be necessary, the reverse policy of keeping the tiles and area dry is the most likely scenario. Furthermore tiles made in the nineteenth century up until the 1930s are rarely uniform in size. Tiles which are ostensibly the same can vary by as much as 3 mm in size, so it is very important to lay out a dummy run of tiles before fixing to establish where the best places for wide or narrow joints between the tiles should occur to allow the design or pattern of the tiles to be properly established, this is particularly true of decorative wall panels. All architectural schemes contain areas where tiles have been, often fairly crudely, trimmed to fit odd shapes or dimensions during their original fixing. It is important to look for these anomalies and either replicate or allow for them when refixing.

If damaged or worn tiles have been removed from within a larger floor or wall area, the tension which existed within the scheme will be broken; this allows the surrounding tile area to relax causing some movement. As a result the space from which the tiles have been removed will measure less than the same area while the tiles were still in place. Consequently new tiles may have to be trimmed to fit to suit the geometry of the scheme.

Previous generations of tile fixers were often far from perfect in the execution of their trade. Chapter 7 includes a detailed case study of two phases of repair to historic floors carried out at Osgoode Hall in Toronto.

Conclusion

Many readers who are familiar with the practices of conservation building techniques may find it strange that lime mortar is not recommended as an adhesive for tiles in all circumstances; there are a number of good reasons for this. One of the advantages of using lime as a mortar for constructing brick or stone walls is its ability to act as a flexible and forgiving cushion to accommodate structural movement, with a greater or lesser degree of adhesion of mortar to brick depending on the type of lime mortar in use. However, when fixing wall tiles the degree of adhesion becomes a crucial issue when choosing a mortar, for the obvious reason that tiles must stay fixed to avoid possible serious damage caused by impact or fracture. Lime mortar requires a controlled drying out or curing time in order to avoid shrinkage and cracking, the risk of cracks appearing in the mortar behind the tiles during the drying period would seriously weaken the overall structure. It should also be remembered that historic tiling relies on design rather than uniformity for its visual impact. Joints between tiles are almost never of a regular width, it is therefore very important that the precise position in the scheme into which a tile is placed in the wet mortar should not be prone to slumping or twisting during drying thus spoiling the geometry and spacing of the design.

With care and attention to detail all of these problems can be relatively easily overcome when fixing floor tiles, as long as complete confidence in the ability of lime mortar to hold and not fail under the repeated stresses and impact of footfall can be assured. The use of lime mortar for resetting historic nineteenth century geometric floor tiles can also result in lime staining in the coloured clay body of the tile (something the manufacturers were anxious to avoid) if the drying period is too prolonged. Church floors can be particularly problematic on that score if the humidity levels within the floor and its substrate are high. Lime staining can be difficult to remove without recourse to acid-based cleaning products though the visual impact of staining will decrease over a period of time.

4 Principals of conservation for architectural tile schemes

Introduction

The centuries old manufacturing history of tiles has ensured that they have often been considered to be so numerous and sometimes commonplace that the most recent examples of their development have usually been regarded as disposable. Additionally techniques of mass production have often left the individual object underappreciated, resulting over the centuries in the loss of the greater mass of ceramic tile material from successive ages of manufacture. A notable exception are the tiles made by William de Morgan at the end of the nineteenth century, which have, rightly so, always been regarded as individual works of ceramic art. In this short chapter I hope to explore the different ways in which, both in the UK and the USA, the principles of conservation ethics, as applied to the built environment rather than the moveable object, can be approached given the range of periods, variations in basic clays and glazes, and diversity of locations and applications, found under the umbrella title of 'architectural tile scheme'.

The society of the middle ages across Europe and the Middle East used tile decoration as an expression of wealth. The material itself, fired earth combined with metal oxide glazes, was cheap and easily available but high standards in craftsmanship and technology were admired. Palaces and temples from Persia to the Iberian peninsula and monasteries and cathedrals across northern Europe where often lavishly decorated in these humble artefacts which could, in skilled hands, become startling in their range of colour and artistry. Throughout the seventeenth and eighteenth centuries, though the technology of tile making had changed relatively little since the middle ages, the Persian style of tile making and decoration moved west through southern Europe and up to the low countries to replace the art of encaustic floor tile making, which although highly prized in early medieval times in northern Europe had fallen into complete decline and was largely lost. By the end of the eighteenth century tin glazed wall tiles were relatively commonplace and the plain tin glazed surface of the tile had become a medium of expression for artistic and painterly endeavour which produced a continuing tradition of beautifully hand painted decoration within a limited palette of colours.

The nineteenth century was the great age of industry and technology, reflected within tile manufacturing in the dramatic diversity in form and colour of tiles available for use in every sphere of the built environment. Tiles were used functionally as well as decoratively, and decoration could be the simple or lavish use of colour combined with mass produced or highly individual design. The technology of production in tiles at the end of the nineteenth century remained much the same up until the mid-twentieth century; however, a much greater importance began to be placed on changing fashions in design with innovations in style taking place virtually every decade. Production technology was revolutionised throughout the later part of the twentieth century with computer generated kiln technology and design enabling fast and ever changing fashions and designs to be at the forefront of an industry creating a disposable product. As with all mediums, however, alongside the mass produced there exists many, many examples of handmade, artist designed and executed tile art. Consequently the value of almost any individual tile or scheme, in terms of continuing conservation, can be found somewhere in the provenance of architecture, design and technology, or culture, art and society.

The three international charters which define and govern our management of the historic environment are the Athens Charter for the Restoration of Historic Monuments of 1931, the Venice Charter for the Conservation and Restoration of Monuments and Sites drawn up in 1964, from which the founding of ICOMMOS was a direct result, and most recently the Charter of Kracow on the Principles for Conservation and Restoration of the Built Heritage of 2000, which was a European Economic Community initiative but was subscribed to by many countries outside the EEC. Each successive charter defined the historic built heritage in greater detail to ultimately cover any building or site 'identified as of worth' though it is not specified by whom.

While the Athens Charter restricted its deliberations to historic monuments, insisting that restoration techniques should be confined to the reuse of authenticated historic material for repair work with any additional new materials being recognisable as such, the Venice Charter says that 'Replacement of missing parts must integrate harmoniously with the whole, but at the same time be distinguishable from the original so that restoration does not falsify artistic or historical evidence.' The Kracow Charter goes further stating that reconstruction can only be carried out 'on condition that it is based on precise and indisputable documentation'. Unfortunately architectural ceramic decoration does not sit easily with these principles. An architectural tile scheme is a decorative design in ceramic made up of a combination of many different but repeating component parts (tiles), sometimes plain, sometimes decorated. Historic schemes often contain areas which are badly damaged or missing leaving the incomplete design difficult to 'read'. It can therefore be problematic to support the use of new ceramic material which is visually distinguishable from the original if to do so will result in loss of integrity of the design as a whole, especially where the design is based on the combination of colour, texture and shape of a variety of component parts. Additionally if authentic techniques are used in the manufacture of replacement parts, then most likely the end product will greatly resemble the original and may only be distinguishable by the expert in the field. The natural aging process may be the only factor which differentiates between the two and in the case of interior ceramics, aging is a very slow process and is greatly affected by a number of pertinent factors, which may or may not be present. The 'indisputable documentation' demanded by the Kracow Charter is a rare commodity indeed associated with most architectural ceramic schemes. They are not often architecturally important enough to carry individual archival documentation but will nevertheless still be part of a long community memory like so many other places and people in our history.

What therefore is our guiding principle for conserving tiles today? Given the diversity of age, location, and provenance found under the heading 'tile' the value of a detailed assessment of all aspects of the individual tile scheme cannot be overestimated, it is the starting point from which decisions can be made and actions taken. As is often the case with architectural fabric, not all historic tile material is of equal importance and distinctions may be made loosely on the basis of age, aesthetic value and provenance. Throughout this text I have attempted to group tiles along those lines. By making distinctions thus I am able to outline the different approaches to conservation treatment which are the most ethically appropriate but are also sustainable in today's marketplace economy. The distinctions I make are open to challenge; fortunately arguing against such divisions can only be positive for the future of historic tiles.

Pre-industrial age

There are no distinctions to be made within the earliest group of manufactured tiles. All pre-industrial age ceramic tiles, fragmented or whole, which have survived thus far into the early twenty-first century, justify preservation whether aesthetically pleasing or not. Our main concerns are how best to serve the interests of the material and the context within which it is seen. We must consider whether particular tiles are too important or too fragile to remain in-situ, when safe storage is available and desirable. If we introduce matching new material must it be to enhance or extend the original only, or can it be used to replace the original if the original is best served by safe storage? Conversely if the interpretation or integrity of the site or location is of primary importance over the fragility of the fabric, it may be essential that the tiles remain in place whatever the cost, including restricting public access or other forms of environmental control.

Once the best interests of the tile fabric, in terms of location, are served, it is our obligation to retain, conserve, and protect all examples of pre-industrial age ceramic tile as part of our wider architectural history. Conservation techniques intended to preserve fabric and delay deterioration are legitimate treatments for medieval tile. Restoration techniques are rarely applicable to medieval material beyond the use of reversible adhesives which will bond fragments of ceramic together to create a whole example or larger part of the tile thereby adding to the sum of knowledge of tile making in the medieval world. However, careful and sympathetic restoration work in conjunction with conservation techniques is acceptable when used to preserve tin glazed delftware tiles of the seventeenth and eighteenth centuries. It is quite common for delftware tile schemes to remain in functional settings where visual continuity of pattern or design and high quality surface appearance are important (Figure 4.1). Restoration techniques can underpin conservation where seventeenth and eighteenth century tiles are still required to be functional as is frequently the case in Holland. Reversibility is the touchstone of conservation and restoration methodology.

Examination and appraisal of the underlying mortar is an important part of the assessment process in almost all circumstances surrounding pre-industrial age tile schemes. The age, composition and condition of the mortar may have a direct bearing on the decision making process which will govern the method of conservation chosen.

Figure 4.1
Late seventeenth century delft tiles reused in a modern setting but performing their traditional function.

Post-industrial age

In terms of any sort of conservation or preservation nineteenth century tiles were largely ignored until the late 1970s except for a few small collections of tiles housed in museums that had a particular connection to the provenance of the tile, which was usually classified as an 'object'. Founded in 1983, the Jackfield Tile Museum in Ironbridge, Shropshire, is a museum of the history of tile manufacture covering the period from 1834 to 1960. In addition to conserving, restoring and displaying the very large collection of tiles and plaster patterns in the usual way, the museum quickly became a focus for the conservation of tiles in the wider context of the built environment.

Figure 4.2
Detail of a hand painted tile panel by
W.B. Simpsons from the Charing
Cross Hospital, London.

Figure 4.3
'Rock a Bye Baby', one of ten nursery
rhyme panels by Carter's of Poole
from Ealing Hospital.

Initially the conservation emphasis was on rescuing and preserving large collections of nineteenth and early twentieth century decorative tile panels or ceramic art which were under immediate threat of destruction by demolition. Notable inclusions were ten pictorial hand painted tile panels by W.B. Simpson from the Charing Cross Hospital (Figure 4.2), a further ten nursery rhyme panels by Carter's of Poole from Ealing Hospital (Figure 4.3), and the ceramic mural by Gilbert Bayes, 'Pottery through the Ages', from Doulton House at Lambeth (Figure 4.4). In all three cases, and many others since, when demolition and complete loss of decorative art panels has been threatened, ruthless but effective methods employing large diamond cutting saws were used to free the ceramic from its setting in Portland cement, necessarily causing damage which required subsequent extensive restoration. The examples of the schemes mentioned above now enjoy permanent exhibition space at Jackfield Tile Museum, with the remainder on display at the new Charing Cross and Ealing hospitals and at the Victoria & Albert Museum respectively.

As time has moved on the threat of destruction from demolition has largely been removed by the protection given to tiles by the listing of buildings throughout the UK combined with the support of conservation minded planning authorities. The opportunity is available to us to question the ethical validity of damaging removal techniques and reinforce the position that important decorative pictorial panels should remain in place and become positive elements of building redesign and refurbishment. The ability of a new generation of architects and designers to combine the old with the new in the revitalisation of brownfield sites is a welcome development in the history of tile conservation.

Figure 4.4
Detail of the ceramic mural by
Gilbert Bayes, 'Pottery through the
Ages' from Doulton House at
Lambeth, London.

Nevertheless there are occasions when important pieces of tile art have to be moved. A recent example of a different approach taken which significantly reduced the probability of damage to the ceramic was the resiting, due to redevelopment in Coventry city centre, of a large tile mural designed by Gordon Cullen, dating from the late 1950s and some 40 feet long. Rather than cutting and separating individual tiles from the cement substrate, the technique used for rescuing tiles from demolition, the panel was cut into just eight large sections measuring approximately 200 cm × 150 cm and moved, still adhered to some 35 cm of precast concrete substrate, using heavy lifting equipment. A great deal of careful preparation and precision work was required to cut, lift and reseat each piece successfully. The outcome, however, was less than 4 per cent damage to the ceramic fabric which represented a considerable improvement on the earlier technique (Figure 4.5).

The examples given here are all tile panels or schemes which have been elevated above the ordinary as examples of tile 'art'. The emphasis during the removal and resiting projects described, and many others like them, was to retain all of the original tile material and seek to protect every individual tile from damage as far as possible within the constraints of technology, time and resources.

The same principles do not always apply, however, for restoration of nineteenth and twentieth century interior tile schemes located in and part of the architectural fabric of working buildings where a more flexible attitude to repairs and alterations is required if the buildings are to remain in use (a redundant building will rapidly deteriorate, losing all its historic fabric, not just the tiles). Many historic interiors

Figure 4.5
Detail of the 1950s panel designed by
Gordon Cullen after resiting and
restoration, Coventry.

are now being restored to their former glory so that they can continue to function well into the twenty-first century, indeed the original beauty and quality of schemes is often fully appreciated by the occupants of the buildings. That said, we also require high standards of cleanliness, functionality and quality of fabric for our public buildings. Chipped, fractured, missing, worn and dirty tiles are considered unacceptable, however grand and splendid the interior in its heyday. In these situations the conservation approach is applied in its broadest sense, and preservation of the scheme as a whole entity takes priority over individual tiles. If a scheme can be retained and admired in the future by replacing the most badly damaged but retaining the best preserved of its individual components then that course is acceptable for all but the most important schemes.

The conservation principle for this group of interior tile schemes may be compared to that of brick (another fired earth material) replacement on external elevations. The basis of this approach is the obligation of replacement material to match the original exactly in terms of size, colour, texture and form, thus avoiding possible misinterpretation or confusion in the future as to the original intention of the design and colour of the scheme. Accurately matched replacement material helps us to visually read the artistic and design realisation of the scheme as a whole.

Artificial ageing is to be avoided as, conversely, there should not be any attempt to disguise that which is new and that which is old. Written or photographic records of all replacement work can be kept and placed in suitable storage for future reference so that it will be possible to distinguish which tiles are new and which are original in the future.

Additionally, care should be taken that original tile material is not removed and replaced unnecessarily if a minor repair will restore its condition back to the realms of acceptability. On-site repairs to individual tiles can and should be carried out if the damage is minor, for example holes caused by obsolete fixtures and fittings. Elaborate mouldings were expensive to produce in the heyday of Victorian manufacture, they were hand made and so were produced in relatively small numbers. Mouldings of this order have historic value so it is much better to repair rather than replace if possible.

Nineteenth century geometric and encaustic tile floors are fairly common. Whether complex and beautiful in design or simple and elegant, they all share a common history of roughly 100 years of dirt and footfall affecting their surface to a greater or lesser degree. Many geometric floors are integral to the overall architectural style of the building in which they are housed. In order to preserve them for the future in the original location, the tiles most seriously affected by severe surface wear, irremovable staining, and fracturing usually in high traffic areas are best replaced with matching new tiles thus not only avoiding accident caused by trip hazards but also increasing the likelihood of longevity for the whole interior and similar restoration works to walls and ceilings. Replacement is not the only available option if the provenance of a particular patterned encaustic tile in a floor scheme makes it especially important; damage can be repaired using coloured polyester resin fillers which are fairly hard wearing and reversible.

Interior glazed wall tile schemes can sometimes fall within the broadest definition of conservation. If changes are not made to parts of the scheme then the whole scheme may be lost because primarily the building must serve the needs of the community; we find that although there may be an onus on the occupants of a building to retain the tile interior within the refurbishment plans, quite often nineteenth century tile schemes simply do not fit with modern ideas about office layout, disabled facilities, or public access. Doorways have to be created, lifts have to be installed, and computer terminal networks have to be established, particularly in hospitals, libraries or municipal buildings. Again the broad brush stroke of conservation is often applied by local authorities as guardians of their local heritage. It has become increasingly acceptable to retain those parts of the scheme which are most decorative and stylistically most important, usually the ground floor, entrance halls and stairwells, while allowing upper floor or basement schemes to be sacrificial and taken down for use as replacement material for the high profile areas. The Exchange building in Birmingham is an example of this type of approach; formerly the GPO Exchange it was originally built as offices of the Bell Edison Company in 1896, and as one of the first two telephone exchanges in the UK, it is of enormous historic importance. Nevertheless it needed to be considerably upgraded if it was to meet modern standards of office space and remain a viable commercial proposition, and though considerable changes were made to the interior tiles scheme as a whole, the ground floor and stairwell areas remain as intended (Figure 4.6).

All interior tile schemes should be judged on their individual merit and it is especially important that an experienced tile conservator is consulted at the early stages of any redevelopment to survey the material and assess its overall condition and architectural significance as well as outlining all the options available for preserving the fabric to the best advantage.

The design mode of art deco schemes dating from the 1930s often relies on a mass of undecorated tiling enhanced by small but significant architectural detail. It could be argued, in some circumstances, that it is the design and style of the interior which is significant rather than the mass produced fabric, sometimes of poor quality, from which it is built. Providing that the exact balance, colour and detail of the

Figure 4.6
The entrance hall of 'The Exchange' building in Birmingham.

Plate 3
The range of colours across tiles at Buildwas Abbey.

Plate 1
Vibrant use of colour in tile and stone at All Saint's
Church, Margaret St, London, by William Butterfield

Plate 2
The author at work on the Neatby scheme, Harrods
meat hall, in 1983

Plate 5
A copy of the tile panel depicting the Bolsward tile factory made at Royal Tichelaar, Makkum. The original was painted by Dirk Danser in 1750 and is in the Rijksmuseum, Amsterdam.

Plate 4
The retro choir pavement at Winchester Cathedral.

Plate 8
Encaustic and geometric floor tiles manufactured in 2004 by Chris Cox of Craven Dunnill Jackfield Ltd. The peacock design is an exact replica of a nineteenth century floor made by Maw & Co. for the Mysore Palace, India.

Plate 6
The central dark panel shows extreme colour variation in early Maw & Co. geometric tiles.

Plate 7
The green glaze on tiles at St Albans Cathedral, originally in all areas now found only in low trafficated areas.

Plate 10
After retouching on a nineteenth century tile panel.

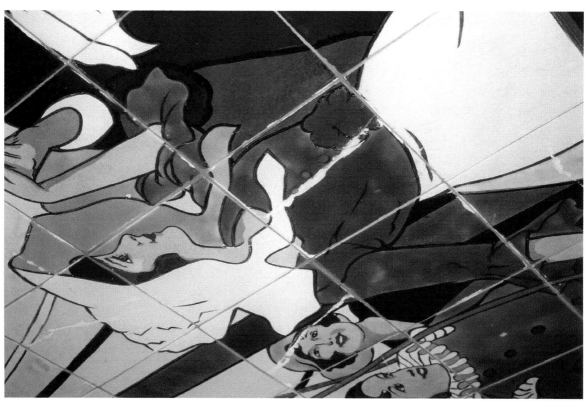

Plate 9
Before retouching on a nineteenth century tile panel.

Figure 4.7
Detail of the entrance foyer tile
scheme at Boots' D6 Building in
Nottingham, designed by
Sir Owen Williams.

scheme are preserved in total, then it is acceptable to replace worn out component parts and in so doing secure its long-term future. The refurbishment of the entrance foyer to Boots' D6 Building in Nottingham (Figure 4.7), a fine art deco building designed by Sir Owen Williams, included all aspects of tile restoration; on-site restoration of original tiles, reusing sacrificial material from upper floors, and manufacture of replacement tiles, to great success and much approval from the occupants.

Maintaining a detailed record of all alterations that have taken place is a vital part of a conservation programme of this type. By contrast some schemes are nationally important, for example the interior of Leighton House in South Kensington, London, or have great artistic, historic or technological merit and must be preserved in their full originality. Whichever route towards preservation is taken it should be our aim to maintain as many historic tile schemes in their original setting as possible.

Conservation in the USA

The latter part of the nineteenth century saw the rise of the tile making industry in the USA. More than likely generated by the steadily increasing popularity for the use of imported encaustic tiles produced in Britain in homes and public buildings in the eastern states, as a statement of both good taste and modernity. Numerous home-grown commercial potteries experimented in their production in response to the popularity of the imported tiles with notable success. John Gardner Low visited the Centennial Exhibition in Philadelphia in 1876, where British and European tiles were on display, and subsequently went on to produce tiles for the Low Art Tile Works, Chelsea, Massachusetts (1877), while F.H. Hall, ceramicist for the American Encaustic Tiling Company of Zanesville, Ohio (1875), was another visitor to the exhibition. Samuel Keys, after a tenuous start, had already founded the Star Encaustic Tile Co. of Pittsburgh, Pennsylvania, in 1871.

The final two decades of the nineteenth century saw the establishment and successful rise of many new manufacturers, though the list is much longer than there is space for here. To name a few: the United States Encaustic Tile Works of Indianapolis and Chicago established by Hall in 1877; the Trent Tile Co., the most important producer in New Jersey; slightly later and less influential the New York Vitrified Tile Works of Brooklyn (NY) established in 1891; and the Beaver Falls Art Tile Co. Ltd of Beaver Falls (Pa) established 1887, demonstrating that late nineteenth century America had an emergent tile industry every bit as productive and inventive as that in Great Britain.

Broadly speaking the product of the early American tile industry in the nineteenth century is British in style and while primarily produced in the eastern states, was transported by rail across the whole of the continent to the western seaboard. By the end of the first decade of the twentieth century the tile legacy of the west coast states began to reflect the Spanish colonial architectural style. A great deal of scholarly work cataloguing, researching archive, and collection of data concerning the history of the American tile industry is carried out by the Tile Heritage Foundation, a non-governmental organisation, alongside similar work by a handful of private individuals.

As in Great Britain, architectural tile schemes are protected by law if they are part of the fabric of a listed historic building recorded in the National Registry of Historic Places, though they have no protection if the building is not listed. In this case responsibility for the protection of architectural schemes depends on the efforts of the individual or groups of individuals in the form of local historic and preservation groups, to lobby either owners or government to facilitate preservation in some form. Historic societies may, and often do, win the support of local museums or city amenity departments in order to carry through successful work to preserve tiles or heighten awareness surrounding the historic or artistic value of threatened schemes. Laws governing protection of fabric vary from place to place, for example California State Law protects against the alteration or destruction of 'fine art' though the situation for tile art is sometimes complicated because it is often an integral part of a structure and does not 'stand alone' therefore it remains vulnerable if the building itself is not listed. The Malibu Lagoon Museum, Malibu, California, undertook a rescue of an important tile scheme in 1990. After being alerted by an individual homeowner to the threat of imminent demolition, museum volunteers with the aid of a local building contractor cut out and removed the tiles over a three day period before placing them into safe museum storage. The Tile Heritage Foundation commented in its new bulletin 'Flash Point' at the time, 'Someone must recognise an inherent value and be sensitive to an imminent threat. From that point on, we have to cross our fingers.'

The Tile Heritage Foundation is just such a preservation group, it is a major national voice for 'the preservation of existing installations of rare and unusual ceramic surfaces'. Its mission statement is broad based, as well as being a resource for the identification of historic tiles it is also committed to fostering appreciation of new tile art on a nationwide basis. It regularly reports on instances of successful preservation of historic tiles in all forms, ranging from the efforts of individuals who have personally undertaken the task of rescuing threatened tiles with little or no experience other than trial and error to, more frequently, using a combination of expertise from building contractors and museum staff.

Campaigning or influencing decision making to preserve historic tiles in their original location is also often community based. The

Urban Corps of San Diego, a community volunteer force, formed under the auspices of the National and Community Service Act of 1990, provided the necessary manpower, guided by local museum staff and college lecturers, with which to develop an archive recording and conservation plan as an aid to preserving the many examples of tile art in the Alcazar Gardens, Balboa Park, in San Diego, a National Historic Landmark dating from 1935 and forming part of San Diego's Second Exposition.

Replacement of damaged fabric forms a large part of the conservation ethic for the preservation of tile schemes in the USA. Manufacture of accurately matching replacement material is usually undertaken by small-scale studio ceramicists or modern tile manufacturers who are willing to experiment with techniques and glazes with which they are not necessarily familiar. Most report unexpected difficulties in achieving the desired results, but at the same time report ultimate success.

In 1987 after six years of pre-production experimentation H.&R. Johnsons of Stoke on Trent, Great Britain, produced encaustic tiles of an acceptable match to enable replacement of 20 per cent of the tile floors in the Capitol building in Washington DC. At that time there was no suitable manufacturing base in America to carry out the project; several large manufacturers were approached but none were willing.

In 1992 the restoration of the glazed tile roof of Los Angeles Central Library used 50 per cent replacement tile, the roof tile scheme was made up of eight different colours and three different finishes forming a multi-coloured extravaganza. Some of the colours were redeveloped to give improved performance which would avoid the mutation of glaze to which the original tiles were prone. More recently the Central Park Conservancy in New York is proceeding slowly and with care, supported by a grant from the Getty Foundation, to investigate ways to conserve and display a large encaustic tile ceiling made by Minton's of Stoke on Trent, which was once part of the decoration in the Bethesda Terrace arcade; the tiles were removed and placed in storage during the 1983 restoration of the terrace. The Central Park Conservancy is a private non-profit making organisation which funds and manages the Park's conservation in conjunction with the City of New York and it is typical of many such organisations nationwide.

As in the UK there are a very small number of specialist conservation studios dedicated to restoration work on historical tile material. One such specialist is the Tile Restoration Center in Seattle, founded by Marie Glass Tappe. This particular company mixes restoration techniques with kiln-based replication and acknowledges that all restorers in the USA develop their own methodologies for which they must be individually ethically responsible. In Great Britain the United Kingdom Institute for Conservation (UKIC) is just one of a number of bodies which fosters professional accreditation and observance of a specified code of ethics and practice for member conservators in both the private and public sectors. UKIC combines with other specialist conservation organisations to form the National Council for Conservation and Restoration whose aim is not only to maintain standards in conservation practice but also to provide a forum for discussion and mechanism with which to influence government on important issues pertaining to conservation.

The structure in place for the protection of architectural fabric in the UK is somewhat different to that of the USA. The systems in place for the protection and conservation of historic tiles in the USA tend to be based on a flexible network of self-help, of which the Tile Heritage Foundation, a volunteer society, is a major resource. They are manifestly successful in their aims. The much more inflexible procedures for protection, governed by local or national authorities, evident in the UK are also, largely, successful in protecting much of our remaining tile heritage. However, probably the most pertinent factors for the successful protection of any architectural heritage is a thriving nucleus of skilled conservators, craftsmen and manufacturers, and the supply of raw materials along with the necessary economic will to support the conservation and restoration sector.

5

Methods of conservation

Introduction

The previous chapters have attempted to explore the history and nature of various types of interior tile schemes with a view to achieving a basic knowledge of the material it is hoped will be conserved for present and future generations. The context in which tile schemes can be found is wide ranging; many tile schemes can lay claim to artistic merit as well as special protection as important historic material, while other tile schemes, albeit historic and possibly highly decorative, are utilitarian with a provenance in mass production and are part of the built environment in which we live and work. These are distinctions which may govern the course of treatment which the conservator advises upon or carries out.

While some historic tile schemes that fall into a class that can boast a provenance of some importance may attract techniques for protection and preservation which follow the recognised patterns of procedure that are common to conservation of ceramics in general, there may be differences in approach by dint of the fact that tile schemes can often be large and are often an integral part of a larger architectural structure. They do not 'stand alone' and are not generally considered to be included in the 'moveable heritage' sector of conservation practice.

The vast majority of tile schemes are unarguably historic material but are still functional in everyday circumstances; a common example would be a tiled floor in a Victorian church. This type of tile scheme still forms part of our living environment and has not yet attained the rarefied status of 'art' or 'architecturally important'. The aim in such circumstances is usually to restore them to a condition which enables continuing usage and in such a way that gives future generations the opportunity to elevate them in status. Encouraging good restoration also encourages admiration of the achievements of recent generations of industrial entrepreneurs and craftsmen. The line between the two approaches is not strictly drawn between 'conservation' and 'restoration' but inevitably tends towards those distinctions.

In this chapter the various practical methods of conserving and restoring for all types of tile schemes are described. The methods explored in this chapter originate in experience accumulated by numerous conservators of architecture over the past three decades, during which time conservation of architectural tiles schemes has gained in importance. The information is not finite or absolute, new experiences are encountered frequently and new treatment methods created, and all conservators have their own methods of preference. Many conservators are extremely innovative, usually successfully, and dissemination of experience and information within the profession is good. Indeed arguments as to 'good and bad' practice or 'right or wrong' methods rage in conservation circles all the time, partly because practitioners often deal with sets of totally new circumstances or constraints. The information that follows I hope will not be contentious, but will gather together basic understanding and practices for the conservation of tiles schemes; its aim is to guide rather that specify treatment.

The information is set out in order of sequence for practical application with chronological subdivisions that apply to the three basic tile types which have been outlined in the previous chapters: medieval pavements, seventeenth and eighteenth century delft tile schemes, and nineteenth and early twentieth century interior tile schemes.

Surveys

The importance of undertaking a full survey of any large and complex tile scheme cannot be overstressed. It should be commissioned and produced at the earliest stages in the conservation programme. A survey will usually fall into two parts relating to current condition and recommended treatment. A good survey can be used for several purposes: as a basis for the programme of work; as an informal document on which to base a specification to tender; as an information document accompanying applications for grant aid; and, just as importantly, as a historical record of the nature and condition of the fabric on a specified date.

Historical context

Ideally a survey should open with a paragraph setting the historical context of the building, the location in which it is set and, if relevant, the architect. Certainly the tiles themselves should be placed in historical context with reference to the time and place of manufacture, if known, whether the design of the material can be attributed or not, or the genre or style into which they can be placed. Information of this nature can be of vital importance in an application for grant aid because it can establish a historical importance to the tiles beyond the immediate environment, or at the very least is a welcome addition to existing archive material relating to a wider area.

Description

Beyond the historical context a tile survey should include a full description of the tile scheme in architectural terms, describing the configuration of dado, panel, frieze, columns, pilasters, arches or whatever features it may contain. A full photographic record of all of the design elements should accompany the description. An inventory of each separate type of tile should be made and recorded as measurement, profile or shape, glaze colour and texture, and design of decorative features if applicable. Several examples of the same types of tile should be measured for comparison and any anomalies recorded. A record of the location of different tile types within the scheme should be included. Judgements pertaining to the porosity, hardness of the clay body and glaze may be given if the tiles conform to a recognisable standard.

Identifying deterioration

The primary function of the survey is to establish the general condition of the scheme and then progress to the detailed condition. All causes of deterioration found within the scheme must be recorded whether visible on the surface or invisible and acting beneath the surface. Commonly found manifestations of deterioration are: impact damage; external stresses such as building load, vibration and thermal movement; dirt; surface abrasion; water ingress causing staining, biological activity or salt crystallisation; manufacturing faults; and unsuitable past treatments. The possible causes of deterioration may be commented upon if they can be confidently ascertained.

Depending on the size of the scheme and the objective of the survey it can either have a detailed written description and photographic record of all damage or deterioration, or it can illustrate typical damage and give quantities and location of similar forms of damage. For example, once a single hole drilled into a Victorian glazed wall tile has been photographed and described it is an unnecessary waste of resources to repeat the exercise if the scheme has 100 or more holes exactly the same in nature (Figure 5.1); however, it is very important to count and locate all such holes as the information has a direct bearing on cost of restoration. Similarly, if the outside edges of a high proportion of delft tiles in a scheme are in a similar state of deterioration (Figure 5.2), as they often are, there is no real benefit to be gained by detailed description of every single example of the problem. Instead it should be illustrated as typical damage and thereafter all

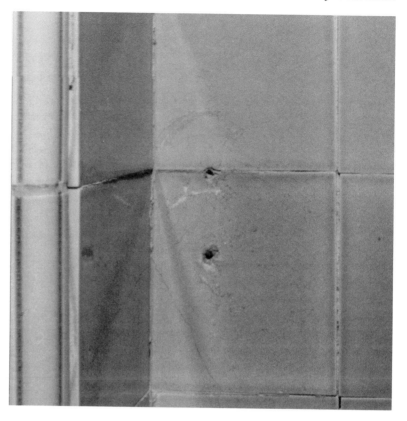

Figure 5.1
Typical damage caused by drilling into glazed tiles.

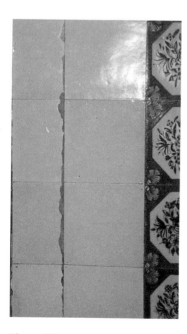

Figure 5.2
Typical damage to the glazed edges of delft tiles.

similar damage located by plan and quantified in terms of length of time needed for cleaning and repair of all examples. All extraordinary damage should be located, photographed and described in detail. Location of damaged tiles can be expressed by description, by means of simple plan or by elevation drawings or photographs.

Similarly all past repairs or unsympathetic replacement material can be located on the plan and by description, including an analysis of the repair materials used. The identification of unsympathetic replacement material should extend to the mortar layer. Tiles which have become detached many decades after their original installation may have been reinstated using much harder or denser mortar which can produce different tensile stresses or moisture absorption rates. Tell-tale evidence can sometimes be seen as different spacing between the tiles as compared to the rest of the scheme (Figure 5.3). Architect's drawings, if made available, can be a useful tool for location purposes but they are not essential.

The presence of salts or other chemical or organic staining including the possible causes of any such conditions should be recorded, as well as an analysis of the general presence and level of dirt.

The type, condition and stability of the mortar substrate and grout should also form part of the condition survey wherever possible. If a mortar sample is available it can be analysed. An indication of the stability of the mortar can be gained by systematic tapping with a small rubber mallet over the whole surface of the scheme, listening for changes in sound. A hollow or rattling sound indicates instability somewhere in the substrate which may have a bearing on the ensuing treatment. If the sounds change from hollow to solid across the surface area, then these changes can be mapped as part of the survey. There may also be a noticeable difference in the sound made by lime mortar and hard Portland cement caused by the difference in density between the two. The type and condition of the grout should be recorded as it may also have a bearing on the stability and treatment of the scheme.

Identifying wear and tear due to natural aging

Certain forms of damage are part of the natural aging process of the tile surface, for example slight 'dishing' of the surface of floor tiles is a result of prolonged wear against low fired body clay (Figure 5.4). The cause of the dishing derives from having a slightly higher fired temperature at the edges of the tile, the clay body becomes harder

Figure 5.3
Unsympathetic replacement material.

Figure 5.4
Typical damage caused by tread.

Figure 5.5
Typical crazing on old glazed tiles.

around the edges than in the centre, which consequently wears away at a faster rate. This condition does not occur with all clay bodies, some tiles wear at an even rate. Almost all historic floors will have some areas where the hardened fire-skin surface of the tile has worn away leaving the softer, permeable, and often pitted inner body clay visible. The inner body clay will be slightly lighter in colour and duller in appearance; it will also have absorbed a higher proportion of dirt. A small percentage of natural wear and tear in the form of damaged edges or shelling of the fire-skin around the edges of floor tiles is acceptable and is part and parcel of the overall appearance of a historic floor.

Glazed wall tile surfaces are always crazed to a greater or lesser extent. The degree to which this effect is visible varies considerably. It is caused by a mismatch in the shrinkage rate of body and glaze during the cooling period directly after firing, and is therefore linked to manufacturing and is part of the natural aging process (Figure 5.5). It is usually left untreated, except in exceptional circumstances where biological micro-organisms may pose a health and safety risk, for example in food service areas or bathing pools.

Nevertheless these kinds of faults, caused by natural aging, should be recorded and included as part of the general condition of the scheme; the appropriate advice generally is that most of the effects of natural aging should remain unaltered unless exceptional circumstances prevail.

Nineteenth and twentieth century schemes can often exhibit fractures caused by structural movement and shifting load due to settlement quite soon after the construction process was completed. The use of Portland cement as both tile adhesive and substrate onto brick structures creates a layered structure with little or no flexibility, which inevitably, if the stresses are too great, causes damage to the weakest element; both ceramic and cement will crack along the same fault lines. Such fractures are often irreparable without considerable loss of surrounding tile material and it may be both expedient and ethically sound to leave damaged material in place (Figure 5.6).

The survey can highlight such problems ahead of the start of the work programme and help create an understanding between the client and conservator which will avoid any difference of opinion as to the level of reinstatement that can or should be achieved as the outcome of restoration. Allowing the dignity of age to shine through the restoration process is a primary concern.

Treatment recommendations within a survey

Treatment recommendations will of course wholly depend on the condition of the scheme, but most survey commissioning agencies will expect guidance as to the best way forward to bring about either

Figure 5.6
Fracturing caused by building load.

stabilisation or improvement in the condition of their tile scheme. There can often be several viable options for treatment when all factors are taken into account; clients should be made aware of all the different possibilities of treatment and their consequences, to enable them to make informed judgements when commissioning a conservation or restoration project. It should be central to the document that treatment recommendations should be seen as guidance to possible treatment not as specifications.

The depth of analysis or extent of material intervention or testing to be carried out as part of the survey is something which should be discussed with the client ahead of the start of the survey, though most schemes can be adequately assessed as a result of visual inspection combined with simple tests. Seeking permission to carry out basic cleaning tests is always worthwhile as the results are often invaluable and the tests are rarely seen as interventionist. As a result of testing, recommendations for an appropriate cleaning regime can then be made. Samples of salts or biological activity can be analysed to give an indication for best possible treatments.

For conservation of early or important historic schemes recommendations for environmental control are appropriate within the treatment section of a survey. The extent of original historical material which can be preserved or restored on site should be identified along with a brief method statement for the repairs. The method statement need only be indicative of the route chosen for treatment as a detailed and final treatment analysis will form the final conservation report which follows completion of the project.

If replacement tile material is being added to the scheme a survey should also quantify and locate the extent of the original tile fabric which is either damaged beyond repair or missing, detailing the colour, size, profile, and quantities of each tile, thus arriving at a list of quantities for new manufacture. It is not appropriate at the survey stage to remove material for use as samples for colour matching or mould making, but the survey should indicate the necessity to do so if the circumstances dictate.

Large restoration projects that encompass areas of tiling of differing status within one building may require detailed assessments of the availability of sacrificial areas of tile identified for use as replacement material and indicate if they require specialist removal or if they are forfeit within the envisaged programme.

Finally most commissioning agencies will require an indication of the length of time required for the recommended works, thus enabling clients, architects or contractors to make full allowances in advance of the start of the project for time and costs relating to the conservation or restoration of valuable tile schemes. In short a tile scheme survey should include in its format all of the information required by the client, architect or conservation officer to adequately instruct the main contractor concerning the commissioning of the appropriate conservation organisation to carry out the conservation or restoration work on the subject tiles. No survey can guarantee that mistakes will not be made or valuable material lost or not catered for, but a good survey will go a long way towards informing the client and thus protecting the tile scheme.

Role of the conservator as consultant

Most conservation companies, because of the specialist nature of the work, tend to be quite small; however, restoration of late Victorian or early twentieth century architectural tile schemes can sometimes require restoration techniques to be applied to several thousand square metres of tiling in a relatively short space of time, for example during major refurbishments of listed building railway stations. In such circumstances there are likely to be strict time schedules and contractual penalties in place.

The role of the conservator in major building refurbishment projects can be solely consultative. The conservator would be expected to produce a series of documents and be available in an advisory capacity, initially to estimate the degree of damage to historic material and then to advise on the appropriate method of restoration – bearing in mind the need to retain as much of the historic fabric as possible while bringing up the overall appearance of the fabric to an acceptable level of cleanliness and sustainability commensurate with everyday use.

Furthermore the conservator can advise which elements of a tile scheme can or should be repaired and which elements are damaged beyond repair and must be replaced; examine all areas tile by tile and make assessments giving actual quantities for repair and replacement. The replacement tile schedule should include quantities for colour, size and profile. The consultant conservator can carry out cleaning trials and assess the degree and type of dirt which has often been accumulating since the beginning of time and make recommendations for the appropriate method of cleaning which is expedient in terms of thoroughness, time/cost ratios, appropriate use of skill base and most importantly non-damaging effects to the tiles. He or she is also well placed to liaise with the conservation officer, architect, quantity surveyor and main contractor at the early stages of the project concerning all these issues.

Prior to the appointment of the main tiling contractor the conservator can provide detailed specifications for the safe removal of individual damaged tiles without causing unnecessary damage to surrounding historic material. If required the conservator can also set up training sessions with tiling contractors which will cover all aspects of the refurbishment including repair of original material and the health and safety issues which specifically pertain to the work in hand. Finally a programme to advise and monitor the ongoing works should be initiated.

Cleaning

The following section looks at appropriate methods of cleaning used for tile schemes. It is important here to recall the different manufacturing processes outlined earlier. The method of manufacture has a direct bearing on the method chosen for cleaning, the important factors being the relative hardness of both glaze and clay body and the stability of both elements. Naturally 'soft' body and glaze tiles are less stable and more prone to damage during the cleaning process than 'hard' body and glaze tiles.

Hard and soft bodies

The clay body typically used for medieval tiles is usually described as lead glazed earthenware. The clay will be naturally occurring from a commonly found source. It is recognised as being low fired at temperatures below 1100 degrees centigrade with possibly only one firing which includes the lead glaze coating, as such both the glaze and the body would be described as 'soft'. Consequently both the glaze and body will abrade very easily and have a high absorption rate of moisture. The glaze may also be only lightly bonded to the surface of the body.

The clay body generally used for delftware tiles is usually clay rich in calcium carbonate, sometimes mixed with marl, dug from selected and specific sources. It is low fired, between 800 to 1000 degrees centigrade, resulting in a 'soft', porous body. The glaze coating is a mix of lead and tin oxide fired at between 800 and 1000 degrees centigrade and produces a soft glaze which is easily abraded and only lightly bonded to the surface of the tile. The glaze is prone to crazing and shedding from the surface of the tile.

The clay bodies used for nineteenth century and early twentieth century tiles were complex and varied. Natural clays were sometimes dug locally to the site of manufacture but also specific clays and minerals were transported great distances if required. Tile bodies were biscuit fired at high temperatures, up to 1200 degrees centigrade, to produce a semi-vitrified body which is described as 'hard'; it is dense, has low porosity and is relatively robust. The firing process produced a fire-skin which resists abrasion for lengthy periods, usually many years; once the fire-skin is worn away the clay bodies become more absorbent to moisture and abrade more easily. Lead glazes used up until the early twentieth century were fired at temperatures up to 1100 degrees and produced a 'soft' glaze. Later, alkaline-based glazes, introduced because they were safer to use, produced a harder glaze. The aim of the manufacturers was to produce a tile where the bond between glaze and clay body is strong. Glazes vary in their susceptibility to abrasion.

Medieval tile pavements

Cleaning medieval tile floors should be carried out only after careful consideration and deliberation, and with the utmost care. The work should not be hurried and constant monitoring of the condition of the fabric of the tile and effect of the chosen method should continue throughout the cleaning process and beyond if possible. Medieval tile floors are most commonly found in ecclesiastical buildings which may be in full use for daily worship or may be scheduled ancient monuments and in full use as visitor attractions. In any circumstances dust and dirt particles will find their way onto the surface of the tiles in considerable quantity. If they are not removed by cleaning, particles will be compressed into the surface of the tile by foot tread causing abrasion and severe wear to the fragile upper surface. Neither are tiles safe even when pedestrians are prevented from walking on medieval floors, although they are plainly at less risk. Birds and bats are often cohabitants of ancient buildings. Acids, nitrates and phosphates found in bird droppings are all harmful to ceramics, and will etch into tile surfaces, particularly when large quantities of droppings are left to build up unchecked under nest sites (Figure 5.7).

Figure 5.7
Debris on medieval tiles underneath a nest site.

Figure 5.8
Lime encrustations on medieval tiles.

Figure 5.9
After cleaning.

Further problems can be encountered on some medieval tile surfaces. Most ancient ecclesiastical buildings are built using lime mortar, some have their original lime wash wall plaster covering the stonework intact, and some have lost their plaster work completely leaving revealed stonework. Whichever the case there will inevitably be a measure of lime in the dust and debris falling from the wall and gathering on the surface of the tiles adjacent to it and often at some distance, possibly half a metre away from the wall. If these conditions are combined with high moisture levels and continuous slow evaporation either within in the tile body or on the surface, the accumulated lime in the dust particles will react with carbon dioxide in the air and the evaporating water and form hard calcium carbonate encrustations. The process is referred to as carbonation (calcium hydroxide, $Ca(OH)_2$, reabsorbs carbon dioxide, CO_2, in moist conditions and reverts to calcium carbonate, $CaCO_3$) – as a result of this chemical change the encrustations are relatively harder than lime mortar itself (Figure 5.8). If the tile surface is dry then the lime mortar particles remain as dust on the surface. The concretion which is formed adheres to the surface of the tile body in exactly the same way as a mortar and is extremely difficult and sometimes impossible to remove without breaking the fragile 'soft' body clay surface to which it is attached. The damage and disfiguration to the tile surface is ruinous. To avoid such irreversible damage regular brushing of the surface of the tile pavement to remove lime mortar dust, using a soft brush, is essential.

However, in some instances the damage is already done and if this is the case, it can be fairly effective to treat the encrusted tile face by pre-wetting with a fine spray mist of distilled water to dampen the surface, then coat with a weak solution of distilled water and detergent. The surface of the ceramic must always be dampened before any additional cleaning agent is applied. Many detergents contain surfactants which may cause irreversible staining if applied directly onto a dry absorbent surface. The detergent most commonly used in ceramics conservation is 'Synperonic A', used mainly because its composition is known and it does not contain many of the added ingredients which perform specific tasks such as bleaching or brightening found in commercial detergent. Generally, most tile cleaning detergents will be based on sulphamic acid (NH_2SO_3H) or phosphoric acid in combination with a surfactant. These products will be acids at ~pH2. Limestone is at ~pH9 so detergents with an acid base are more effective at softening the carbonated lime. The solution may be left in place for up to ten minutes and then the surface steam cleaned using a low pressure steam cleaner; a sponge may be used to collect the residual moisture. The softened encrustations can then be scraped away manually with a scalpel blade. As the carbonated lime dries it becomes hard again, and it may be necessary to repeat this process seven or eight times. At the end of the procedure the floor should be sponged with distilled water until the pH level of the surface is close to neutral. The results can be reasonably successful though the process is lengthy and labour intensive (Figure 5.9).

Steam is also an effective method of removing bird droppings, once the greater amount of dried droppings have been carefully scraped away using plastic spatulas. The remaining residue left behind can be softened using steam and then sponged off the tile surface.

Excessive build up of old waxes and linseed oil is also a fairly frequently encountered problem on medieval floors, particularly in churches. Beeswax and linseed oil were favoured coatings for tiles in the past, both substances actively attract dirt, and consequently tend to blacken with age; wax will turn yellow over a period of time as the natural process of oxidation takes place. They also contain natural fatty acids which may in some instances have a detrimental effect on the ceramic over a period of time; although this has not yet been shown to be definitely the case, the risk is there. Wax impregnation can prevent further more desirable treatments from being effective and is very difficult to remove; the older the coating is, the more resistant it is to solvents. Steaming can be a fairly effective means of softening the wax, before applying a neutral pH soft soap mixed with a little white spirit. The mixture is gently agitated into the tile, so long as the surface is not friable, using a firm but not stiff bristle brush and then sponged off with distilled water. The aromatic type hydrocarbon solvents are most successful in removing wax, though the stronger, more effective ones such as toluene and xylene carry health and safety implications which make their use difficult to control in the necessary quantities needed, particularly in public places. Alternatively dichloromethane-based paint strippers can be effective especially when heat is applied in the form of steam at the same time, though the use of such products carries the same health and safety warnings. Thorough rinsing with distilled water is also required.

The amount of water applied to medieval tiles should always be kept to a minimum, for fear of setting up a reaction of salt crystal growth. Distilled or deionised water is preferable to tap water. Though tap water may be used in the initial stages of cleaning the final rinse is with purified water. Sponges should always be squeezed to almost dry before applying to the surface. It is much preferable to repeat the sponging several times rather than soak floors excessively.

Providing the surface is not friable, the surface of the tile pavement can be brushed with a soft nylon brush and sponged with distilled water to remove any build-up of dust and debris that may have accumulated in the natural progress of time. Once dry, the floor can be buffed using a soft cotton cloth.

If the tile surface is friable, then it is debatable whether a floor should be cleaned at all, because a small quantity of tile material will always be lifted along with the dirt whatever method is used. However, the surface loss can be minimal and may be balanced against the advantage of removing damaging surface accretions or debris which may abrade the surface under the impact of footfall.

In such cases soft brushing should be carried out carefully using a small squirrel hair paint brush 2 or 3 cm wide. The surface of each tile is lightly brushed to dislodge the dirt, a damp sponge is then placed over the surface and lifted off quickly, two or three times in a dabbing motion rather than wiping. The damp sponge picks up the dirt off the surface; the sponge is rinsed clean between uses on each tile. Each tile is given attention in this way while constantly checking the level of surface loss; excessive surface loss will show up as red dust on the damp sponge.

Some conservators may prefer to use a variable speed museum vacuum cleaner to remove the dust from medieval pavement floors. However, there is a danger of dislocation or loss of loose medieval mortar from between the tiles when using vacuum cleaners, which must be avoided. Some pavements are in situations without easy access to power.

How often medieval tile floors should be cleaned is a matter for careful consideration, and the answer is usually as little as possible.

Seventeenth and eighteenth century glazed wall tiles

The particular type of tile we are referring to here are 'delft style' tiles, which although predominantly date from the seventeenth and eighteenth centuries, continued in production by the same method right through the nineteenth century up to the present day. They are tin glazed with a relatively soft body and as such are highly permeable and prone to absorption of all types of organic staining. They are often found in fire surrounds or kitchen and dairy locations where the less than robust tin glaze may have been subjected to a good deal of impact damage resulting in pitting of the surface or wear and tear and loss of glaze around the edges of the tile. Loss of glaze leaves the soft permeable body exposed which will then easily absorb dirt and stains (Figure 5.10).

The glazed coating of the tile may be cleaned with a solution of distilled water and a neutral pH, non-ionic detergent, such as Synperonic A, applied with a well-squeezed sponge over the surface. The application of too much moisture may be detrimental, it could cause the lime plaster adhesive to soften or it could initiate salt crystallisation so it is important to keep moisture levels as low as possible.

Areas of tile where the glaze is missing and the clay body exposed are best cleaned locally, first by pre-wetting the area with clean distilled water. With a stronger solution of distilled water and detergent than used in the previous first phase clean, apply with a toothbrush

Figure 5.10
Delft tiles taken from a fireplace showing soot blackening of the edges.

and agitate gently, then sponge clean with clear distilled water. Be aware that glaze near the edges of the tile, or where tiles have become fractured, may be fragile or loose; care must be taken not to dislodge glaze fragments. If glaze fragments are disturbed it is best to suspend the cleaning operation until the fragments can be consolidated. When dry, gently buff with dry cotton wool or a soft cloth.

Fire surrounds especially suffer from soot blackening at the edges of tiles; the worst effects of this can usually be removed as described but sometimes the lime plaster grout between the tiles remains blackened and visually unappealing. In such cases the best option is to remove the old grout altogether and replace with new. First soften with distilled water and then carefully pick out the old grout using a scalpel or fine pick, taking care not to scratch the adjoining glaze.

Localised staining is often difficult to remove from tiles while they remain in-situ mainly because the application of stain removing agents should be preceded by soaking the whole tile body in distilled water. If the body is dry the stain may be drawn further into the tile by the application of stain removing agents in liquid form.

However, if it is possible to wet the tile sufficiently first, rust stains can sometimes be removed by gently cleaning the affected area with a cotton bud dipped in a rust inhibitor that contains phosphoric acid. Rinse in distilled water afterwards. By the same token, if it is possible to carry out a preliminary wetting, many organic stains can be removed with a poultice of hydrogen peroxide 20:100 volume, or alternatively a solution of citric acid dissolved in distilled water applied as a poultice. It is unwise to use household chloride bleaches, as they may cause crystallisation under the glaze. The ability to rinse away thoroughly any cleaning agent is all important. It is worth noting that all stains are difficult to remove, and some may be permanent.

Nineteenth and twentieth century tiles

Glazed wall tiles

Nineteenth and twentieth century glazed tiles are usually, though by no means always, considerably more robust than delft tiles because the body clay is harder and less permeable. However, as a general rule the same cleaning methods apply, although less damage is likely to be caused by absorption of excessive amounts of unfriendly stain removing agents because of the harder body. Nevertheless it is always better to err on the side of caution and restrict the use of cleaning agents to gentle non-ionic detergents with a neutral pH to combat normal levels of accumulated dirt. The less permeable body clay and glaze coating also means that the use of distilled water only is not always necessary, tap water may be substituted. Problems due to salt crystallisation are more likely to be caused by other factors in hard body tiles rather than reaction from possible chemical additives present in tap water.

Glazes on nineteenth century tiles are sometimes a variant on lead and tin glaze and therefore very prone to surface abrasion, but if they were produced at the end of the century or later they are more likely to be alkaline glazes which tend to be harder, more robust and resistant to scratching. Either way it is worth avoiding abrasive techniques of any kind for fear of damaging the glaze surface; nothing harder than a bristle scrubbing brush should be used on glazes tiles, and only then after a small test area has been cleaned and checked for possible surface damage. Surface accretions such as paint splashes are best removed with a scalpel blade.

It is important to use neutral pH detergents because some historic glazes can be unstable. Alkaline-based cleaning products may affect particular turquoise blue glazes and acid-based cleaning products can affect certain orange red glazes, in both instances causing colour change. Acid-based cleaners can etch into soft glaze if left in contact too long with the surface. Etching will result in a dulling of the surface gloss.

White spirit will safely remove adhesive residue from sticky tapes, while industrial methylated spirit is an excellent degreasant if tiles have been in an environment used for smoking, for example a bar or hotel lounge where there may be a brown tar film over the surface. Industrial methylated spirit can only be used under licence from HM Customs and Excise in the UK; it is a mix of ethanol, a small amount of methanol and water. Methylated spirit bought from hardware stores will contain a purple dye which may stain porous bodies. Once again there are health and safety implications for the use of ethanol, a highly flammable substance in on-site circumstances which may be a construction site or may be a historically sensitive interior. If smoke and tar residues can be removed with detergent applications without resorting to solvents then so much the better.

Conservators often feel compelled to establish a faster cleaning regime for large-scale architectural tile schemes when the full-time and cost implications of cleaning by hand are established. It can be hard to convince commissioning agents that careful hand cleaning will yield the best results and be the safest option for the tiles. As in all conservation disciplines a great deal of irreversible damage can be done by ill advised cleaning methods.

Pressurised steam cleaning is unlikely to cause any damage to glazed wall tiles though it is not always completely effective as it will often leave behind a residue which must be finished off by hand cleaning. High pressure water washing is undesirable in most instances because there is an inherent danger of excessive water penetrating behind the tiles and lifting them away from the substrate. Both the JOS system of cleaning and laser cleaning are effective for glazed ceramics; however, both systems are costly and require a good deal of trained expertise in their use. At present the costs outweigh the benefits. Both systems are very effective in removing black sulphate deposits, caused by the reaction of acid rain or other atmospheric pollutions, from exterior glazed surfaces which would otherwise have to be removed mechanically using scalpel blades. However, the use of either system has not yet been thoroughly established as being the effective way forward in the cleaning of all glazed tile surfaces.

On-site use of laser technology carries serious and expensive health and safety implications which must be in place in order to safeguard other workers from possible damage to eyesight by casual intrusion during the cleaning operation.

The JOS system uses air and cold water mixed with a variety of abrasives under pressure. The equipment uses nozzles which produce a rotary spray which has a buffing and dislodging effect on dirt rather than a blasting and impacting effect. The distance of the nozzle from the ceramic, the size of nozzle, the volume of water and amount of air pressure, and the choice of abrasive can all be varied depending on the degree and type of soiling. The choices are very relevant and require some expertise as much damage can be done in the wrong hands. If the surface of the ceramic is at all friable then this system is not advisable. A mild abrasive such as powdered limestone is used in many instances in the cleaning of stonework. It is in the cleaning of stonework that this system has proved its worth.

Most architectural schemes will need two phases of cleaning, the first as a preliminary exercise to remove the worst effects of years of neglect and establish the real extent of the damage to be repaired, and second, a gentle finishing clean and polish to bring back the beauty and lustre of the glaze. Buffing with a soft cotton cloth is usually all that is required to bring a final deep shine to Victorian glazed tiles.

Victorian encaustic and geometric floor tiles

Victorian encaustic and geometric floor tiles are usually the most robust of the architectural ceramic family; they are hard body, semi- or fully vitrified and in their newly manufactured state have a hard fire skin. However, any cleaning treatment on old floors is always experimental and is not bound to be successful or without problems, so with that in mind, finding an unobtrusive corner in which to test a method or product is a valuable and important first step before establishing a cleaning regime.

Victorian floor tiles, though they are high fired with a semi- or fully vitrified clay body, more often than not, especially in high traffic areas, have lost the fine fire-skin through wear, which protected the slightly more absorbent body clay. The surface will often be finely pitted because of the granular texture of the fired clay. The pitted surface will hold dirt deposits which will also have, to some degree, absorbed into the body clay. The most common problems encountered are:

- dull dirty appearance caused by over 100 years of wear and tear
- paint spills and encrustations of other coatings
- grease, oil or rust stains
- ancient and discoloured coatings of wax and linseed oil which have absorbed into the body of the tiles
- dirty or missing cement grouting.

Semi-industrial pressure steam cleaning can sometimes be a useful first phase before hand cleaning on large floor areas in public buildings especially if the floor is in particularly bad condition, though there should be no other vulnerable building fabric in the vicinity which may be affected by the high humidity created by the steam. Usually for domestic or ecclesiastical buildings the best method of cleaning is by hand.

For the most part there is little problem attached to using product ranges which have been specifically designed for use with modern floor tiles as cleaning agents. However, there are varying degrees of aggressive qualities attached to every cleaning product and careful examination of the integrity of the tile body should precede the choice of a cleaning agent. It is also wise to start the product testing process with the mildest agent first, and if unsuccessful move up the scale until a product equal to the task is found. All manufacturers will supply a product data sheet, which will give information about the basic formula of the product, although they are never completely definitive. The product data sheet will also give all of the relevant health and safety criteria.

All products should be non-ionic. Conservation cleaning detergents and soaps will have a balanced pH. Detergents are preferable to soaps because they are less prone to forming scum on the surface of the tiles, which is difficult to remove. Commercial detergents used for removing heavy deposits of dirt and cement or lime stains will contain acids in dilute, usually between 15 and 30 per cent, solution in combination with a surfactant. Commonly used acids are hydrochloric, phosphoric or sulphamic. Detergents formulated for removing grease or oil stains are alkali based, usually containing sodium hydroxide. The decisive factor in using any product is to rinse as thoroughly as possible after use.

Whichever product is chosen it should be applied neat onto the pre-wetted surface of the tile and agitated manually, left for 10 to 20 minutes, and then thoroughly rinsed off. The cleaning agent should never be left to dry on the surface of the tile as it may cause staining. Each tile should be given individual attention.

To agitate the detergent use green nylon pan scourers (the type usually used for washing dishes in domestic kitchens); made of nylon material they are abrasive enough to work the liquid into the body of the tile, but will not scratch the surface. Never use wire wool or any hard abrasive material. Hardened substances, such as paint splashes, which are on the surface of the tile, may be removed using a 'Stanley' blade held at a 45 degree angle in a plastic holder; specifically designed for removing paint splashes from glass they also work very well on tiles. Experienced conservators carrying out bench work cleaning of historic materials may prefer to use a scalpel blade rather than a 'Stanley' blade for mechanical cleaning because they are more controllable. A 'Stanley' blade in a plastic handle is a better tool for the purpose of removing paint or other encrustations on Victorian tile floors because of the combination of the expanse of material involved and the robustness of the ceramic body. Few contract commissioners would tolerate the time scales involved in cleaning large areas of floor with a scalpel blade. A 'Stanley' blade is also a more appropriate tool for use by an amateur.

The same methods and stain removing agents that are used for delft tiles apply also to Victorian floor tiles (see the section on cleaning seventeenth and eighteenth century tiles). Localised staining is often difficult to remove from tiles which remain in-situ mainly because any application of a stain removing agent should be preceded by soaking the tile body in water first before applying the stain removing liquid or poultice; if the body is dry the stain may be drawn further into the tile.

It is often possible to wet floor tiles sufficiently first, so the application of a rust inhibitor that contains phosphoric acid will usually remove rust stains after several applications. Rinse in distilled water afterwards. The ability to rinse away thoroughly any cleaning agent is all important. It is worth noting that all stains are difficult to remove, and some may be permanent.

Some clay bodies are prone to iron staining which is caused by complex chemical reaction within the body associated with poor clay preparation combined with excess moisture and salt action, which has forced the natural iron already present in the clay to resurface as staining. The resulting discolouration is permanent.

When the tiles are cleaned, regrouting is often a good idea. Clean, new grout will often give the tiles a visual lift; it will also protect the edges of the tiles in areas of heavy tread. Cement-based grouting mix or lime mortar grout may be used depending on the environment of the rest of the building.

The choice of protective coating is problematical as coatings should be easily reversible and harmless. Coatings are advantageous because they help to prevent the further absorption of dirt into the tile body, but as we have seen waxes are difficult to remove. Non-yellowing micro-crystalline wax applied lightly offers the best opportunity for reversibility, though it does not provide that all important 'shine' which most clients find desirable and it tends to leave a slippery surface finish which is quite inappropriate if floors are in continued use. Bees wax or linseed oil, in the long run, are detrimental because again they are difficult to remove and darken and discolour with age which will spoil the aesthetic effect of the coloured geometric or encaustic tile. There are new floor tile coating products available that claim reversibility which largely comprise of complex chains of cross-linked polymers suspended in an emulsion; the effects in the long term on semi-vitrified bodies is as yet undetermined.

Wearing rubber gloves, eye protection and, if necessary, protection against the inhalation of fumes is recommended during cleaning processes.

Paint removal from glazed tiles

Before removing paint layers on old tiles, particularly those found in public buildings, it is worth considering that the paint layer will have been considered an expedient method of refurbishment in the past. Usually the tiles found underneath the paint will be dirty, worn and damaged, and will rarely live up to expectation. Inevitably the tile scheme which is revealed may have many positive and valuable features but will be in sore need of expensive restoration. In some instances

Figure 5.11
Nineteenth century tiles which have
been covered with paint.

Figure 5.12
A sample after paint removal.

layers of old paint have provided a means of preserving the glazed surface from wear and tear and have been applied simply as a statement of changing fashions. (Figure 5.11).

Paint removal from tile or glazed surfaces is a relatively straightforward process. Dichloromethane-based paint strippers, which are water soluble, are recognised as reliable for conservation use. However, some products carry health and safety implications for use in confined areas in which case adequate ventilation or air extraction should be provided, or the correct breather masks used.

Once the paint coating has softened after the application of paint stripper, plastic spatula tools only should be used to scrape away the paint. Under no circumstances should wire wool, wire brushes or metal scrapers be used as they will inevitably scratch or scour the glazed surface of the tile and permanently damage the glaze. (Figure 5.12).

Paint may be left behind in the grout lines. Further applications of paint stripper can be applied. After each application the grout lines may be brushed out with a nylon or bristle scrubbing brush. For removing paint from delicately moulded tile faces, wooden cocktail sticks can prove very useful.

The tiles should be thoroughly washed down with clean water, preferably distilled, after all of the paint has been removed. The surface of the tiles may be tested for pH levels after washing if necessary.

Wearing rubber gloves, eye protection and, if necessary, protection against the inhalation of fumes is recommended during paint removing processes.

Salts

The damaging effect of salt crystal growth in ceramic bodies is well documented (Buys and Oakley, 1993). Broadly speaking, salts of various types, most commonly chlorides, nitrates, and phosphates, are naturally present in either the tile body itself or the underlying material of the substrate, whatever it may be, or in both. For the most part they will remain as soluble salts within the body and do no harm as long as both the tile and the substrate remain in a stable atmosphere, either humid or dry. When rapid changes of humidity occur, in the case of tile schemes this usually means excessive amounts of moisture ingress after a prolonged period of dryness. The soluble salts will then begin to recrystallise thereby expanding and creating stresses within the clay, exerting pressure which forces the clay to disintegrate resulting in exfoliation. If the expanding crystals, or subflorescence, remain below the surface the effects are extremely damaging, in a way not dissimilar to the effect caused by frost action. (Figure 5.13). If the salt crystals have penetrated right through the body gathering on the surface of the

Figure 5.13
Exfoliation caused by salt action on
floor tiles caused by moisture
leaching from below.

Figure 5.14
Salt damage to the surface of glazed
tiles caused by constant leaching of
water from above.

tiles and are left unmolested they will harden preventing further evaporation of moisture and cause areas of fine disintegration of either the fire-
skin or glaze just below the encrustation. The visual effect will have the
appearance of etching, completely destroying the surface (Figure 5.14).
Salt crystals will often appear at the place where high moisture levels in
the body reach the area where evaporation is successfully taking place.
Ashurst (1988) refers to this as the 'evaporation zone' (Figure 5.15). The
damaged areas can also become permanently stained black by the effect
of metallic salts such as iron or lead sulphides.

Fortunately nineteenth and twentieth century tiles are not generally
prone to such unstable conditions. Whether this is due to better building techniques or better tile production is unclear, because once crystallisation has occurred it is exceptionally difficult, if not impossible, to
correct in fixed tile schemes. However, occasionally unstable conditions which will produce salt crystal damage can be brought about
from excessive and prolonged water penetration from below in floor
tiles, and from above in wall tiles. The occurrence of the effects of
crystallisation on medieval tile floors is generally due to excessive
water penetration; for example, in low lying ecclesiastical buildings,
with no damp course, that are subject to a rising water table.

Dutch tiles, particularly early examples, tend to be more prone to
salt crystallisation than other types of tile as a result of high body
porosity. The problem of glaze loss is further compounded by the
relatively poor glaze bond found in tin glazed tiles.

The only course of action on fixed tile schemes is to manually scrape
the salts from the surface with a sharp blade and address the cause of
the water penetration.

Figure 5.15
Residue of salt damage caused by
slow evaporation.

Soft white salt powdery crystals or efflorescence will sometimes
form very rapidly on tiles if they have been saturated using tap water
as a cleaning agent after a prolonged period of dryness, followed by
slow evaporation. The effect is very similar to the efflorescence sometimes found on new brick; it is disfiguring and probably harmful to
some extent but does not cause the same level of material damage as
subflorescence. It should be dry brushed away as soon as possible.

Continuing care of historic and restored glazed tile schemes

Advice to others

As part of the contract completion process, conservators engaged in
works which are part of a larger building restoration programme are
required to submit continuing care data to contractors. The data forms
part of a legal requirement in the client and main contractor agree-
ment. The advice contained in the document is meant to highlight any
particular maintenance required for the greater longevity or better performance of materials used as part of the building refurbishment. In
the main this is a good idea, and if the advice given is followed rather
than flouted, then we can reasonably expect that good conservation
work, using reversible materials, will last as long as can be usefully
predicted given the nature of the materials used.

Continuing care of glazed tiles mainly centres around the cleaning
regime, particularly in the environment of public buildings where

Figure 5.16
Severe surface pollution.

contracted out cleaning companies may be responsible for day to day environmental health procedures. Experienced conservators will have an understanding of both the historic fabric and the additional materials they have been working with and their tolerances. It may be that the historic material has been found to be in such a severe state of surface pollution, decay or damage (Figure 5.16) that the conservator has decided to act with some robustness to bring it back to a state which will be considered acceptable within the context of the building's proposed use. However, advice on continuing care which is to be passed forward must assume that the recipient will have no experience with the material at all, and must be absolutely foolproof.

Advice on tiles can often be best communicated by outlining a list of 'don'ts' which will help to avoid some of the worst and most common effects of casual or inexperienced cleaning regimes along with easily communicated reasons 'why not'.

It should contain most of the following points:

- The surface glaze on historic and restored tiles is usually fragile. It should therefore be treated with some care.
- Abrasive action will permanently damage the glaze; it is unacceptable and unnecessary to use any form of abrasive cleaner or scouring cloth. Never use wire wool.
- Acid-based cleaners can permanently damage red glazes. Alkaline-based cleaners can permanently damage blue or green glazes. No form of chemical or industrial cleaners should be used at all.
- Glazed tile surfaces need only to be lightly dusted with a soft cloth periodically.
- Should the tiles become splashed from spills or the weather, wash with a dilution of a mild detergent and a soft cloth. Allow to dry then buff with a soft dry cloth.

For decorative tile panels which have been restored the advice for continuing care pertaining to cleaning should contain the following messages:

- A percentage of the surface area has been restored, these areas are very fragile.
- The restored areas are spread about the surface of the mural and many of them are not easily detectable. The restored areas may easily be damaged by even normal cleaning methods.
- Routine cleaning of the tile panel must consist only of a light dusting with a soft cloth or cotton duster.
- Do not wet clean.
- Do not use any cleaning products.
- Do not apply any solvents.

- Do not apply any waxes or polishes.
- To remove any splashes, such as food or drink, from organic substances, spot clean with warm water and a mild detergent, using a soft cloth.
- Graffiti must be removed immediately using the appropriate solvent for the purpose.
- Most graffiti solvents will not harm ceramic in the short term. If the unfortunate circumstance arises where the graffiti appears over a restored area, then the solvent will also remove the restoration, in which case the restoration should be reinstated by a conservator.

Consolidation of mortar

Consolidation procedures covering architectural tile schemes fall into two distinct materials skills base: consolidation of the mortar substrate and the ceramic itself.

Consolidation of the mortar substrate is usually achieved by introducing a material homogeneous with the substrate itself in a liquid or semi-liquid consistency which will bind the degraded or fragmented mortar, fill voids, and adhere to the adjacent surfaces, and in so doing, stabilise the degraded substrate which threatened the security of the ceramic layer. It also implies the use of a treatment method which will avoid the wholesale, and potentially damaging, lifting and removal of tiles in order to replace the original mortar substrate with new.

Degradation and consolidation of medieval mortar

A combination of lime, sand and pozzolanic aggregate of varying quantities and qualities makes up the constituent parts of medieval lime mortar mixes. They can degrade from any number of causes or combination of factors including ingress of water, frost action, impact damage or chemical change. The result is often manifest as crumbling, fissures and fractures, or voids which will allow tiles to become loose or unseated. If the underlying mortar is degraded or damaged to any great extent valuable tiles are vulnerable to damaged or worn edges, fractures, or in worst cases, complete loss.

The aim of consolidation is to refix loose tiles and provide a sound substrate while at the same time preserve the original medieval mortar. It is unwise to lift or move loose tiles from their original position as it is rarely possible to reseat them exactly as before, unless tiles have strayed so far from their original location as to make it beneficial to lift and reset.

As no two medieval mortar mixes are exactly alike it is essential to carry out a few simple trials to devise a slurry mix of hydraulic lime and water, with the possible addition of a little fine sand, which will

Figure 5.17
Mortar trials.

adequately flow far enough to fill voids beneath the tiles and give a good bond and set between mortar and tiles. Slurry would be described as a thick mixture but one which retains fluidity. Using a slurry rather than the standard stiff mortar mix used for pointing has the advantage that the tiles are less likely to become unseated during the works.

Tests may be devised by setting out a series of wooden boxes in which a close replication of the original substrate mortar is mixed and left to set; voids and fissures in the substrate can be replicated using a drill fixed with a masonry bit, or hammer and chisel (Figure 5.17). Pieces of broken earthenware or cut brick of similar texture can be used to represent the tiles and placed at intervals on the substrate. After pre-wetting the set mortar, various proportions of water to hydraulic lime can then be made up into different slurry mixes and each one either poured slowly or gravity fed through copper tubes into the trays at various places deemed best for filling all the necessary voids. Fine sand may be an appropriate addition to the slurries in order to aid setting, but it may also impede flow into all crevices between and below the tiles, so again trials with and without sand are useful. Labelling each tray with the ratio of lime sand and water of the slurry mix, followed by recording of the setting time, tendency towards shrinkage and adhesion qualities are essential data to be gathered by trials.

We have found during our own trials that a mix of four parts natural hydraulic lime (NHL3.5) to three parts water by volume has provided a good flow rate, a reasonably fast set and has bonded together the tiles and fractured mortar in most, though not all, instances. Where the lime and water slurry mix has adequately repaired the cracks in the mortar substrate and provided a sound base but has failed to bond the tiles, the addition of a little fine sand to the same ratio slurry mix will make a grouting mix which can then be poured in between tiles to aid consolidation.

In order for the consolidating mortar slurry to have a chance of adhering to medieval mortar and to tiles, all loose dust and small size debris must be carefully cleared from spaces between the tiles and also from visible voids and fissures in the mortar.

The voids must be very carefully wetted first using the minimum of water to allow the slurry to adhere to the original mortar. The amount of water must be carefully judged in order not to cause further damage to adjacent tiles, which may have only a fragile bond, by allowing too much water ingress. In line with common practice all lime mortars should be kept damp and protected from frost until set.

Causes of degradation in seventeenth and eighteenth century mortars

Thermal shock is a common cause of degradation in lime plaster mortars used as adhesives for seventeenth and eighteenth century delft

Figure 5.18
Degraded lime plaster adhesive in
a delft tile fireplace.

style tin glaze tiles, for example around fireplaces. A further cause is
water penetration by capillary action, for example rising damp, which
creates pressure within the mortar. In both instances the mortar will
first expand and then shrink on cooling or drying respectively, occa-
sioning cracked mortar or complete detachment from the ceramic
which has expanded and contracted at a different rate (Figure 5.18).
Very often, although the mortar behind the tiles has failed, the tiles
may remain in place by continuing adhesion around each tile, effectively bonding tile to tile. Failed mortar can be diagnosed by a hollow
or rattling sound emanating from behind the tile surface when tapped
gently. The surface plane of the tiles may have bulged outward and
be seen to move when slight pressure is placed on the outside face.
Corroded ironwork within or adjacent to the mortar may also cause
fracturing due to expansion of the ironwork. Corrosion can also
cause staining from iron oxides leaching into the mortar and becoming evident on the surface in the joints between tiles. Chemical changes
resulting from salt crystallisation may also degrade lime plaster causing
it to soften and crumble.

Consolidating seventeenth and eighteenth century mortars

Leaving aside the option of dismantling and the replacing the mortar with new, as described in Chapter 3, the alternative is to consolidate the original mortar by introducing an adhesive liquid which will creep into voids as far as possible and thereby give additional adhesion between tiles and mortar. The advantage is that both the tiles and the original mortar are left largely undisturbed except for the intrusion of the adhesive liquid. The disadvantage is the near impossibility of complete re-adhesion as there will always be some areas to which the liquid will not spread. Materials' compatibility and reversibility are important considerations when choosing a consolidant; it must not be stronger or harder than the ceramic tile, and as delft tiles have a relatively weak body, then the choice of consolidating materials is quite small.

A weak mix of conservation grade polyvinyl acetate emulsion (PVAC) and water is favoured by many conservators. The ratio of PVAC to water should be kept quite low, say four parts water to one part PVAC. This ensures that the mix will be less strong than the tile body, with the addition of a filler material, which will fill the voids. For this the fine grade, acrylic and calcium carbonate-based range of filler pastes (normally used for small repairs in plaster wall coatings) gives added adhesion. The consistency of the mix depends on the size of the voids to be filled and the distance to which the liquid must spread.

Introduction of the liquid adhesive to the gaps behind the tiles can be difficult and must be approached with care. In the first instance all tiles must be temporarily secured in place with an adhesive masking tape to prevent a mass fall or dislocation of tiles during the works, the tape must also remain in place until the adhesive, mortar and tiles are completely dry. Residue from the tape can be removed with a solvent such as acetone.

Gradually the grout between the tiles on the top row of the scheme can be softened with water, applied with a small brush, and carefully removed with a small pick. When all of the old grout on the top row is removed, the spaces between the tiles should be given a fine spray with water which will aid capillary action and help the adhesive to spread evenly between and behind the tiles rather than being absorbed too quickly, stopping short and forming a blockage. The adhesive mix can then be introduced into the gaps using a small paintbrush or pipette, whichever suits the situation best. Allow a drying time of at least 20 minutes, longer if possible, and then proceed down to subsequent rows and repeat the process until the bottom row of tiles is reached.

After the area of tiles and mortar have been allowed to dry completely regrouting may be carried out using a mix of feebly hydraulic lime (NHL2) and very fine silver sand at ratios of 1:1 or 1:2 depending on the textural quality of the original grouting mix. The amount of water added to the mix should be quite low as it is an advantage to have a fairly dry mix which can be pushed into the joint using the fingers (protected by a plastic glove) and then tamped firmly in using a small bristle brush. Any residue of mortar on the surface of the tile is best wiped off immediately.

Causes of degradation in nineteenth and twentieth century mortars

Visual and audio diagnosis of failed mortar in nineteenth and twentieth century tile schemes is very much the same as in tile schemes dating from the seventeenth and eighteenth centuries; bulging surface planes and a hollow sound when tapped. The causes are somewhat different; thermal shock is less likely as the commonly used adhesive, Portland cement, is less prone to thermal shock except in extreme conditions such as fire damage. The most likely effect of normal fireside temperatures with continuous heating and cooling is loosening of tiles from the mortar bed.

Excessive amounts of water following flood damage will often cause the adhesion properties of the mortar to fail while leaving the structure of the grout intact, commonly resulting in a void behind the tiles though they remain adhered to each other. Although the same conditions can arise solely due to shifting load, if ingress of water is also present then the situation is usually exacerbated. The breakdown of mortar adhesion combined with external stress, for example footfall or vibration, or continuing settling or subsidence, can have disastrous effects on the tile layer in the form of fracturing or spalling around the edges of the tiles, and even complete structural collapse (Figure 5.19).

Figure 5.19
Complete collapse of a tiled floor after severe water penetration.

In early Victorian upper floors, constructed with timber subframes, dislocation of the mortar substrate can be caused by shrinkage of the timber joists, thus creating voids which will result in uneven pressure on the mortar under the strain of load or footfall. Consequently the mortar is liable to crack or crumble and eventually unseat the tile layer (Figure 5.20).

While the adhesive layer in most nineteenth century tile schemes is usually Portland cement, very often, especially if the scheme is a pre-1870 floor construction, or there has been a Victorian tile floor laid on top of an earlier foundation subfloor, there may be an element of lime mortar either in the substrate or foundation layer in the form of packed rough mortar and aggregate. Improperly slaked lime contained within the hardcore aggregate in the form of raw burnt lime can remain active, resulting in expansion and build-up of pressure in different directions. The adhesive Portland cement layer can fail under such circumstances without the reasons being entirely obvious on first inspection.

Traditionally, the ratios used to blend a cement or lime mortar mix have never been an exact science when executed on site during the construction phase. The human element involved in the gauging of the ratios of sand to cement to water plays a large part in explaining why some areas of tile schemes will be affected by external or environmental changes that have taken place and other parts of a scheme which are subject to similar circumstances are not affected.

In Victorian or early twentieth century schemes the grout bond between the tiles will often be a cement mix which is harder than the adhesive layer, usually a one to one sand and cement slurry as advised by the tile manufacturers; it will also be a very narrow joint in most,

Figure 5.20
Crumbling lime mortar in a subfloor due to shrinkage of the timber joists.

Figure 5.21
Spalled edges of tiles due to tensile
pressure.

though not all, circumstances. Quite commonly wall tiles can stay
adhered to each other with immensely strong grout joints while not
being fixed to the cement screed beneath for many years without any
problem. The void between tiles and substrate only becomes a problem if other factors come into play, for example changes of load stress
or vibration associated with adjacent works.

The same problem in floor tiles is less benign. Where tiles are
tightly and strongly butt jointed with hard Portland cement but are not
fixed to the substrate, the whole tile layer will tend to 'bounce' under
footfall; even if the movement is only slight the result over a period of
time will be spalling and shelling of the ceramic surface around the
edges of the tile (Figure 5.21). The ceramic fails before the cement
grout joint because it is the weaker material; those tiles with the weakest body clay will be the first to suffer.

Consolidation of nineteenth and twentieth century mortars

The aim of the consolidation process is to fill the voids behind or
underneath the tiles and provide a new adhesion between the tiles
and the substrate without dismantling large parts of the whole scheme
and thereby unsettling, changing and causing unnecessarily excessive damage. However, this is rarely possible without the removal of
some tile material to facilitate the introduction of a new slurry mix
which will bond all the elements together. Removal of tile material
without damage to adjacent material will be discussed later in this
chapter, but there are obvious factors to take into account when
choosing which tiles to remove and which to leave in place. They
must be well spaced and infrequent enough not to effect more
changes to the overall scheme than necessary, but close enough to
allow the newly bonded areas to be adjacent in spread; however, an
effective consolidation can be achieved even if some gaps in the
bonding remain. Plainly it is preferable to remove a damaged tile than
a perfect example if there is a choice to be had, and, again if there is
a choice, it is always best to forfeit undecorated tiles in colours and
textures which are most easily replicated.

The cement-based slurry mix which is introduced should be weak
in structure, usually one part Portland cement to four parts of very fine
sand; one part hydrated lime may also be added if there is lime element
in the original mix. After the usual careful pre-wetting, the mix can be
introduced into the voids by means of narrow copper pipes, either
gravity fed or hand pressure pumped. Copper pipes are preferable to
plastic tubes because they are rigid, but can be curved into useful
shapes, and one end of the tube may be flattened to reach into the
voids as far as possible. Feeding mortar slurry down narrow copper
tubes is a painstakingly slow process, some might say akin to watching
paint dry. New mortar must be mixed frequently as once the hardening

process has begun it is impossible to feed down the pipes, indeed it will easily harden inside the pipes rendering them useless; a good supply of copper piping is essential. There are no standard or easily available tools to carry out this task, so it is often up to the conservators to engineer their own devices to suit the situation. The process can be fraught with technical difficulties relating to the degree of pre-wetting, the component parts and ratios of the slurry mix and the use of gravity or pressure to force the mix down the tubes. The diameter and length of the tubes also has a bearing on the success or otherwise of the exercise. However, if the alternative option is to completely lift and reset an entire scheme then it is well worth the time and effort spent in preparing test boxes, similar to those described for medieval mortar consolidation, in which to carry out trials to perfect the technique to suit the location.

The importance of grout

It is debatable whether, historically, medieval tile pavements and early delftware tiles were grouted as a separate task from the setting process, certainly the same mortar mixes were used for both purposes. There are ethical questions on the level of historical importance attached to the original grout in the overall scheme. It surely has some importance and if it is to be removed and replaced completely then samples should be retained as archive material; however, grout has a vital utility function and must be in good condition for the greater protection of the tile scheme as a whole. In most instances the conservation of a tile scheme will involve the replacement of only that part of the original grouting material which has failed and is no longer protecting the tiles. If the grout between the tiles is loose, then it has failed and should be removed and replaced.

Sound mortar grouting helps to prevent further stress movement by providing equal pressure around the individual tiles, it also protects the vulnerable edges of tiles; it is a vital part of protecting historic floors which are subject to foot traffic. Grouting is an important part of the consolidating process.

The choice of grout for use with historic tiles should either match or be closely compatible with the adhesive material, it should never be stronger.

Medieval tiles, delftware tiles and other soft bodied tiles may be grouted with a mix of feebly hydraulic lime (NHL2) and very fine silver sand at ratios of 1:1 or 1:2 depending on the textural quality of the original grouting mix. The amount of water added to the mix should be quite low as it is an advantage to have a fairly dry mix which can be pushed into the joint using the fingers (protected by a plastic glove) and then tamped in firmly using a small bristle brush until an even level just below the surface of the tile is attained. Any residue of mortar on the surface of the tile is best wiped off immediately using a slightly dampened cloth. The grout must be kept slightly damp until it has set to avoid shrinkage.

Mortar used for grouting in nineteenth and early twentieth century tile schemes is the same mortar as used for fixing and it will vary in hardness, colour and texture from scheme to scheme. Grout and adhesives were not separated as different materials with different qualities until the late 1950s. The intention in the construction of nineteenth century tile schemes was that the tiles should be 'butt' jointed (i.e. abutting each other) leaving no grout showing, nevertheless the mortar used for grouting is usually in evidence in some part of the scheme. By the 1930s designs had changed and mortar filled joints between tiles were more in evidence.

Following the conservation principle of 'replacing like with like', nineteenth and early twentieth century schemes should, correctly, be grouted using a 1:1 Portland cement and sand mix; however, as discussed, such a mix is too hard, lacks permeability and in itself presents a threat to the longevity of the tile scheme. Commercially available hydraulic cement-based grouts have a cement content of, typically, 35 per cent, making them considerably weaker than typical Victorian and early twentieth century mortar grouts. For conservation purposes the ratio of cement to very fine or silica sand may be reduced further to one part cement to four parts sand. White cement may be used if pigments are to be added.

Commercially available epoxy grouts are unsuitable because of their hardness and lack of permeability.

Matching the colour of new grout to blend in with original grout is all important for the overall finish to the consolidation work on any historic scheme; this can be done either by careful selection of sand in the case of lime or cement mixes, or the introduction of pigments of the correct colour. Commercially available pigments used for mortar which may be blended to the correct shade are readily available for large areas of grouting, but for smaller areas artist's powder pigment or acrylic paints may be used.

It is difficult if not almost impossible to remove nineteenth century grout without unacceptable levels of damage to the edges of the tiles, particularly if the tiles are glazed, because of the exceptional hardness of the typical mortar used for the purpose. Therefore it is far preferable to improve the visual impact of the scheme as a whole by careful cleaning of the grout. A solution of distilled water and non-ionic detergent agitated into the surface of the grout with a folded green nylon scouring pad (the type usually used for washing dishes in domestic kitchens), followed by thorough rinsing, will usually suffice to bring about an enhancement. The level of abrasiveness of the nylon pad should first be tested against the edges of glazed tiles, where they occur, in an unobtrusive corner of the scheme, to ensure that the glaze is robust enough to withstand such treatment. If there is any doubt a toothbrush can be substituted for the nylon pads.

Consolidation of ceramic tiles in-situ

Further to consolidation of the mortar substrate, conservation treatments of architectural tile schemes should include methods for consolidation of ceramic material suitably adapted for application at the site of the scheme and away from the controlled environment of the studio, laboratory or workshop. Consolidation is necessary when tile material is fragile to the point of threatening loss of original material; by implication the tiles are damaged in some way. Consolidation is generally considered to be a conservation technique that does not include restoration.

Causes of damage to in-situ tiles

Damage to in-situ ceramic tiles manifests as fractures, delamination, and spalling. The causes stem from several sources which may act on the material alone or collectively; poor manufacture, water ingress and temperature change which lead to frost or salt crystallisation damage, impact, load shift, vibration, or expansion of corroded metalwork integral to the tile scheme.

Poor manufacture can have a contributory effect towards delamination when combined with other forces such as water, frost, salt crystallisation, and sometimes impact. Improperly wedged plastic clay can leave behind folds or air pockets within the tile body which, when underfired, result in fault lines or weaknesses. These weak spots are susceptible when combined with attack from those external forces already listed. Water penetration, whether from behind the tile or from surface moisture, will naturally gather in the fault lines and will either expend its own pressure to force the layers apart or combine with temperature or humidity changes to allow frost or salt crystals to form and exert enough pressure to force the surface layer of the ceramic to part from the main body. The tile's surface may not always become completely detached from the main body but will sometimes form a horizontal split through the tile leaving it especially vulnerable under further stress of impact or vibration. Delamination linked to poor manufacture can be found in tiles from all periods of tile making (Figure 5.22).

Spalling or shelling are terms often used to describe the condition where 'shell'-shaped flakes of surface fire-skin or glaze spontaneously burst away from the surface exposing the body of the ceramic

Figure 5.22
Delamination due to frost action.

Figure 5.23
Spontaneous shedding of glaze due to tensile pressure.

Figure 5.24
Fracturing caused by corrosion
expansion.

Figure 5.25
Compressive tension and shifting causing fracturing and
misalignment.

underneath (Figure 5.23). This condition is indicative of extreme compressive or tensile force on the edges of tiles, usually the result of building load shift, though it can also be caused by corrosion and expansion of ironwork used structurally within the tile scheme. Complete delamination as described above can also result from the same types of external pressure. The edges of tiles are usually worst affected though glaze fragments can also detach from over the whole surface (Figures 5.24 and 5.25). The same compressive or tensile forces can also result in fracturing of the whole tile body and forcing a shift out of alignment between the fractured parts.

Consolidation treatments for free-standing ceramic objects are explained admirably by Buys and Oakley (1993). The treatment of ceramic tile as an integral part of an architectural scheme differs only in those aspects which relate to conditions which are found where the tile is not detached from its surroundings. Consolidation of tiles in-situ usually refers to bonding together loose fragments of tile material, or parts of tile, either glaze or body, which have a potential for further fragmentation and loss. Options for treatment must therefore take into account environmental and causal issues as well as the possible effects of contiguous materials.

Consolidating medieval tiles

Consolidation of medieval tiles will generally be covered by the practice of bonding loose or fragmented parts of ceramic tile back into the position from whence they came. A good adhesive bond relies on the surface planes to which the adhesive is to be applied being clean, dry and dust free. No surface found in ancient buildings can ever be made completely dry and free of dust; there will inevitably be a level of humidity present as well as an accumulation of dust particles in the location of the damage. However, some effort must be made to remove dust and dirt from the surfaces to be bonded. The fractured areas should be brushed with a small, dry, soft paintbrush to remove loose debris, and then patted lightly over with a soft cloth dipped in a degreasing solvent such as acetone or industrial methylated spirit.

Adhesives used on historic tiles should be easily reversible and should not form a bond which is stronger than the ceramic material. Use of an overly strong adhesive presents a real danger of further fragmentation of the ceramic alongside the bonded joint if it is subjected to subsequent added pressure. Paraloid B72 (USA Acryloid B72) is very suited to site work, it is fast drying, taking only 24 hours to harden and performs well in all but the most extreme low temperatures. It is stable over long periods of time but easily reversible in acetone and requires only light contact pressure to give a good bond when it is applied to both surfaces of the joint. Paraloid B72 has been shown to remain transparent in colour for a greater length of time than many other adhesives and can also be diluted in acetone and drizzled in between delaminated surfaces which have not completely parted.

Larger voids in tile bodies, or missing parts of whole tiles, can be infilled with a weak mix of lime mortar, if there exists a threat of further fragmentation due to unavoidable effects of the immediate environment, for example vibration, impact from footfall, movement

Figure 5.26
Lime mortar infill in medieval tiles.

Figure 5.27
Plaster infill in eighteenth century tiles.

Figure 5.28
Full restoration on delft tiles.

stress or other circumstances which may cause pressure on the fragile clay body. Mortar infilling will help to produce a more solid and sound surface area which in itself helps to protect the tiles. However, the advantages of stability gained by infilling tiles may need to be balanced against the, sometimes unappealing, visual impact of lime mortar used as a filler material. (Figure 5.26).

Consolidating seventeenth and eighteenth century tiles

Fragile glaze surfaces frequently present the need for consolidation in delft or tin glazed tiles; exfoliation has a number of causes, mostly inherent, as discussed in Chapter 2, and further exacerbated by age and environment. Fracturing and delamination as a result of pressure from corroded ironwork is also frequently found around fireplaces, the first response should be to remove the cause of any increased pressure by treating the corrosion.

Paraloid B72 can be used as a standard consolidant adhesive for delft tiles and other soft bodied tiles; it may be applied, diluted in acetone, with a fine paintbrush around the fragile edges of distressed glaze and over vulnerable crazed areas. Excess solution left on the surface of the glaze is removable using a soft cloth dipped in acetone. Broken fragments of tile can be rebonded with an adhesive strength solution of Paraloid B72 in acetone after the edges of the fragments have been cleaned of dust, dirt and grease. The edges of fragmented tiles around fireplaces are often blackened with the effects of soot and smoke and must be cleaned as thoroughly as possible. Frequently wet cleaning, as described earlier in this chapter, is needed in order to reduce the soot blackening as much as possible, the edges of the fracture must be thoroughly dry before bonding can take place.

Filling missing areas of glaze or body clay is preferable to leaving damaged edges and surfaces uncovered and therefore unprotected. Exposed body clay and fragmented glaze will be subject to dirt ingress, further glaze exfoliation or continued delamination and fracturing in uncontrolled environments. The original material of the tile will be better preserved if there is a sound surface area. The introduction of a white plaster of Paris infill will not greatly detract from the overall visual aesthetic of the pale blue or shades of white, which are the dominant ground colour in delftware. Plaster, provided it is not high density and therefore too hard and prone to shrinkage, is also the best material to use as filler as it complements the body clay in terms of absorption of humidity and tensile strength. Once it has hardened it is not soluble, but will soften and expand slightly when fully wetted to enable removal by manual scraping with a scalpel. If the intention is to restore the colour and decoration to the fragmented areas then it is advisable to use an acrylic and calcium carbonate-based fine surface filler as a final finishing layer to the plaster infill as it will provide a smoother denser surface finish for paint application (Figures 5.27 and 5.28).

Consolidating nineteenth and twentieth century tiles

The treatment for rebonding and consolidation of fragmented glaze, delamination or fractured ceramic body affecting nineteenth and twentieth century tiles is more or less identical to the treatment given to delft tiles, although the causes of exfoliation and loss of glaze are slightly different to those presented in soft bodied tiles, being more usually external rather than inherent. Broken fragments of tile can be rebonded with an adhesive strength solution of Paraloid B72 in acetone after the edges of the fragments have been cleaned of dust, dirt and grease. Wet cleaning of fracture edges is usually only necessary if the break is old and has absorbed such a degree of dirt as to jeopardise the bonding mechanism. Exfoliation and loss of glaze can be consolidated using the same method as described for delft tiles.

Infilling of missing parts of fragmented tiles is equally important for hard body semi-vitreous tiles as tiles with soft body clay and glaze. It protects the damaged edges of ceramic body and glaze thereby avoiding dirt ingress. Infilling of voids resulting from missing fragments helps to displace uneven pressure and check possible further shifting and fracturing, it also prevents further impact or abrasion damage to fragile edges.

Ceramic conservators have many options of filler pastes available for use with hard body ceramics at their disposal; however, they are not all suitable for in-situ repairs on architectural schemes. Plaster or acrylic-based fillers will not provide the material longevity required for most nineteenth and twentieth century schemes where the tile surface is expected to perform as a robust wall or floor surface which is subject to normal environmental wear and tear, including regular cleaning regimes which are not under the control or management of a conservator. Some filler products require constant and controlled temperatures over several hours to allow curing to occur, inevitably restricting their use on busy construction sites where most in-situ architectural tile conservation projects take place. Two part epoxy-based fillers can be too hard in their final cured state to be compatible with the body of the ceramic. Some epoxy fillers also take considerable time and effort, because of their hardness, to cut back to a suitably detailed, finely finished, profile. All products will be subject to varying degrees of colour change or moisture degradation over long periods of time especially where there is no control over exposure to ultraviolet rays or humidity levels.

Polyester resin paste mixed with 2 per cent peroxide hardener or initiator provides the best compromise for on-site use, as it gives a fast cure in all but the very lowest of temperatures, and it will also cure in humid conditions. Its hardened state is less hard than most hard bodied ceramic and at the same time is reversible using a dichloromethane-based disintegrator. It will cut back to profile relatively easily, giving a harder, smoother finish than plaster. Over a period of time oxidisation resulting in yellowing will occur, although it has good resistance to colour change and can remain stable in favourable light level conditions for up to 20 years, though it is not guaranteed to do so. The base colour of commercially available polyester resin is usually pale grey so it must be mixed with colorants or pigments to make an appropriate matching colour for the infill. Once hardened it is cut back to profile using a sharp blade or scalpel before finally smoothing with a succession of fine to ultra-fine grade abrasive papers, cloths or creams. The use of abrasive papers must be carefully controlled with the fingertip as any scouring action over the actual ceramic glaze or body clay will cause irreparable damage.

While polyester resin paste offers the best compromise as a consolidating filler for in-situ conservation to tiles in architectural schemes where longevity, strength, speed and ease of use are overarching factors, when deciding which materials to opt for, museum display work is probably best served by using acrylic and calcium carbonate-based fine surface filler paste. Ultimately conserved or restored tiles destined for museum display will be in a protected and controlled environment, not subject to rigorous cleaning regimes or threatened impact, abrasion or shifting. Plaster and acrylic-based fillers tend to give greater immunity to colour change and are much more easily reversed.

Painting or retouching

The purpose of painting or retouching the filler material with a coating, which matches not just the colour but also the opacity and texture of the surrounding ceramic, is to smooth over and diminish the visual impact of the damaged area. For the same reason we introduce carefully colour and texture matched replacement new tile, we attempt to match with added colour enhancement the usually neutral colour of the filler material. Colour retouching helps us to visually read the artistic and design realisation of the scheme as a whole.

The use of unretouched neutral colour fillers is appropriate and correct for archaeological material and medieval tiles. Plain white plaster fills can in some instances be visually suited for delft tile schemes because they are most commonly made up of a series of related but individually designed tiles, although there are many examples in the Netherlands of large high status panels or wall schemes where the hand painted design is carried over many tiles. The practice there is to use painted retouching on filler material to complete the design, and it is generally to be recommended as visually enhancing to the scheme as a whole.

Similarly, art tile panels of the nineteenth and twentieth centuries benefit from colour retouching of the filler material on the basis that reading the design as a complete entity is unrewarding if damage remains prominent to the eye (Plates 9 and 10).

A full and detailed explanation of the practice of retouching is ably and authoritatively described in *The Conservation and Restoration of Ceramics* (Buys and Oakley, 1993). The practice of retouching damaged ceramics is highly skilled and should not be attempted by the untrained hand.

Our interest in this text centres on retouching only in a broad sense. As with filler materials there are many different paint systems which conservators and restorers use to achieve the finish they require which will blend in sympathetically with the surrounding ceramic. Each practitioner also has their own favoured technique, partly because the skill is somewhere near an art form.

Restoration retouching as an integral part of site work when tiles remain in location has its own special technical difficulties and parameters which affect the ease at which the work can advance, the final result, and the future longevity of the painted material. They include low temperatures, high humidity, dust, poor light, limited contract time and difficult access. Therefore when choosing a paint system for on-site retouching, it must include qualities of reversibility, a hard finish, ease of use in all temperatures, be fast drying and possess a reasonable degree of colour permanence.

Reversibility is the touchstone of conservation ethics and providing retouching is confined to the area of filler material only; the paint should only travel over onto the ceramic enough to blend the two parts together visually, then the other requirements of hard finish, to provide robust longevity, and fast drying, because no construction site is ever dust free, can be met. Urea-formaldehyde-based resin glaze used with an acid catalyst and mixed with dry pigments provides all of the above properties but has a poor reputation for colour permanence, though in all other respects it performs well. The resin glaze is available in two forms: clear and white. The glazes are the same, the white having the addition of titanium dioxide. The choice of which to use depends on the colour or opacity of the desired end colour. Small amounts of glaze, thinner and catalyst are decanted onto an artist's paint palette with separate dished compartments. Dry powder artist's pigments of the desired colour are added to the glaze in small amounts until a perfect match with the original ceramic glaze is attained. Once the colour match is perfected then the catalyst is added with an eyedropper to no more than 2 per cent by volume. More than 2 per cent will result in instability of colour. The glaze may then be painted directly onto the filler using a small artist's sable hair paintbrush. The glaze may be added layer upon layer if necessary allowing an interval drying time in between layers. The drying time depends upon prevalent conditions. Once dry each layer may be sanded to obviate the appearance of brush strokes using very find grade abrasive papers or creams. While the glaze will be fully dry in a matter of hours it will require between two weeks to one month to properly harden.

The properties required in a paint system used under studio conditions and destined for museum display fall into an altogether wider set of parameters: ease of reversibility standing virtually alone at the top of the list of priorities, alongside colour permanence. Hardness of finish, speed of drying and longevity are properties which have less relevance in the controlled environment of studio or museum.

Whichever paint system is chosen the end result should be a perfectly colour and texture matched infill which provides a neat and tidy repair that is not necessarily invisible, but which is compatible and sympathetic to the eye.

Safe removal of damaged historic tiles

Medieval tiles

In this section we will make a distinction between medieval and later material. Most medieval tiles are located within Scheduled Ancient Monuments or listed buildings and are protected by law. There may be occasions when damaged medieval tiles must be lifted and relocated in pursuit of the greater good. However, actions of this sort, with far reaching consequences, are best carried out by fully experienced conservators or archaeologists. It is usually considered best practice first to investigate thoroughly the nature of the ceramic, mortar and location, and thereafter make a written report of the findings that takes into account the known history and future life of the site and any other factors which may have a bearing on the decision making process. The final report should be followed by a detailed consultation with whoever is the governing body or individual that is in control of the whole site. The decision to lift and relocate medieval tiles or mortar should never be taken alone.

Eighteenth century and later tiles

There are many instances when the introduction of new replacement tiles into a scheme is necessary and beneficial. The continued inclusion of tiles within a scheme which may be worn or damaged beyond repair represents a threat to the life of the scheme as a whole if replacement tiles are not introduced which bring the overall condition to a more favourable aspect. The aim of such an exercise is to remove historic tile material which is damaged beyond repair in readiness for replacement with new, without incurring further damage to adjacent or surrounding historic material in the process.

Floor schemes are the most obvious example, where damaged and dangerous areas of heavy tread must be renewed in order to make normal pedestrian movement safe (Figure 5.29). Frequently Victorian

Figure 5.29
Damage forming a trip hazard in floor tiles at the entrance to a church.

glazed wall schemes display a flamboyance of colour and design in near perfect condition on the upper parts of the wall area but have suffered neglect and damage over the lower half, while the formerly utilitarian, but now greatly prized, eighteenth century fireplace or dairy scheme is unusual if its condition is complete.

Most importantly the appropriate replacement tiles must be at hand before removal work begins. To calculate the number of tiles which need to be available to complete the replacement work all tiles scheduled for replacement should be identified. A list of the sizes and colours should be compiled and an inventory made of the quantities of each type of tile present in the scheme. A calculated 10 per cent of each of those numbers should be in-built into the quantities list, this will put in place the appropriate number of each type of tile to cover the designated repair works and any accidental damage caused to adjacent tiles, it will also allow a small stock of tiles for any possible future damage or failure.

As discussed in Chapter 3, grouting material in historic tile schemes, dating from before 1950, is almost always made up of the same lime or cement-based mortar as used to fix the tiles to the substrate. Victorian and early twentieth century grout, being cement based, is more often than not particularly strong and will have bonded adjacent tiles together to the extent that they have, to all intents and purposes, become one object. Victorian tiles are generally found to be closely pushed against one another with little or no space between, and are referred to as 'butt jointed'.

Uncontrolled impact from a hammer and chisel against a damaged tile will cause shockwaves to run through the ceramic at random thereby causing fractures to run in any direction, often across cement grout lines and into sound adjacent tiling. The damaged tile must be separated from its neighbours first, before any shockwaves have the opportunity to cross the grout line.

Damaged tile material can be extracted quickly and easily using the following method; however, it is important to note that these activities should only be carried out by those who have been fully trained in the use of power cutting tools and are fully acquainted with current health and safety requirements and procedures. Once these are in place:

Test the wall or floor area first for any possible steelwork or live electric cables hidden beneath the surface which may represent a hazard; this is easily carried out by sweeping the wall or floor area with a battery operated cable detector alarm. If steelwork or live cables are present do not continue with the damaged tile removal process.

Soundings can be taken across wall areas by tapping gently with a rubber mallet to determine if the damaged tiles are located within a larger area of wall tiles which are no longer fixed to the substrate but

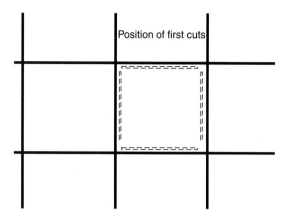

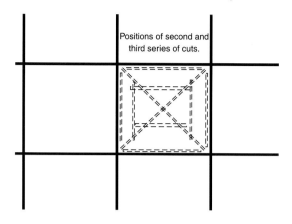

Figure 5.30
Diagram to illustrate removal of damaged historic tiles.

Figure 5.31
Diagram to illustrate removal of damaged historic tiles.

are held in place only by tension and the cement grout which bonds them to each other. A hollow sound will emanate if there is a void somewhere beneath the tile layer. If so, it is essential that all of the tiles which surround the damaged tile should be taped horizontally and vertically to each other to avoid collapse when the tension is broken by cutting. Ordinary masking tape will suffice as its use is only temporary.

Tile dust is hazardous to health so all personal protective equipment and safety measures should be put in place prior to carrying out cutting operations. A health and safety risk assessment should be carried out and surrounding building fabric or furnishings should be protected from dust. The use of air extraction or an industrial vacuum cleaner is advisable to contain and collect the volume of cement and tile dust that will be airborne as a result of the cutting process. Goggles or safety glasses must be worn to protect eyes from flying debris. Masks must be worn to protect from hazardous dust and ear defenders to protect the ears from excessive noise levels, plus any other personal safety equipment deemed necessary. Co-workers must also be protected from hazards.

Using a small hand-held angle grinder fitted with a diamond edged cutting blade, 11 cm in diameter, cut width no greater than 2 mm, make cuts around the perimeter of the damaged tile, at a distance of between 3 and 4 mm *inside* the grout line. The cut must penetrate the full depth of the tile. Avoid going closely into the corners as any over-run of the cut will damage the next tile (Figure 5.30).

The cuts are made inside the grout line in order to avoid damaging the edges of the adjacent tile, cutting along the grout line is likely to take at least 1 mm off the edge of the adjacent tile and thus create roughened edges and an overall space which is larger than the replacement tile.

Make a second series of cuts to the same depth diagonally across the tile. Make a third series of cuts across each of these diagonals (Figure 5.31).

Taking a flat 2 inch cold chisel and a hammer starting at the centre of the tile and working outwards begin to knock away all of the parts of the tile until all that remains is the 3–4 mm of tile which is around the edge. Change to a 1 inch chisel with a thin blade and carefully tap along the grout line holding the chisel at 90 degrees to the tile face. The remaining tile should fall away.

If more depth space is required on the revealed cement bed, because the replacement tile is either of the same thickness or thicker than the original, then excess concrete can be removed by the same means. Every bit of excess grout left at the edges of the cleared space must be completely cleaned back using a selection of small chisels and light hammer work.

This principal of tile removal can be used for any size or type of tile.

The methods described above for removal of damaged tiles should only be carried out by those who have undergone full health and safety training in the use of powered rotary cutting tools and are fully acquainted with current health and safety requirements and procedures.

Removal of steel pins

It is rare to find an interior wall tile scheme which has not at some time in its history been affected by fixtures, fittings or services having been attached directly into the glazed tile surface by means of drilling and screwing or even hammer and nails. Where the interior is prone to dampness or high humidity levels all unnecessary steel pins found in tile schemes should be removed before either replacement or repair of the damaged tile is realised. Steel or iron left in place below the surface of the replacement tile will eventually corrode, iron oxide stains will, at first, permeate the body of the new tile from behind and then on through to the surface. As the corrosion continues, expansion will take place causing enough pressure to fracture the tile. The same applies to resin repairs which have been made over the top of undisturbed steel screws or nails.

Removing a pin by simply knocking, prising or levering will cause the ceramic surface to spall and break away in quite large quantities around the pre-existing hole; damage may travel across the grout line into adjacent tiles (Figure 5.32).

Always attempt to unscrew all screwed in fixtures, never prise nails or screws out of tiles without extreme care; empty rawl plugs can be drilled out using a masonry drill bit or preferably a diamond coated drill bit. Really stubborn steel pins can only be removed by drilling holes into the ceramic and substrate all around the steel to a greater depth and thereby loosening the pin. Successfully releasing stubborn steel pins is very difficult to achieve without threatening to render the tile so badly damaged that it becomes a candidate for replacement rather than repair.

Figure 5.32
Steel fixings left in glazed tiles.

If a tile must be removed because it has been damaged by the insertion of steel screws which are still in place, follow the same method as described above; placing the second and third series of cuts in such positions as to isolate only a small proportion of the tile surrounding the screw or nail, which then can be levered without damage to surrounding tiles.

Relocation of eighteenth century decorative tile panels and schemes

Eighteenth century tile schemes in their original location are typically fixed to the substrate with a lime-based plaster or mortar which would be described as 'soft'. Water, in sufficient volume and over sufficient length of time, will penetrate small fissures in the granular structure of the mortar causing it to swell slightly, enough to facilitate careful removal. The water may be sprayed or drizzled down the surface of the tiles; removing the grout material between the tiles will facilitate water penetration. Grout can be softened with water and removed either manually with a sharp knife or, if the tiles are spaced far enough apart, more than 1.5 mm, by using a power tool fixed with a fine edged oscillating diamond blade. It is important, however, not to place any stress against the tile until water has penetrated the reverse of the tile completely. After removing all of the grout and achieving complete saturation, gentle tapping around the edge of each tile between the adhesive layer and the substrate using a flat, wide edged glazing knife and lightweight mallet will often be enough to cause a separation between the layers. A second pair of hands is required to cover the tile and prevent it from falling. As each tile is removed more water should be allowed to soak into the substrate of the adjacent tiles. Surrounding areas, hearths, floors etc. must be protected from quantities of water. Strong polythene sheets and frequent use of a wet-vacuum appliance are recommended.

After releasing the tile from the substrate excess plaster can be removed from the reverse by soaking in water and manually scraping the tile with a scalpel or sharp blade.

Relocation of nineteenth and twentieth century decorative tile panels and schemes

Ethical considerations

Dismantling and moving nineteenth and twentieth century tile panels or schemes is difficult and will almost certainly result in damage to the ceramic to some degree. All alternative avenues should be explored

Figure 5.33
Redevelopment of a baby cereal
factory building leaving the original
tiled façade in place.

before the final decision is made to relocate. Determination and a willingness to incorporate historic tiles within well-designed architecture can overcome many of the obstacles related to leaving tiles in their original location. In the context of social history a tile scheme can beneficially provide a visual link with the past life of a building whose function may be altered completely (Figure 5.33). With this in mind many planners and local conservation agencies rightly encourage the integration of historic material and new functions.

Nevertheless commonly found situations arise where decorative tile schemes must be moved or relocated to avoid total loss. Many public spaces designed in the late 1950s and early 1960s are now being considered for redevelopment. A greater awareness of planning for enjoyment of urban spaces integrated with safety and security means that tiles used as decorative elements for underpasses or poorly designed public spaces are, of necessity, being relocated. The artistic merit of twentieth century tile design and the durability of the material are recognised as valuable assets worth retaining, but often the original location does not do them justice.

In addition there are numerous late Victorian and early Edwardian buildings, institutional in function and with no great architectural worth which have now come to the end of their useful lives perhaps as hospitals or schools. They are either being demolished or redeveloped to serve other functions but are often decorated with tile panels depicting nursery rhymes or poetic scenes which have great social and sentimental value within the local community. Wealthy nineteenth century philanthropists frequently saw endowment of tile schemes in hospitals and schools as a valuable gesture towards the betterment of the community at large, as tiles provided a clean, hygienic and cheerful interior for children to inhabit. Often a groundswell of public opinion to which local authorities are now sensitive will demand that tile schemes are relocated to other public buildings as part of the continuity of community.

There are also, of course, occasions when tiles must be removed and relocated to facilitate important structural repairs which will ultimately prolong the life of the building as a whole. However, the decision to remove and relocate decorative tile schemes should never be taken lightly or in a cavalier fashion.

Practice of relocation

As previously noted, schemes from the late Victorian period and later are invariably adhered to the substrate with dense Portland cement mortar. The mortar mix will inevitably be stronger than the ceramic body of the tile and as both materials – ceramic and Portland cement – are inflexible and unforgiving in the extreme there is little opportunity for relocating tiles without some degree of damage. Any method used for relocation is best viewed as successful only in terms of damage limitation. Separating securely bonded tiles from the adhesive substrate layer is fraught with difficulty and potential for damage.

Portland cement is insoluble in water or solvents and while there are some positive effects to be gained by water penetration the volume of water and length of time required for water to significantly affect the bond between tile and substrate is sometimes impractical to attain. Continuous water penetration will eventually loosen the bond between tile and substrate but it will take a long time to do so. Similarly hydrochloric acid has the ability to dissolve low-level cement accretions on the surface of tiles but it will not affect the bond in volumes or solutions low enough to have no deleterious effect on the ceramic.

The most effective and least damaging method of relocation, if the structural circumstances permit and the resources are available, is to move tiles en bloc in large sections while still attached to the wall and substrate. This method of relocation is only possible where the surrounding structures are earmarked for demolition and can only be pursued, for obvious reasons of safety, with the full approval and under the supervision of qualified structural engineers.

There is no definitive method for relocating large tile murals as each situation will be different and have a range of mitigating factors which must be taken into account to ensure safe relocation with least damage to the tile fabric. There are nevertheless some characteristics common to most projects which, if given careful consideration, can contribute to success.

The most successful relocation projects are usually the result of team effort, where each part of the process is carried out only by those who are qualified as experts in their field. For example, the conservation adviser may be best placed to carry out the initial photographic recording and advise on the best cladding material to cushion and protect the ceramic face, but the heavy lifting must be under the control of those qualified to carry out that procedure.

A successful example of this method of relocation is the Gordon Cullen tile mural in the Lower Precinct, Coventry, described in Chapter 4. The success of the project relied not only upon accurate measurements and precision cutting but also that the tiles were set upon a sizable precast concrete structure which gave great stability to the cut sections during the lifting process. However, many tile murals are set onto brickwork which may be of dubious stability. The brick-work will not give the necessary stability to the tile panel which has no structural integrity of its own. Therefore each section of the mural designated for lifting must be completely supported on the face and rear to avoid flexing and cracking. The supporting structures may be in the form of timber battens and plywood boards, or specially con-structed steel cradles. The tile sections can be drilled, if necessary, to fix supporting boards and timber battens used to avoid flexing. Though drilling through the face of the ceramic will cause obvious damage, the damage can be restored once relocation is complete.

An alternative to drilling through the tile face to fix the supporting timber battens is to bond the battens to the tile face with an adhesive; however, the adhesive must be relatively strong, have a good surface bond and must be reversible. The drawback of adhesive fixing is the possibility that the glaze face of the tile can suffer unless great care is taken to thoroughly reverse the adhesive before attempting to remove the battens during the restoration phase. Most methods of fixing a sup-port system to the tile sections have a downside and the choice to be made is one of damage limitation in the specific circumstances.

Support battens must be evenly spaced apart to avoid any flexing and cracking when the panels are manoeuvred. The ceramic face should be padded with a layer of cushioning material before the support boards and battens are fixed.

The precise technology and equipment used for the lifting should be left to the judgement of qualified heavy lifting engineers, whose input and skill is vital to success.

The decision where to make the cuts that will divide the mural into suitable sections for lifting is best made in advance of the works accompanied by a drawn plan. The panels should be as large as pos-sible within the bounds of safe practice as this will reduce the amount of damage to the mural caused by cutting. The decision where to make the cuts should be taken jointly between the structural engineer in charge of the works and the conservation adviser. The structural engineer is qualified to determine the ideal dimension and weight for the safety and security of the lifting, while the conservation adviser can determine the best line of cut to preserve the most important parts of the design from any possible damage. The last word should be with the structural engineer.

It is beneficial to engage an expert diamond cutting team to carry out the work of dividing the mural into sections; they should first demonstrate their ability to carry out detailed, accurate cutting. The operative must be able to make narrow cuts no greater than 2 mm wide on the face of the mural accurately following along the line of grout joint, through the Portland cement adhesive and render coat to the brickwork. The operative must then follow the exact path of the cuts which were made on the face at the rear of the wall, through the brickwork to coincide with the cuts to the face, so that both sets of cuts meet up exactly causing a vertical division. The structural engineer is best qualified to measure and mark up the paths the cut lines should take.

The complete stability of the designated sections must, of course, be ensured before any cutting takes place in order to prevent any uncontrolled shifting or movement of the, inevitably very heavy, panels made up of tile, brick, and timber, which could present a danger to the cutting operatives.

If the successfully divided and lifted sections of the mural are to be placed in storage in readiness for restoration work, they are best stored face down to facilitate removal of the unwanted brickwork without recourse to expensive and difficult turning manoeuvres. The brickwork can be removed in a controlled fashion in workshop conditions or can remain in place and incorporated into the new location.

Dismantling walls wholesale is not always technically possible or desirable and some tile schemes are of course decorative floors. An alternative method for removing tiles from their original setting is to detach them individually from the supporting substrate. However, it cannot be overstressed that uncontrolled impact from hammer and chisel in an attempt to remove tiles from walls or floors will only result in disaster, causing shockwaves to move indiscriminately through tile and adhesive resulting in fracturing. Nineteenth and twentieth century tile schemes, as we have discussed in previous chapters, will be made up of three distinct layers: the tile; the cement bonding layer, often twice the thickness of the tile; and the substrate which may be brick in the case of walls or a rough aggregate foundation layer in the case of floors. The principle of successful removal lies in separating the cement bonding layer away from the substrate, thus giving the ceramic tile the extra thickness and strength of the attached cement adhesive, which can be removed later with workshop-based facilities.

Before commencement of cutting processes it is important to test the wall or floor area first for any possible steelwork or live electric cables hidden beneath the surface which may represent a hazard; this is easily carried out by sweeping the wall or floor area with a battery operated cable detector alarm. If live cables are present do not continue with the tile removal process.

The tiles which are intended for careful removal must first be isolated from the immediately surrounding structure or material, which is likely to be a contributing factor towards keeping them in place. This can be achieved by cutting a careful line around the perimeter edge of the mural or scheme using cutting machinery fitted with either a rotary or oscillating diamond coated blade.

Diamond coated wheels or blades have now become available in a wide variety of sizes and qualities. The technology of applying the diamonds to the edge of the metal wheel or blade is also highly developed and frequently changing, with specific blades designed for specific tasks. Blades are available in a variety of diameters; the width of the cut that the blade will make will also vary depending on size from about 1.3 mm at the smallest and upwards. Machinery and power tools are available that will hold either a rotary or oscillating blade. The advantage of the oscillating blade is that it is more easily controlled and will cut into corners, whereas a rotary blade will not; however, rotary blades are faster and more powerful and will cut harder material more easily. Blades with segmented rims will give a faster, rougher cut, while a blade with a continuous rim will give a smoother cut, but will wear out more quickly. Blades with embedded diamonds around the rim are more likely to last longer than blades where the rim is coated. Blades may also be water cooled or dry cut. It is important to research the correct type and size of machine and blade for the task in hand with the manufacturers.

Having cleared the plaster, cement render or sacrificial tile work back to the substrate above or to the side of the tile scheme using a hammer and chisel, the process of separating each tile from its neighbours, which will prevent giving shockwaves the opportunity to cross the grout line, can begin.

Some considerable skill and care are required to cut along the lines of the grout joints both horizontally and vertically using the narrowest cut of blade available but which will also penetrate deeply enough to cut the cement bonding layer through completely at all points right back to the brick substrate.

The cutting process separates each tile from its neighbour and thus prevents shockwaves from travelling across from one tile to the next. It will also release the tension which may be present across the whole panel of tiles. Starting with a tile located at a corner of the panel, because it will have two edges where the substrate and brickwork are now visible, careful tapping with a thin blade cold chisel and hammer along the visible joints between the mortar and the brick will almost

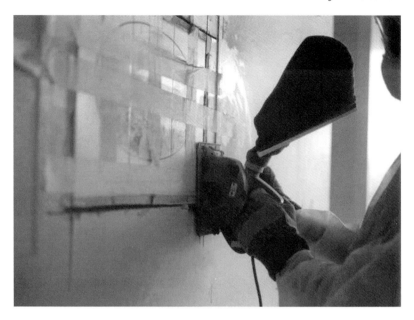

Figure 5.34
Cutting around the perimeter of a
tiled panel in preparation for
removal.

Figure 5.35
Isolating each tile.

always release the tile, along with its adhesive layer still attached, from
the substrate (Figures 5.34–5.36).

The most important point to make here is that although the above
method *will almost always release the tile* there is definitely no
guarantee that the division between adhesive and substrate will be
made successfully. There may be overriding factors: the bond may be
too strong; the cement adhesive layer may be embedded too deeply
and securely into the pointing between the brickwork; and the bricks
themselves may be too hard. But with careful cutting and handling the
division between the brickwork and the cement layer can be made.

Figure 5.36
Releasing tiles from the substrate with mortar attached.

The above method of removal also carries with it the damage which will result from the process of cutting the tiles to provide the necessary separation. At least 1 mm will be lost from the edges of all tiles, which will not only destroy the proper edges of the tile but also reduce their size. In the case of geometric or encaustic floor tiles this is not such a serious proposal as once the floor is relaid and regrouted the overall loss both visually and dimensionally is not of great consequence. However, glazed decorative panels will suffer far more seriously as the original glazed edge of each tile will be lost, along with whatever elements of linear design that cross over from tile to tile. Any more serious damage such as fractured tiles from glazed decorative wall murals can be restored, while damaged floor tiles can be replaced with matching new ones if necessary. Restoration techniques can cover this loss, but it is nevertheless irretrievable and must be weighed into the equation when making the decision to relocate tiles and which methods to choose.

The methods described above for relocation of tiles should only be carried out by those who have undergone full health and safety training in the use of powered rotary cutting tools and are fully acquainted with current health and safety requirements and procedures.

Preparing for reuse or display

Tiles which have been released from their original location often have a thickness of mortar or adhesive attached to the rear. Non-water resistant acrylic-based tile adhesive can be removed by soaking in water for approximately 24 hours and then scraping using a sharp

'Stanley' blade or scalpel. Lime mortar residues will often respond to the same treatment but may have to be removed using a small hand-held angle grinder power tool fitted with a stone cutting wheel or diamond cutting wheel as described below for Portland cement. The risk of fracturing the tiles is then greatly diminished.

Most tile conservation workshops will have specialist cutting equipment specifically used for removing mortar from the reverse of tiles. Without specialist equipment the process is more labour intensive but not difficult. Mortar may be removed by fixing the tile securely into a vice or Workmate face downwards and grinding the mortar away to the reverse of the ceramic using a small angle grinder with stone grinding wheel attached. Alternatively the mortar may be cross-hatched with vertical cuts at 2 cm intervals, to within 2 mm of the reverse of the tile using an angle grinder fitted with a diamond rimmed wheel. The mortar can then be knocked away using a hammer and chisel. Using hammer and chisel techniques on fragile glazed wall tiles can risk fracturing but floor tiles are relatively robust. Keeping the chisel at an acute rather than a vertical angle and placing the tile in a sand box while using a hammer and chisel can significantly reduce the effect of the shockwaves. The rough residue of cement can then be ground smooth.

Dividing large blocks of tiles which have mortar attached into single tile units is best attempted by scoring through the mortar using an angle grinder fitted with a rotary diamond wheel of appropriate size and power on the reverse of the block along the length of the grout lines to the depth of the tile back. The tiles will then separate neatly without damage to the edges. Excess mortar adhered to the edges of tiles may be cleaned off using a hand file if tiles are to be reused or displayed.

Tile conservation workshops will generally be equipped with a bench mounted mortar and stone cutting saw fitted with a large diamond blade which is water cooled. The tiles are held vertically in a steel jig allowing the blade to move forward and downwards in a slicing action to remove the excess mortar from the reverse of the tile.

Increasingly as historians and researchers take more of an interest in tiles and Victorian manufacturing techniques in general, the question arises about preserving the identifying manufacturer's back stamp on the reverse of the tile. Tile enthusiasts would advocate leaving a thin residue of mortar covering the maker's mark, leaving it intact for future research, arguing that the maker's mark on the reverse is as important as the design on the face. At the very least the maker's mark should be recorded, photographed and form part of the final conservation treatment report.

There may be a significant reason for research interest in the discarded mortar which is not immediately obvious, Portland cement being ubiquitous as a building material from the mid-Victorian era. If the mortar dates from the pre-Portland cement era there is often good reason to preserve a sample, which may be put forward for analysis. If there is any doubt then a sample of the mortar may be packaged and stored as part of the conservation treatment report. Interest in old mortars is not universal at the present time.

Displaying tile panels

The choice of method and materials on which to display decorative tile panels depends on a variety of factors. The immediate environment is an important issue. Is it protected from wear and tear, vandalism and theft? Is it meant to be displayed in a permanent fashion as one complete object or do the tiles have an intrinsic value as individual objects which may be separated in the future? Is the display meant to be permanent or should it be a moveable feast? How easy should 'reversible' be, should it be a specialist task or can it be made simple for the non-specialist?

Given that the tiles under discussion have by definition already undergone a process of relocation which will have been either easy or difficult and expensive, it is reasonable to suppose that the tiles have already assumed a degree of value as community, artistic, or historic artefacts. If this is the case we can also assume that they are likely to continue to hold value, which may even increase as they become more antique. It is also possible that at some time in the future those among us who assume the roles of great, good and powerful in society will be of the opinion that wherever the current location may be it can be improved upon, and the tiles will be moved again.

Conservators have an obligation to ensure that future relocation of decorative tile panels be relatively simple to achieve without threat to the fabric of the tiles. It should also be an easily understood method under visual examination. Conservation treatment reports, however thorough, do not always remain with the object they report on. Materials whose long-term effects are unknown should be avoided, though traditional materials also have drawbacks; most of them are well understood and if they begin to fail then at least the reasons are usually also understood. For this reason we intend to describe two suggested methods which have timber as the basic structural material rather than resins, metals or other materials. Though timber is not a particularly stable or inert material, very few materials are, it has the advantage that it is easily understood by the non-specialist and can be dismantled using the most common of tools and skills, which in its way helps to protect the tile panel for the future.

There is no one correct way to display tile panels. All of the major museums in Europe devise their own methods for the display of tile panels, some of them good, some of them not so good, nevertheless museums are a good source of information on display techniques. Preserving and displaying objects is their business and a lot can be learned by examining the display methods as well as the object when visiting, though not so closely as to attract attention from security staff. Detailed information about display methods can usually be gained from conservation departments on request.

The following suggested method is suitable for tiles which are in a continuously protected environment, where the tiles have value as individual components in the whole, and where the panel must have the advantage of being easily dismantled by the non-specialist for removal to another location. The method was first devised by the resident technician at Stoke-on-Trent Museum and Art Gallery some 15 years ago and, so far, has stood the test of time.

Cut a 3/4 inch thick piece of plywood, block board or a similarly least flexible board to a size a little larger than the tile panel. Cover the face of the board with strips of balsa wood, glued with a wood adhesive at intervals corresponding to the joints in the tile panel. The balsa wood should be at least 3 inches wide to allow the edges of adjoining tiles to fit comfortably over the balsa. The tiles can then be secured to the balsa with a small amount of reversible glue or adhesive at each corner. When set, cover the edges of the panel with framing material in the usual manner. Make sure that the hanging device for the completed panel is completely secure and will withstand the weight of the complete panel.

To remove the tiles from the panel, take away the frame, and using a scalpel blade with a handle or a craft knife, slice into the sacrificial balsa wood layer at the points where the tiles are glued. Lift off the tiles and either carefully trim away any glue and balsa from the back of the tile with your scalpel, or soften and remove the glue with a solvent.

The second method was devised by the conservation department at the Jackfield Tile Museum in the early 1980s and has also stood the test of time. It is well suited to environments which are under cover, open to the public but not permanently guarded, where the intention is to display a decorative tile panel as a complete object in a semi-permanent situation. It is also suited to panels which are very large in size. Use of good quality timber is advisable throughout.

A piece of 3/4 inch thick plywood, block board or a similarly least flexible board is cut to the same size as the tile panel. Medium density fibre board is not suitable because of its excessive weight and inability to take threaded screws securely. The board should be braced on the reverse with a suitably sized timber framework around the edges and across the centre of the panel. The bracing frame should be glued and screwed to the reverse of the board (Figure 5.37).

The tiles may then be fixed to the board using an adhesive that will give strength, flexibility and breathability. Modern adhesives are available which are based on a sand and cement mix with the addition

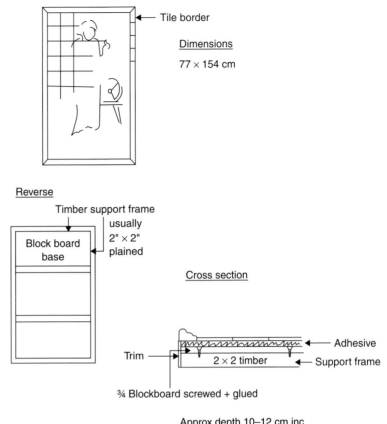

Figure 5.37
Illustration for mounting a large tile panel.

of rubber granules in a PVA solution. The completed panel may then be framed to cover the edges of the tiles and supporting structure. The hanging devices usually include a load bearing bar or bracket fixed securely into the wall and must be fully supportive of the weight of the whole panel.

This method of mounting is designed for displays which are expected to last a considerable length of time. It is not meant for quick or easy reversibility but can be dismantled from the reverse by carefully unscrewing and taking apart the supporting timber frame and cutting the board into tile size squares using ordinary carpentry tools. The remaining timber can be removed from the reverse of the tile with a sharp wood chisel and mallet, leaving the rubberised adhesive which may be peeled away using a sharp 'Stanley' blade or scalpel.

Conservation treatment reports

There is little to say concerning conservation treatment reports other than that they should contain a complete record of all treatment carried out to conserve the historic material and all changes brought about as a result of restoration work; it should also include samples of any discarded material and if necessary all of the fragments of historic tiles which have been replaced during the works. It should be a follow-on document from the initial condition survey and both documents should be lodged together in the most appropriate archive, which, if the building does not have its own, may be the local records library or museum.

6

Tools, products, and health and safety

Introduction

This short chapter is designed with the intention of aiding new conservators of architectural tile schemes in the task of equipping their workshops with the basic necessities of the trade. The chapter also alerts them to some of the issues relating to conservation outside of the studio, and some of those which are studio based but are characteristic of conservation of tile schemes.

The following information is not meant to be a comprehensive list of products and tools to cover all eventualities, neither is it an analysis of the use and effects of materials used in conservation. For more in-depth studies into the subject of materials for conservation and the practice of studio ceramics conservation there are two excellent books published in this series which are invaluable workshop tools in themselves: *Materials for Conservation*, (Horie, 1987) Butterworth-Heinemann Ltd, and *The Conservation and Restoration of Ceramics* (Buys and Oakley, 1993) and also published by Butterworth-Heinemann Ltd.

On-site work

The practice of conservation and restoration of architectural tile schemes not only covers a wide skill base but also the willingness, ability and resources to carry out both studio and site-based conservation. The continuing and welcome trend for retaining historic tiles in their original location makes on-site work the most frequent and likely scenario for practising conservation or restoration work. Site-based work more often than not is situated within operational construction sites, but it can also be based in sensitive historic interiors. Consequently conservators engaged in site work must make sure they have assessed the terms and conditions of the proposed site work correctly.

In some instances conservators may be engaged directly by the client to carry out conservation work in a sensitive historic interior such as a church or historic house where there are no other repairs or alterations taking place. In this case it is the responsibility of the conservator to clarify who is accountable for the protection of adjoining fabric which may suffer in some way as a direct result of conservation work to the tiles. If the client takes on responsibility for protection of fabric, the conservator has a duty to make sure that the client is fully aware of the processes that are to take place and the likely or possible fallout from those processes to enable the client to adequately protect the adjoining furnishings and fittings. If the conservator is made responsible for protecting adjoining fabric then the responsibility is his and the costs for protective material must be included in the overall fee for the works.

The conservator must also be responsible for his own on-site health and safety; this may include not working alone if power tools or scaffolding are part of the process. There should also be some provision of water, adequate lighting, a power source if necessary, and a contact person for either problems or emergencies.

Access can sometimes be an issue. The conservator must establish in advance if there is the possibility of difficulties which are to be overcome. There may be specific times during the day over which work cannot be carried out, requiring the conservator to work unsocial hours. Access may be physically difficult consequently adding time and extra effort into the equation, both of which can be reflected in the scale of charges. Some historic site managements require security checks to be run on applicants for all non-routine access which may take a significant time to process.

The works may also be scheduled for a public place, in which case the conservator must establish who is responsible for information and safety to the general public. Common sense on the part of the conservator, adequate barriers and clear warning notices are necessary inclusions when considering on-site conservation in public places. It is worth remembering that many people will be curious as to the nature of the work being carried out on what may be an integral and well-known part of the community landscape; they will stop to ask questions if there is an opportunity to do so.

Unequivocally the most important issue for the conservator to address is the necessity for adequate insurance cover for both personal and public safety, and additional financial cover for the value of the historic fabric in the care of the conservator in the event of some unforeseen difficulty.

Some of the issues highlighted above will automatically be the responsibility of the main contractor if the conservation work to be undertaken is part of a wider package of works on an operational construction site. The conservator must be aware of his own responsibilities towards the main contractor and other subcontractors when carrying out his work, especially in terms of health and safety; noise and dust pollution being a particular area for concern. The conservator will usually be required to supply the main contractor with a method statement, a health and safety assessment document, an electrical equipment safety check certificate and copies of insurance cover details. The main contractor will also normally require attendance at a safety induction meeting where he will go through all the relevant health and safety procedures and requirements for that specific site. Personal protective equipment is the responsibility of the conservator, some of which – for example, face masks, gloves, and overalls – will be specific to the conservator's own work processes, but others such as hard hats, work boots and reflective jackets will be necessary equipment to gain access to the site. All work at height should be performed from scaffold rather than ladder, which should be erected by a professional scaffolding company. Any procedures carried out from scaffold must be assessed for risk within the health and safety plan.

Having all of the necessary equipment to hand on site in order to complete the project is, however, a very important aspect of on-site conservation, especially when much of the equipment is specialist and not easily available at a nearby hardware store. Some larger conservation companies will be able to duplicate their studio equipment in a 'travelling' vehicle-based studio which can be kept stocked and ready to travel to site. Smaller conservation companies will have recourse to repeated packing and unpacking of tools and equipment.

It is a great advantage to devise a standard tools and equipment checklist which can be used repeatedly, and against which all items can be considered and checked as part of the packing process. It can also be a help towards assessing the step-by-step programme of work for the project in hand.

On-site tools and materials checklist

Tools

transformer	extension lead 240 V
extension leads 110 V	lights
angle grinder or oscillating cutting tool	diamond blades
drill	drill bits
hammers	chisels
screwdriver	adjustable spanner
metal files	mole grips
hacksaws	pincers
tile files	vacuum cleaner
spirit level/steel rule	trowels

Personal protective equipment

hard hats	overalls
safety glasses	work gloves
ear defenders	masks
first aid kit	paper suits
kneeling mats	rubber gloves

General equipment

broom/hand brush	buckets
ladder	notebook
packing material	shovel
black plastic bags	masking tape
cloths/wet/dry/soft	pencils/marker
polythene	plumb line
camera	film

Conservation equipment

mortar	grout
pots for mixing	knives for mixing
spatulas/spreaders	filler paste
hardener	cleaning solutions
pigments for glazes and fillers	paper towel
palettes	'Stanley' blades/scalpels
files/rifflers	abrasive papers/pastes
glazes white/clear	wax
acetone	brushes
thinners	industrial methylated spirits
conservation adhesive	

The choice of which ceramics conservation materials are best suited to site work is personal to the conservator. Most materials and products have both advantages and disadvantages but some are more adaptable to the special and sometimes difficult circumstances encountered on site. Cold, damp or dusty conditions with poor light are common environmental problems which must be negotiated and overcome on some sites. Additionally some restoration projects require the use of materials which offer longevity and durability. The sections in Chapter 5 which cover 'consolidation of ceramic' and 'painting and retouching' explain in more detail why some materials are preferable to others for use on site.

Studio equipment

Studio-based conservation allows a much greater freedom of choice for materials with which to conserve and restore architectural ceramics. The studio environment will, hopefully, be dry, light, airy and with a constant controllable temperature as well as the advantage of air extraction facilities, either portable or fixed. It will have benches at the correct height for working comfortably and facilities in which to leave materials to cure, or dry, for the recommended time at the recommended temperature. Individual tiles can easily and safely be allowed to soak to make possible cleaning, stain removal or desalination and achieve the best results. Well-equipped studios will also have equipment for magnifying and analysis. All of these advantages allow the conservator to follow the methods and use the materials of their choice.

There are few pieces of equipment that are specific to architectural tile conservation which are over and above those needed for object conservation. Space is a necessity. Decorative tile panels are often large in size and need to be laid out, initially to record and ascertain damage and treatment and, after treatment, to either pack in sequence or redisplay. There should be at least one large flat table on which to lay tiles in sequence which should be strong enough to take the weight of large numbers of tiles. Benches should be moveable rather than fixed to allow changes in the workshop configuration for a more versatile use of space.

Collections of tiles are heavy, for example one ceramic industry standard size box measuring 15 cm × 15 cm × 35 cm when packed with tiles weighs 8.5 kilos. Equipment and training to aid moving and lifting heavy weights are essential health and safety requirements.

Diamond cutting tools will be required for some purposes; a bench saw to cut unwanted mortar from ceramic or to separate panels of tiles into individual component parts, as well as hand-held cutting tools, are probably the most essential. Hand-held power tools with an oscillating cutting action provide the necessary control required to tackle removal of mortar grout in awkward corners and narrow joints. Bench mounted buffing wheels with expanding rubber drums and fitted with diamond coated belts are used to clean cement grout from the edges of tiles and can be a useful investment in addition to a selection of diamond coated files. Industrial diamond tool technology is constantly changing and improving, therefore it is essential to keep up to date with the sources of information for those changes.

The same is true of all products, materials and equipment used for conservation. The most valuable tool is a willingness to source, enquire about and exchange information, then evaluate new or different techniques and materials which are available to colleagues and suppliers within the conservation profession or on the wider market outside. Continuing professional development is the new twenty-first century mantra in many areas of public and private sector services and industries. It is one to be recommended and pursued.

7

Case studies

The conservation of the historic tile floors at Ontario State Courthouse, Osgoode Hall, Toronto

Historic context

In September 1999, the Toronto Provincial Government, on the advice of Jill Taylor of Taylor Hazell Architects, Toronto, commissioned a full condition survey into the current and future conservation of the historic courthouse floor. At first glance the floors gave the impression of being of outstanding architectural importance. The floors are a series of complex geometric layouts emanating from one of Britain's most important Victorian tile factories, namely Maw & Co., Broseley, Shropshire, England.

The restoration planning for the historic floor in the Ontario State Courthouse, Osgoode Hall, Toronto, has produced some interesting parallels with another historic floor at Benthall Hall, Shropshire, UK.

When the main courthouse for Ontario was redeveloped in 1858, impressive arrays of floor layouts were commissioned to complement this important stone building. The company that won that commission was the Shropshire firm of Maw & Co. based in the Ironbridge Gorge. This large area of geometric patterns was assembled in two phases, with the largest portion of the works being completed in 1858, with later additions completed in 1910. The most impressive areas are undoubtedly those of the central ground floor atrium and the lobbies above.

The distinctive feature of the atrium floor is the novel curved junction detail and banding used to structure the overall design (Figure 7.1). It is this detail which intriguingly draws comparison with the floor laid in 1859, one year later than the Toronto floor, in the main hall at Benthall Hall (Figure 7.2). Given that the tenant of Benthall Hall at the time was George Maw, owner and co-director of the Maw & Co. tile works, we can only guess at the degree of involvement of George Maw himself in the design and construction of both floors. Maw is

Figure 7.1
The atrium floor, Osgoode Hall, showing the curved detail.

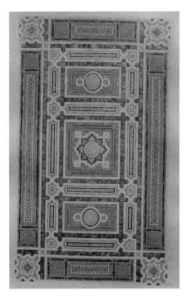

Figure 7.2
Drawing of the floor at Benthall Hall.

known to have taken an active interest in both individual tile designs and extensive layouts.

The dates 1858 to 1859 were still quite early days for a company that had only come into existence in 1850, moving to the Gorge in 1852. Within 30 years the company had become the largest manufacturer of tiles in the world and exported its tiles for use in some of the most important buildings in the British Empire. We can justifiably speculate on the importance of the Ontario courthouse atrium floor for the future of the company, and its appearance in the home of George Maw.

The later 1910 to 1920 phase of work in Osgoode Hall is also of some importance given the continued use of Maw & Co.'s product. These areas are a fine example of developing technological change within mass production. The tiles and their layouts show much finer detailed precision of manufacture, and consistency of material quality, colour and size.

At the end of 1998, after researching the source of the original tiles, Jill Taylor came to Jackfield Tile Museum, Ironbridge, Shropshire, situated only 200 yards upriver from the original Maws factory, to investigate the availability of tiles to match the Osgoode floors.

Discussions at that first meeting centred on the belief that while all of the floors were generally in excellent condition for their age, there was a case for replacing the most severely damaged tiles in this most busy and public of buildings. To this end the provincial government eventually commissioned the special development of clay colours from Chris Cox at Craven Dunnill Jackfield Ltd (a rival company to Maw & Co. at the time of the original manufacture) in order to manufacture, once again in the Ironbridge Gorge, matching tiles for

Osgoode Hall, Toronto. The visit was timely as Jackfield Conservation Studio had also just completed a very similar, though much smaller, project at the Royal Courts of Justice, The Strand, London, which concerned itself with the conservation of original tiles, while also consolidating the lime substrate and providing new replacement tiles where necessary. At the end of 2001 Jackfield Conservation Studio and Taylor Hazell Architects completed the full conservation programme of works to the historically valuable atrium floor.

Condition survey, September 1999

The condition survey with recommendations for treatment was commissioned from Jackfield Conservation Studio for September 1999. The report itself was detailed enough to include a tile by tile assessment, written and photographic, of damage throughout the whole of the Osgoode Hall schemes, possible causes and possible treatments. The following is a synopsis of the main findings and conclusions.

The general condition of the floor tiles throughout was exceptionally good given their age and the amount of foot traffic in the building. There were, however, some factors concerning their condition which were common to many areas of the tiled floors, both from a visual aspect and their continuing survival as an important architectural feature within the building.

The floor had, in many places, a build-up of old wax and lacquer which, over the years, had absorbed dirt and grease giving the floor a rather dull and dirty appearance (Figure 7.3). Grout between the tiles had broken down and been replaced through natural movement with dirt. Because the edges of the tiles are unprotected by grout they had, in many places, become ragged and rough. A programme of careful conservation cleaning and regrouting would give the tiles a visual lift and better protect the edges of the tiles.

Some areas suffer greater foot and trolley traffic than others, and as with other buildings which have comparable high status historically, its users must at some stage give consideration to the importance of the fabric over everyday routine use. Possible re-routing of traffic was suggested in detail (Figure 7.4).

The material found directly underneath the tiles was lime mortar, the tiles had become detached from the mortar over almost the whole of the tiled floors. In many instances the tiles were loose enough to move, they therefore were at risk from impact fracture (where tiles had fractured, this was the cause) (Figure 7.5). In other instances the tiles were detached from the mortar but, because of movement in the building, had been forced together, creating a pressure on the edges of the tiles causing spalling of the ceramic. The lime mortar, which may have been poorly or at least haphazardly specified initially, possibly without enough sharp sand to make a good set, or using unwashed sand from

Figure 7.3
Old and dirty lacquer coating.

Figure 7.4
Damage caused by use of heavy
trolleys over the atrium floor.

Figure 7.5
Impact fracture.

the bay thereby setting up an inevitable chemical chain reaction, was not as strong as it could have been. However, with the likely shifting or sinking of the building over time the lime mortar had, in effect, been the contributing factor in the tiles themselves remaining in good condition. The lime mortar bed had been the sacrificial layer which had given way, rather than the tiles themselves, which is exactly the purpose of lime mortar. The mortar could be heard to crack under foot all over the building. It is not unlikely that the lime mortar, after 150 years, had now begun to degrade and crumble coming to the end of its natural life.

There were many instances of badly colour matched and unsympathetic replacement tiles having been introduced during various attempts at restoration in the past. Poor colour matching or inattention to the logic of the designs had resulted in the bad pattern making to be found in many areas (Figure 7.6). These were the factors which we found common to a greater or lesser degree in all areas.

Repairs to the hallway floor (Room 242), August 2000

The year 2000 saw the necessary and urgent repair to part of the lower ground hallway floor. Damage to the floor had been caused by a sudden and severe downpour of rainwater during repair work on the roof. The required repairs were unavoidable and urgent, but they also gave us the opportunity not only to demonstrate the techniques for repair, but also to take advantage of exploratory works relating to future work on the more important atrium floor.

It is always important when approaching repair works to historic tiling to examine in detail the pattern in which the tiles are set, to try

Figure 7.6
Poor colour matching and inattention
to the logic of the design during
previous repairs.

to ascertain in what order and direction they were set originally. This can often give strong clues as to where the likely stresses and pressures will be found, which in turn will help to reduce further damage during the lifting.

The hallway floor comprised of a repeating pattern of nine 4 inch × 4 inch (102 mm × 102 mm) tiles set in a square, surrounded by three rows of 4 inch × 1½ inch (102 mm × 37 mm) tiles set in tramlines. All tiles were set diagonally across the room.

Purpose and aims

Our purpose was to carry out limited patch repairs to the damaged area assessed in our report of October 1999, i.e. an area of tiling that had become delaminated and raised due to water ingress from a leaking roof. In the course of doing so we were able to ascertain how the floor was constructed and some of the inherent structural problems in the floor, all of which will help to point the way forward for future repairs. During the works a core sample of the substrate was taken. After examining the core sample we were able to make a more informed decision as to the required mortar mix for refixing.

Condition

The area of raised or 'bubbled' floor tiles had fractured since our previous visit, probably due to pedestrian foot traffic.

This had caused tiles to become loose and fractured not only in the immediate area of the 'bubble' but also at some considerable distance from the original area of damage (Figure 7.7).

Spalling of the edges of some tiles had occurred all over the damaged area, caused by uneven pressures and movements between the tiles. The buff colour tiles seemed to be most affected, indicating that

Figure 7.7
Damage to hallway floor.

Figure 7.8
Differing sizes found in original tiling
which had been cut to fit.

they were probably made from a softer clay body. The loose tiles had
no mortar residue on the reverse showing that adhesion had always
been poor. Though a number of tiles were loose, where the 'bubble'
had collapsed, there was also a large area of flooring which had lifted
approximately 2 cm off the screed bed with the tiles still firmly adhered
to each other, a hard mortar grout holding them under tension.

We estimated that an area approximately 240 cm × 195 cm was
under tension and not adhered to the screed.

Close examination of the damaged area before any tiles were moved
showed that the area that contained one row of alternate red and
mushroom tiles had been reduced in size by cutting during the original
laying process in 1910. The row extended to the middle of the floor
and was no doubt an expedient measure in order to make the design
fit what was probably not a square room. The tiles had been reduced
by 6 mm down one side (Figure 7.8).

Overall damage to tiles in the area was estimated at approximately
3 per cent.

Treatment
Lifting the tiles
The tiles were loose enough over approximately one third of the area
to either simply pick up or gently tap with a rubber mallet until free.

A point was reached whereby the tension at the apex of the diagonal lines was so tight that tiles would not loosen without spalling
damage to their edges. There was still a gap of 5 mm between the
underside of the tiles and the screed, it was decided that it was necessary to continue to lift tiles until a place was reached where all tiles
were laying flat to the screed bed. The situation also demonstrated
that the floor had originally been laid diagonally as we suspected.

To release the tension and loosen the tiles we cut along the grout line of one tile at the apex. We continued this for each row, cutting in opposite directions on each row. An area of tiles approximately 2 m × 3 m was lifted before all tiles were flat to the screed (Figure 7.9).

A significant series of fractures in the substrate was revealed when the tiles were lifted. The first core sample showed that there were two layers of screed, a bedding compound, approximately 1.5 cm deep, not fixed to the lower screed, which was of a courser texture. Drilling showed that the lower screed was approximately 20 cm deep, and that the fracture was running directly over a steel beam. A further core sample was taken to give an exact example of the make-up of the entire floor construction (Figure 7.10). At the place where the new core sample was taken, approximately 60 cm distance from the first, the upper bedding compound was firmly fixed to the lower screed. But at a depth of about 10 cm the lower screed became a loose rubble type consistency, which broke up. When examined, the construction of the floor was shown to be at least 20 cm of a lime, probably cement (judging by the colour), and sand mix of which the lower part was heavier in aggregate and rubble. The lower part broke up due to the high quantity of rubble which contained chunks of limestone. The top part of the mix contained quite course aggregate but no rubble.

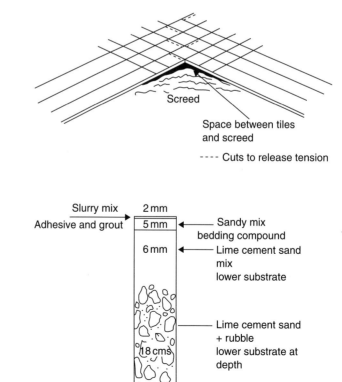

Figure 7.9
Diagram of the cuts used in the tile work under tension.

Figure 7.10
Diagram of the substrate.

The upper bedding mix was a sandier mix with lime and again probably cement. The tiles had then been fixed with a Portland cement slurry, probably a 1:1 mix with fine sand. These conclusions were arrived at by visual evidence only; the core was taken for laboratory analysis.

Preparation and consolidation of the screed

In order to protect the surrounding tiles from damage through vibration during the works, a line was cut, with an angle grinder fitted with a diamond blade, down through the screed at a distance of about 2 cm from the tile edge all around the area. The tiles were also taped firmly together with masking tape.

The intention was to remove, using a small power nibbler chisel, the top 4 mm of the upper screed in order to make a space for new adhesive; to facilitate this, cuts in screed were scored to a depth of 5 mm across the area. This was achieved around the edges of the area. However, nearer to the fracture the upper bedding compound layer proved to be completely detached from the lower substrate. All loose material had to be taken up.

Underneath the loose upper layer, the lower substrate was shown to be much more severely fractured along the line of the steel beam than was at first visible directly beneath the damaged tiles (Figure 7.11). For the replacement mortar mix it was decided that a minimum of Portland cement be added to the mix, this was comparable with the substrate we had just lifted and was replacing like with like. The local building sand which was available for the project was high in clay content, which was not wholly desirable, as it had the potential to weaken the mix and prevent it from going 'off' easily. For

Figure 7.11
Fracturing in the lower screed.

the further works envisaged in the atrium it would be important to source a supply of sharp sand with grains 30 to 60 microns.

Our mix was:

Bedding compound   1 lime hydrate : 1 Portland cement : 6 sand.

Slurry adhesive and grout   1 lime hydrate : 3 Portland cement : 4 flint silica.

The bottom of the core hole was filled with washed limestone chunks and covered with the bedding mix. The lower screed was wetted and the mixed mortar was spread evenly over the area to a level 5 mm below the original bed level. It was left 24 hours to go off.

Refixing the tiles

All mortar attached to the edges of original tiles, including those tiles around the edge of the area, was removed. It came away easily using a knife after soaking the tiles in water. The bed was wetted prior to laying, and the tiles were soaked in water. Each line of tiles was laid out on a 'dummy' run before fixing, to ascertain whether the tiles would fit in their allotted space, and, if not, which tiles required trimming and by how much. It was important to keep the 'tramlines' going in the correct alignment to meet up with their opposite numbers, and at the same time to keep the central motif as a square; these two elements formed the most eye-catching part of the design.

The thin slurry was spread to a depth of about 2 mm over an area for laying one row of tiles. The tiles were tapped in place using a rubber mallet. The levels and directions were checked constantly. The same slurry mix was then used for grouting purposes. The tile laying process took place over three evening shifts. The tiles were not 'place specific' in this instance, if trimming was required we tended to use the new replacement tiles for that purpose. The whole area was polished with several coats of wax polish to enable it to blend with its surroundings.

Relevance to further works

The reports on the repair to the hallway floor were able to highlight some important factors to be taken into consideration in the preparation for the repair work to the atrium floor.

The time scales for the whole project were:

Recording and photographing	2 hours
Lifting tiles	6 hours
Cleaning tiles	5 hours
Screed lifting and preparation	16 hours
Laying tiles	20 hours

Grouting and polishing   4 hours

Reports   20 hours

Total loss of original tile material was 5 per cent. Three per cent of material was damaged at the outset, and a further 2 per cent was inevitable damage caused by the lifting process.

Greater importance needed to be given to the types of sand and lime used in any further works. A different type of sand may need to be imported from elsewhere to give greater integrity to the mortar.

In addition to information gleaned which would be useful for the atrium works, we were able to infer a number of conditions which applied not only to the future of the hallway floor itself, but, the evidence showed, also to future works on a corresponding floor, the upper hallway floor, above.

The upper bedding compound being unfixed to the lower substrate over such a large area around the steel beams was significant for the rest of the floor. Our reassessment of the floor subsequent to the works was that most tiles, at present, remain fixed to the upper bedding. The rattling and hollow sound from the floor when tapped or walked upon comes from the space between upper and lower screed. The tiles have significant areas of damage or previous repairs which, most likely, run concurrent with the steel beams.

Due to vibrations or shifts in the building the lower substrate around the beams has become cracked and broken down, it has also shifted away from the upper substrate. This movement has in turn caused significant spalling and fracturing of the tiles as the three layers have moved in opposing directions. It could therefore be reasonably supposed that any patch repairs to damaged areas of tiling could be expected to include the lifting of tiles and repair and consolidation to the screed over a significantly wider area than visually apparent from the surface.

There should be no real reason to lift the whole floor in the future, as much of the floor and screed is sound, and the undesirability of damage caused to tiles in the lifting process far outweighs any benefits gained in renewing the screed. There is, however, every good reason to pursue a programme of proper patch repairs which includes the consolidation of areas of fractured screed in much the same way as has been demonstrated by these works.

The atrium floor

The conservation approach

The atrium floor is an extraordinary example of early Victorian tile flooring. It is not only of the highest quality, it also has importance in terms of the design of the interior of the building and the history of tile making. Any work on the atrium floor therefore required an

Figure 7.12
The atrium floor.

approach embodying the greatest of care, deliberation and forward planning (Figure 7.12)

The approach to the work was conservation based, that is, there was a criteria to preserve the original material to the greatest possible extent. It was self-evident that some of the original material had failed in some way and therefore must be replaced, for example the lime mortar substrate had failed, as a result tiles were missing or broken. As was shown in the work to the hallway floor, lifting damaged tiles would almost certainly reveal extensive and necessary consolidation of the lime mortar substrate. Careful lifting can and should keep damage to a minimum, and it is a measure of the success of the job that as little new material is used as possible.

The appropriate replacement materials must be in place before work starts. While Victorian floor tiles have a relatively robust clay body, the surface fire-skin can be very fragile and prone to 'shelling' or 'spalling' around the edges, it is prudent therefore to have in place appropriate replacement tiles for all eventualities extending beyond the immediate damage area. All projects should begin with a tile inventory which lists the measurement, profile and colour of every type of tile in the scheme to be used as a reference and identification document.

The approximate area for repair should be identified. Referring to the tile inventory, a list should be prepared of the sizes and colours of tiles which make up that area. After counting how many of each type of tile are used in the area, calculate 20 per cent of each of those numbers. This will put in place the appropriate number of each type of tile to cover repair works and allow a small stock of tiles for any future possible damage or failure.

Preparation

The conservation team were supplied with an accurate drawing of the atrium floor by the architect's office. These are not always necessary and can be costly to produce, but when accurate, they can prove to be an extremely useful tool for identification and record keeping. On important and high profile schemes they are to be recommended.

For the purposes of identification of damaged areas the atrium floor was divided into quadrants as per the architect's drawings; key plan 1, **A B C D**.

Using the drawing as a working document, all areas which had been designated for replacement tiles by the architect were outlined in heavy black and each tile earmarked for replacement within that area infilled in black on the plan.

The conservation team identified the areas marked on the plan against the in-situ tiles and either confirmed the architect's decision, extended the area for replacement, or redesignated it as an area for resin filler repair. All changes to the preliminary designations were marked on the drawing.

Each area was given a letter corresponding with the quadrant letter and a number with which to identify it. The conservation team then outlined and numbered each area to be worked on directly onto the floor using masking tape.

Lifting

The first areas to be lifted were chosen for investigation purposes, on the basis that they were the areas most likely to require consolidation of the lime mortar bed.

The same method for lifting tiles was used in all areas. The grout around each damaged tile was cut using a *fein cutting tool*, the reciprocating action of the diamond blade allows grout to be cut away into each corner of the tile without damaging the adjacent tile; the diamond blade is only 1.5 mm thick so can be used on the narrowest of grout lines without excessive damage. The damaged tile was then cut diagonally from opposite corners using a small rotary diamond blade. Each piece of tile was then carefully tapped away with a chisel and mallet.

Area **A12** was lifted first and found to have a significant void, approximately 5 cm deep in some places, between the original adhesive layer and the setting bed. Area **A1** was lifted and found to have the same problem but the void was much less, down to about 4 mm.

It was observed that a large area in the south west corner was hollow sounding. In conjunction with the architect, the conservation team decided to lift area **A15** on the basis that tiles could be lifted at intermittent spacing in order to allow using a liquid lime, gravity fed, infill beneath the surface of the tiles, with the purpose of consolidating quite large areas of tiling and filling the potentially damaging voids beneath the tiles. However, when tile **A15** was lifted it was found that the void in this area was between the tile and the adhesive layer and was no more than 1 mm deep.

The results of the investigation showed that the problems caused by degradation of the mortar bed were not consistent over the whole floor. Therefore each damaged area should be treated as a separate entity and treated according to its own problems.

Resetting

In order to minimise the introduction of new tile material, any damaged original tile material, which was large enough, was recut to smaller sizes and used in other areas where possible. In areas where the lifted tiles were found to be on degraded mortar only, with no significant voids, the original mortar bed was removed and the tiles reset using the specified mortar mix of two parts NHL5 hydraulic lime to five parts sand.

In areas where there was found to be a significant void a gravity fed lime slurry was passed through copper pipes of varying diameters into the voids and left to go off. The voids were very carefully wetted first using the minimum of water to allow the slurry to adhere to the original mortar. The amount of water used was carefully judged in order not to cause further damage to an already fragile bond on adjacent tiles by allowing too much water ingress.

The lime slurry mix was four parts NHL5 hydraulic lime to three parts water.

In line with common practice all new lime mortar was kept damp until set.

A similar problem was discovered in the north west corner extending 90 cm $\times$ 300 cm from the stone pillar. The void was found to be at least 8 cm deep. The potential for further damage in this instance was considered to be so great that selected yellow tiles around the perimeter of the area were designated as sacrificial and lifted to allow tubes to be inserted at given intervals for consolidation to take place.

Tests were carried out to ascertain whether the slurry mix was likely to adhere to the original mortar. Wooden trays were filled with a basic lime sand mix and allowed to go off. Cores were drilled out of the centre of the mortar slabs about 8 cm in diameter and the slurry mix, in various proportions of water to lime, was poured into the core holes.

We found that the specified mix went off fastest with the required strength, but that none of the mixes adhered well to the mortar slab. The conclusion was that although our slurry mix will have hardened and filled the voids adequately it is unlikely to have adhered to the original underfloor mortar.

New replacement tiles

The 'off-the-peg' availability of Victorian style floor tiles is nowadays severely limited, only a few colours are generally available within large-scale manufacturing, and only black could be said to match original tiles with confidence; however, we found that within the Osgoode schemes we were able to match red, dark blue, pale mushroom and dark mushroom from a readily available range of tiles. The remaining colours were specially developed at Jackfield Tile Museum, Ironbridge, Shropshire, UK. They were identified as dark red brown, pale yellow, cream, white, pale blue, and biscuit.

Dark red brown and biscuit proved difficult to manufacture because of the unavailability of the correct raw materials to match those used in the nineteenth century. Many nineteenth century tiles are dust pressed; this was a new innovation which made tile production much faster and more reliable than using wet clay. Body clays are made by mixing clays and oxides in dust form and pressing to remove excess moisture. In the Victorian era the oxides were milled to a lesser degree of refinement than those currently available, resulting in body colours which are comprised of small speckles of varying hues which make up the colour. This particular effect is difficult to replicate. In addition some of the raw materials used in the nineteenth century are now illegal, among them are lead, cadmium, antimony and arsenic. Consequently a closely approximate match was accepted for both colours after many weeks of clay colour testing.

Resin repairs

It had been agreed by the architect's office and the conservation team at the outset, that the floor contained a great deal of material with only slight damage that did not warrant replacement. The conservation approach had always been to retain as much original material as possible. There was in the region of 1000 tiles that required resin repair. Much of the damage was very slight, usually between 2 and 5 mm diameter chips or pock-marks, but the accumulative effect of repair would visually enhance the overall condition of the floor. Although not usual practice, we chose to remove dirt from the fractures using a small masonry drill bit. The high number of repairs and the need to provide an absolutely clean surface on very small repair areas was important. Many of the repairs were to the edges of tiles; good adhesion of the resin filler was important for longevity of the repair. A mix of polyester resin and colour matched pigments was applied to the cleaned surface of the clay body, left to go off, and then cut back with a sharp blade to the correct profile. The surface was polished with very fine grade emery paper, to bring the resin to a respectable textural match to the surrounding tile.

Cleaning

The atrium floor had a plastic coating which had degraded and become dirty over the years. It gave the floor a visually very poor appearance and had to be removed. Tests were carried out using a variety of mild detergent cleaners usually used for floor tiles. None were successful. A sodium hydroxide-based coating stripper was eventually used, albeit reluctantly. The stripper was applied and left for 10 to 20 minutes, during which time the coating was softened, it could then be scraped off by hand using sharp blades in holders. The process had to be carried out twice, followed by thorough rinsing and was extremely labour intensive. The whole area of the atrium took three men four nights of work to completely clean. The results were good. The tiles were cleaned back to their original colour allowing the new tiles to match correctly. The tiles were sealed with a natural look penetrating sealer and coated with a non-slip natural wax.

Conclusion

The overall results of the work carried out on the atrium floor were good. Some problems remained, however; the discolouration of the grout was not properly dealt with. The old plastic sealer had penetrated the mortar of the grout, sealing in dirt causing blackening of the joint.

Removal of the sealant off the grout to reveal the correct lime mortar colour is a hand mechanical operation; some grout areas could be cleaned, some would have to be taken out and replaced with new mortar grout, all of which is labour intensive. While most of the underfloor damage to the original mortar was corrected and consolidated, there are undoubtedly further areas which, while not apparent at the present time, will inevitably reveal deterioration in the future. However, this project has now established a good working practice for repairs which can be carried out piecemeal as and when required.

The conservation and restoration of Pugin tiles at the House of Commons, London

After a lengthy and complex restoration programme set in motion on 12 July 1994, the Terrace Cafeteria of the House of Commons was officially opened by Madam Speaker, the Rt Hon. Betty Boothroyd MP, on 13 November, 1996. Research into the archives kept by the House of Lords Records Office had provided documentary evidence of the existence of important early Victorian wall tiles, designed by Augustus W.N. Pugin and made by Henry Minton of Stoke on Trent, of dado height around the perimeter of the room which had originally been the Stranger's Smoking Room. However, it was not until the mock Tudor panelling dating from 1914 was removed could the condition of the tiles be ascertained.

What was revealed was both good and bad. On the positive side almost the whole of the original scheme was still in place except for areas where heating ducts had been fitted and new doorways had been knocked through, probably in the 1960s (Figure 7.13). To counterbalance this, the tiles had suffered severe damage resulting from the hammering of steel pins into the tiles the whole height and length of the dado to provide crude fixings for the oak panelling at about 30 cm intervals. This had left holes with deep shelling of the ceramic about 3–5 cm in diameter (Figure 7.14). Added to this the majority of the bottom row of tiles were badly – damaged, probably caused by rough and ready removal of a Victorian timber skirting board in order to facilitate the fitting of the 1914 panelling.

In consultation with English Heritage, the architects Cecil Denny Highton and Partners decided first to establish the provenance of the tiles. This they did by contacting tile historian and author Chris Blanchett, who confirmed that the tiles were indeed examples of the earliest block printed tiles made by Minton's using the Collins and Reynold's 'New Press' printing technique patented in 1848, and that they were stylistically certain to have been designed by Augustus Welby Northmore Pugin, first appearing in the Minton Catalogue in 1850.

Figure 7.13
Damage to scheme caused by the letting in of heating ducts to walls.

Figure 7.14
Damage caused by steel pins hammered into tiles.

However, while it was agreed by all concerned that conservation and restoration of as much of the original tile material as possible was desirable, it quickly became apparent that there was a need for a considerable number of new examples of these complex, highly decorative and colourful tiles in order to: fill in missing areas; replace tiles too badly damaged to be restored; and decorate new walls which were being reinstated according to the original building plan. The architects contacted the Decorative Tile Works at Jackfield Tile Museum for advice as to the possibility of manufacturing tiles which would be an exact copy of colour and manufacturing technique of the originals. The Decorative Tile Works and Jackfield Conservation Studio responded jointly to provide a manufacturing and conservation service for the project under the control of Michael Kay of Decorative Tile Works.

Manufacture

There were three different tile designs which required manufacture: tile A, a polychrome tile 130 mm × 130 mm self-contained design used at the head of each drop of border tiles. Tile C, polychrome, 130 mm × 130 mm, a frieze design which formed the border and drops which surrounded each panel of the predominant design. Tile B, white ground with a green gothic style design which formed the main component of the overall scheme.

The majority of the tile B type are 206 mm × 206 mm except for two small areas near the entrance of the Smoking Room where the same design had been either stretched or reduced onto tiles measuring 206 mm × 219 mm and 178 mm × 178 mm respectively in order to fit precisely into an odd corner of the room. This is an unusual detail which is generally not found in later schemes, where standard size tiles will simply be cut to fit, irrespective of how reduced size tiles will sit visually within a scheme. The likelihood is that this fine tuning was demanded by the designer, Pugin. We also found during the on-site conservation works that these non-standard size tiles were not two colour glazed; the white ground was indeed glaze, but the green design was in fact oil-based paint, indicating that although Pugin demanded additional sizes, Henry Minton was not prepared to pay the cost of additional blocks for such a small number of tiles.

Separate silk screens were made for each component of all three designs, with extra hand finishing needed for the corners of the stretched design for tile B. The colours were developed from the standard range of on-glaze colours from Cookson Matthey of Stoke on Trent by a process of mixing and testing. The forward planning for the delivery of the tiles took well over 12 months.

All tiles were first hand dipped in a Victorian white glaze and fired. The solid colours were then individually screen printed on top of the white. Two of the colours, pink and green, also needed further hand painting on top of the printing in order to gain the necessary finish to the glaze texture. Each colour underwent a drying process before the next application, finishing with a final enamel firing at 820 degrees centigrade for two hours (Figure 2.36).

A strict timetable was absolutely necessary in order to complete this complex manufacturing process on time as all on-site works on the project had to be completed within the 12 weeks of the Parliament summer recess. But the best laid plans of mice and men will often go awry, and several days into the on-site conservation work an accidental but fortuitous discovery was made.

The existing brickwork behind the panelling on the six window reveals had always posed something of a problem which had been noted on the original tile survey – they were bare of tiles, presumed missing. The dimensions of the exposed brick bore no relation to the sizing of the rest of the tiles in the scheme. In order to fit tiles onto the brick it would have been necessary to cut our new tiles; as we have noted there was no precedent for such a solution anywhere else in the room. For a long time this obvious inconsistency was ignored; however, an accident with a scaffolding pole on the night shift knocked a small piece of brick out of place on one of the reveals, exposing to view the familiar green and white glaze of tile pattern B. The brickwork on all of the reveals was carefully taken down exposing a well-preserved original tile scheme running up to the stone architrave. There were, however, a handful of tile B type missing and astonishingly these were yet again of a different size, this time 178 mm × 196 mm. Another screen was commissioned and the manufacturing process restarted as a matter of urgency!

On-site conservation

The conservation team consisted of a senior conservator and two assistants, but because of the constraints imposed by the 12 week time schedule, work on the tiles had to be carried out alongside and around all other craftsmen and contractors, stonemasons, plasterers, electricians and demolition. Dusty conditions and poor lighting were sometimes not conducive to fine detail restoration work. However, the main contractors made every effort to provide the best conditions possible for all concerned.

Before any restoration work could begin a programme of conservation cleaning was required. The tiles were covered with a thick coating of a brown tar substance, no doubt left over from the many years used as a smoking room. The grout was a lime plaster mix, which had originally been white in colour; it was now a very dirty dark brown. Some discussions centred on whether the grout should be retained as part of the original building fabric, but visually it was poor. Additionally the proposed use for the room was to be a food serving area, with all the implications for cleanliness and health and safety considerations to be taken into account. By the same token any tiles which were considered to be too contaminated with absorbed organic staining into the clay body were to be replaced. Fortunately there were very few.

The tiles were washed with a non-ionic detergent diluted 60 ml: 5 litres distilled water using soft cloths and a minimum of water. The grout was softened with water and then scraped out by hand. Finally the tiles were buffed to a dry shine with soft cloths.

All damaged areas of ceramic then had to be made good with polyester resin coloured with a white pigment (Figure 7.15). The hardened resin was smoothed or shaped to a perfect profile. When this was complete, the missing parts of design on the tiles were hand drawn with the aid of a series of stencils made from a sample tile. We frequently found that the stencils did not quite line up, showing that the manufacturers, Minton's, had originally used a number of different blocks, not all of which were exactly the same. The next stage was to fill in the missing colours by hand using a cold epoxy glaze coloured with artist's pigments. The colours had to be remixed for each tile as the originals had a wide variance of colour tone from tile to tile. Layers of colour also had to be built up in order to gain the right depth and translucency. New white grouting replaced the old, which gave the scheme a brightness and coherence. The tiles were finally coated with two coats of microcrystalline wax in order to seal and protect them.

Figure 7.15
Polyester resin filler being applied to damage.

Ordinarily most tiles are sufficiently protected by the hardness of the glaze itself, but in this instance, the extra protection given by waxing was thought to be expedient because of the nature of the working environment.

The restoration works took three to four weeks, with a final visit and check on the works immediately prior to the opening of the restaurant. This was an unusual but sensible precaution undertaken by the contractors, which enabled the conservators not only to correct any further damage caused by installation of new fixtures and fittings, but also to review the quality of the conservation work itself and make improvements.

The manufacturing and restoration programmes on these important tiles was considered to be a success, a good balance was struck between the necessities of the building and its users and retaining the historical integrity of the original materials and interior design.

Appendix

In 2002 we had, by chance, the opportunity to revisit the Terrace Restaurant where we found the restoration works to be in good order with no obvious visible changes.

Conservation of medieval tile pavements in an outdoor environment (1998–2001)

Introduction

It is now generally accepted that medieval tiles in unprotected outdoor sites, which are exposed to weather, visitors, and various unwanted attention in the form of theft and vandalism, are possessed of an in-built inevitability towards deterioration. Our aim as conservators is to find ways of slowing down that inevitable process.

The 12 priory or abbey sites, in the guardianship of English Heritage, included in our project in the Midlands and East Anglia regions have within them, on the whole, collections of fairly low status tiles, all of which have numerous examples of the same, recorded and in storage. Some 50 per cent of the areas we are currently working on are out of doors and completely exposed, others are partially protected by standing ruins, and some are sited indoors and are completely protected. This case study deals with those pavements which are out of doors and unprotected. Most of the pavements are fairly small, and the majority, with one or two exceptions, have been set down in Portland cement at some time between the 1930s and the 1950s; they are all surrounded by lush grass which is cut on a regular basis. Their value to the individual sites is as an aid for visual interpretation of the once colourful and sometimes lavish interiors. By remaining in place they provide a link between the grass covered ruins we see today and the ecclesiastical interior of the past.

We know that deterioration does occur; the causes are, in general terms, the natural environment, the weather, visitors, and vandalism. Our aim is to establish to what degree and over what time span each of these elements contributes to the material degradation of the tiles and find ways of arresting that process. The means to these ends had to be low budget, because of the volume of material involved, and 'low tech' in order to include the option that, on some sites at least, regular housekeeping could eventually take the place of specialised conservation programmes.

Background to the project

The medieval tile pavements at Buildwas Abbey, Shropshire, were the subject of an archaeological assessment in 1995 (Chadderton and Moore, non-published report EH). The Jackfield Conservation Studio was consulted to advise on possible in-situ conservation treatments or options for lifting the pavements for preservation in storage. It was within this document that the possibility of lifting and storing the tiles was rejected as being potentially too damaging, costly and undesirable; however, 14 of the 16 separate tile pavements were found to have at least 20 to 40 per cent of their surface area buried under earth, weeds and grass with the remaining areas completely exposed to the elements.

Our recommendations for conservation treatment at that time were: to remove all vegetation from the surface and of the tiles; to remove all debris and clean the surface; and to cut back an area of grass away from the tiles and replace it with a lime mortar surround (or 'buffer' zone) at least 10 cm wide which would prevent further incursion of weeds and grass. We also advised that the tiles should be covered in the winter months and that cleaning and weeding the surface of the tiles should take place annually. This document, along with the preliminary surveys on the other 11 sites carried out by Sandra Davidson (1995–96), provided the basis of the programme of work which was the English Heritage Medieval Tile Project – Phase II carried out in 1996–97, and the current Medieval Tile Project – Conservation Maintenance started in 1998 and to run on until February 2001.

The natural environment

It quickly became clear that weed and grass incursion into the pavement areas, along with the growth of moss and lichen on the surface of the tiles, had a more damaging effect than the merely unkempt appearance which resulted from a policy of non-intervention.

The combination of worn glaze and a low temperature, fired body clay leave the tile vulnerable to the fine root systems of grass and moss penetrating into the soft clay body causing it to break up. Moss is particularly insidious, its fine root systems can penetrate up to, and sometimes over, 1 cm deep, disrupting surface layers and creating small, deep craters that hold water, which in turn will freeze during cold spells, causing enough expansion to make the crater larger thus creating more space for the moss to penetrate. Accumulations of moss, lichen, algae and earth deposits provide a foothold for higher plant life. Not only do weeds, grass and moss cause direct crumbling of the clay body, they have a secondary effect of clogging up the pores in the ceramic and holding water around root systems which penetrates into the tiles. When combined with low temperatures this has a devastating effect. The larger the root system is, for example grass, the more drastic the effect, causing complete fracturing of the tile. The harder the clay body the more easily these effects are resisted, but it is well known that within any tile pavement the differences in density, purity and vitrification of the clay covers the complete spectrum from very hard to very soft. We therefore reasoned that it is important to clear the pavements of vegetation and the pockets of earth, onto which plant life attaches itself, annually before the first frosts.

This, of course, is stating the case a little too simplistically; there are considerable site specific differences in the type and degree of damage caused by vegetation which depend on the immediate environment. Buildwas Abbey, in the western region, is substantially more prone to moss and lichen – it is low lying, close to the River Severn and has a water retaining loam subsoil – than say Thetford Priory in the east which suffers relatively very little moss damage and almost none from lichen growth due to its situation on a light, sandy, well-drained subsoil. However, on the sandy soil severe damage is caused by grass and weed incursion, particularly those weeds which are spread by root systems (e.g. buttercups and potentillas) which will run fast and easily into joints between the tiles, or even into fissures within the clay body causing fractures, and underneath the tile forcing them upwards or apart (Figure 7.16). The detrimental effects of the higher developed vegetation are much more easily assessed than those of algae or lichen, but some lichens produce organic acids which are harmful to lead-based glaze; they also penetrate the material and cause physical distressing of the surface. The material breakdown is slow but ruinous, causing small pits across the surface of the tile. The specific effects of the various lower orders of plant life on fired clay require microscopic analysis which was not part of our brief for the project. We decided, however, to remove algae and lichens from the surface of the tiles by mechanical cleaning in order to monitor the speed at which they might reoccur.

We are also recording how efficient the use of a simple non-ionic detergent is as a cleaning agent, in terms of recolonisation of algae

Figure 7.16
Damage caused by weed growth.

and lichen. We are also critically aware of the surface damage to soft bodied tiles which could result from repeated mechanical removal of moss, lichen and algae and would like to see more analysis of the effects of chemical algaecides on tile bodies, and whether their controlled regular use is actually less damaging to surfaces than mechanical action. Both methods rely on regular maintenance to be effective and there are also cost and health and safety implications attached to the use of algaecides. The widespread surface algae found at Buildwas Abbey is disfiguring and makes the decoration on some tiles difficult to read (Figure 7.17).

Treatment methods

Hand weeding is the first stage. Weeds with long root systems can only be pulled with care. If the roots have penetrated into or around the tiles to the point where they will cause severe disturbance by pulling, they are best cut off below the crown of the plant and left to die back. Moss, lichen and algae are removed by brushing, or using a hard edged hand tool (preferably made of plastic to avoid damaging the tile surface) in order to loosen moss or collections of earth and small root systems from crevices and pitting in the tiles. The final stage is to wash the tiles with non-ionic detergent and distilled water, this final stage may eventually be shown to be unnecessary but we are hoping by the end of the project to determine whether the detergent has any useful effect in deterring the regrowth of algae and lichen.

Figure 7.17
Algae on tiles.

Figure 7.17
Algae on tiles.

Figure 7.18
Lime mortar 'buffer' zone.

Hand weeding and cleaning can only be effective as a conservation measure if it is carried out on an annual basis.

As a preventive measure against grass incursion particularly, we have put in place around every tile pavement a mortar 'buffer' zone. After cutting back the grass from the edges of the tiles to an approximate width of 12 cm we laid down a lime mortar border around the perimeter of each pavement about 10 cm wide (it was at this juncture that we were able to determine which pavements were set on concrete and which pavements were on possible original lime mortar). We used a 2:5 mix of moderately hydraulic lime with 60 per cent local and 40 per cent sharp sand and have found that the mortar has become hard enough to resist invasion by grass roots. The annual growth rate of the grass on the wettest sites covers the mortar without reaching the vulnerable edges of the pavements. Thus the tiles are protected from root penetration; each year the grass is cut back again to the further edge of the 'buffer' zone (Figure 7.18). In addition we have found that the mortar acts as a protective edging against careless use of grass cutting machinery.

During Medieval Tile Project – Phase II we used the Buildwas Abbey site as a test for the effectiveness of grouting the tiles as a protection from self-seeding weed growth between tiles. We have found it generally effective in reducing the number of weeds in the pavements. Lime mortar grouting is labour intensive, so with cost in mind we are only gradually extending the areas of grouted tiles each season. Weighing in against the outlined advantages of lime mortar protection is the tendency for lime to attract its own moss and lichen growth.

Pockets of earth or sand which have blown or been carried by rain-water into crevices on the surface of tile pavements will inevitably attract more weed growth. It seems important therefore, at least once a year, preferably in the spring, to brush tile pavements clean of sur-face earth and sand.

The weather

The most obvious and devastating effect of the weather on exposed tile pavements is frost. Frost causes large flakes of surface glaze and ceramic body to break away from the surface of the tiles resulting in loss of decoration and exposure of the softer inner body of the tile to more damage. Delamination of the surface leaves the tiles no longer flat or smooth allowing more dirt and debris to collect, in turn attract-ing further weed growth.

The recording survey carried out by Birmingham Field Archaeology Unit in 1996–97 on all sites shows that a large proportion, possibly 30 per cent, of tiles exposed to the weather have lost their flat surface due to frost damage. The presbytery area at Thetford Abbey, in par-ticular, has only about one third of the body of each tile left in place. The surface of the pavement is completely lost while the lower part of each tile remains adhered to the concrete base (Figure 7.19).

Therein lies a major problem. With the exception of one or two pavements, all areas were, at sometime in the past (probably in the 1950s), laid on Portland cement. The non-porous cement holds the rainwater within the clay body of the tiles, which when frozen expands and bursts the surface of the tiles. If we assume that when these tile pavements were laid onto the cement they were whole and in good condition (there would be no real reason to display damaged tiles) then we can easily see the rate of damage caused by frost over a mere 40 to 50 years. Protecting vulnerable cement-based pavements from saturating rainwater will go a long way to prevent surface exfoliation.

Pavements situated in exposed central areas of sites, away from protecting walls, suffer worst from frost. Many tile pavements, notably at Binham Abbey, have walls immediately adjacent or even surround-ing them; these, often low, walls offer considerable protection. Tiles situated close to walls usually have retained their glaze or decoration and are in visibly better condition than those at a further distance from protection. It is also apparent that there is little difference between north and south facing walls, both offer good protection. South facing walls stay warmer for longer periods, while north facing walls, though subject to much colder temperatures, tend not to heat up quickly, so neither situation is subject to rapid temperature changes. However, tiles positioned away from the protection of the walls are subject to

Figure 7.19
Frost damage on tiles, the result of many years' exposure.

rapid changes in temperature and therefore tend to suffer the most damage. A rapid temperature change causes a disparity between the temperature on the surface of the tiles and the temperature within the inner body which results in thermal shock. If we couple these conditions with the fact that many medieval tiles have inherent fault lines within their structure, probably caused by insufficient 'wedging' or folding of the clay, then the two forces, poor clay body and rapid temperature change, will combine to cause fracturing and spalling. Tiles from the Bawsey kilns in Norfolk seem particularly susceptible to these conditions.

We have already discussed the further possible damage from frost caused by the accumulation of moisture around weed and grass roots. It therefore seems impossible to avoid the conclusion that winter covers will protect tiles from the combined action of rainwater and low temperatures, and are essential to the longevity of tiles on site. A variety of different cover types have been put into service over the years on some sites in the eastern region, but there are considerable difficulties governing their effectiveness which relate less to the type of cover but more to either their handling or to problems of vandalism.

The method of winter cover protection recommended in Medieval Tile Project – Phase II Conservation 1997 was a box type construction built specifically to fit each pavement either as a whole cover or as a number of component parts for larger pavements (Figure 7.20). It was designed to be put in place in the autumn and lifted again in spring. Though excellent for protecting tiles, and working successfully so far at one site, they have failed on another because of interference at the hands of vandals. Fixing covers to the ground presents some difficulties in ancient scheduled monuments where archaeology must not be disturbed without prior consent.

For many years tiles on some sites had been covered with sand, we found this to be damaging and ineffective. The sand layer was not

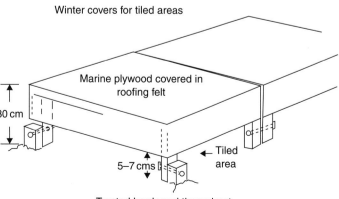

Figure 7.20
Diagram of winter covers.

deep enough to keep out frost, it kept tiles in a wet condition and was often removed in the spring in an inadequate and damaging way. There is also some evidence that it leaves an orange stain on the tiles along with the probability that it imparts salts into the body of the covered tiles.

Visitors

There is no doubt that the continuing tread of feet over pavements causes surface wear. Gravel from adjacent paths finds its way onto pavements resulting in the abrading of the surface of the tiles by pedestrian traffic. Tiles can become loosened by the impact of feet if the tiles are set on a soft lime mortar and the edges of tiles can become worn or damaged. In many instances, tiles can be protected by the simple expedient of guiding the flow of visitors around pavements rather than over them. While there is no doubt that this type of damage can and does occur, within our three year programme of inspections and maintenance the impact of damage of this sort has been slight, particularly when compared with damage caused every year by the weather and natural environment.

Vandalism

Wanton vandalism is a problem to all sites, especially open unmanned sites; it manifests itself as graffiti, destruction and interference with winter covers, casual dislodging of tiles and theft. Very little can be done to prevent determined theft; however, good maintenance can have a deterrent effect on casual vandalism. Tile pavements which are regularly maintained with sound mortar and grout are less likely to be casually dislodged. A well-maintained pavement also has an appearance of being in ownership and cared for and is less likely to be treated negligently.

Conclusion

Our programme of work so far has highlighted certain aspects of tile deterioration on outdoor sites. The causes of deterioration have long been well known, but our maintenance programme has shown us how the most serious damage occurs and therefore where money can be well spent to reduce the effects of the damage. The two main causes of serious deterioration are the natural environment, meaning factors which encourage damaging weed growth, and the weather.

The encroachment of plant life is unstoppable, but its damaging effects can be much reduced if it is not allowed to take hold; annual maintenance can prevent this happening.

Damage from the weather is mainly caused by the freeze–thaw cycle, every year since the 1950s. A mere 50 years in the 700 year old history of many of the tiles have seen substantial amounts of material lost to bad weather conditions. Proper use of winter covers would cut this loss at a stroke. We have established that visitors have caused little in the way of damage over the years by comparison. It is useless to pretend that measures taken to protect tiles in-situ are a cheap option, regular maintenance costs money, but more people who care for our outdoor built heritage are finding that maintenance works as a protection, and that there is no such thing as a quick 'one-off' solution.

Appendix
Conservation of medieval tile pavements in an outdoor environment (2001–04)

From the autumn, winter season of 2001–02 until autumn, winter season 2003–04 the conservation maintenance regime for all sites will be governed by the standard of minimal intervention based on an assessment which takes into account all environmental and site specific factors. At the end of three years the results regarding the overall condition of the tiles will be assessed. We are particularly looking at the effect of winter covers on tiles. At the end of the first three year maintenance project, 1998–2001, winter covers were put in place on many sites. We are monitoring their effectiveness within an ongoing maintenance regime at Buildwas Abbey, Shropshire, and Castle Acre Priory, Norfolk. There are no winter covers in place at Thetford Priory which will be used as a comparison against which to judge their effectiveness.

All outdoor areas will be carefully weeded, the moss removed and the grass edges cut back away from the tiles. They will be cleaned with a dry brush except where green algae occurs, in which instance they will be washed with distilled water only with no added detergent. Mortar repairs will be carried out as necessary.

Use of detergent cleaners (2001–04)

The change in the cleaning regime has proved instructive. We have found that if pavements are well drained and in full sunlight they tend to attract little in the way of algae or lichen growth, therefore they do not require any type of wet cleaning or cleaning agent; dry brushing is sufficient to clean the tiles, leaving no specific change in the overall look of the pavement.

However, if pavements are situated in shady areas they tend to grow more algae which must be wet cleaned in order to remove the green coating presented by the algae. The amount of algae growth seems to be determined by the wetness of the season. We have also determined that the absence of any detergent cleaning agent in the water acts as a check for the algae but is allowing a regrowth of lichens, which was not occurring when detergent was used in conjunction with distilled water.

Our previous three year maintenance programme included a small amount of mild detergent in the cleaning water which significantly reduced the presence of lichen. Removing the detergent from the cleaning water has seen the re-emergence of lichens.

Winter covers (2001–04)

The importance of protection by winter covers for outdoor pavements cannot be overstated. The tiles at Castle Acre Priory are the only site in the eastern region which has the benefit of the specified cover regime, as a result there has been no damage by frost action to the tiles or mortar at that site over the three year period, but there has been considerable damage at Thetford Priory where there were no covers over the same period. The old sand winter cover regime which was in place at Thetford Abbey is no longer an option as a protection, as it is widely recognised to cause damage to tiles in its own right; its presence also attracts vandalism. However, the specified covering regime should be retained at Castle Acre as it has been shown to be beneficial. Tiles at Binham Abbey do not have winter covers but they tend not to suffer from frost conditions as the site is close to the coast and all of the pavements are surrounded by protecting walls.

All tile pavements at Buildwas Abbey showed improvement in condition, due to the protection of winter covers. There was no frost damage despite a severe cold spell during January 2001. We have experienced a drastic fall in the numbers of tiles damaged by frost and a general improvement in the condition of the tiles year on year since the introduction of winter covers.

Weed and moss growth (2001–04)

Weed and moss growth are also less of a problem where pavements are covered in the winter months. The winter covers may help to check moss growth as they allow the tiles to stay relatively dry throughout February which is the main time for moss growth. Area 16 at Buildwas Abbey, which does not have winter covers, suffered considerably more moss and weed growth than all other pavements in the same vicinity, though it is protected from frost by high walls. All tile areas showed improvement in condition, probably due to the protection of winter covers. We are observing a lessening in the amount of weed and moss growth accumulating each year.

Both Castle Acre and Thetford Priories have been the subject of weed killing routines around and over the stonework, carried out by the technical teams who work to protect the ruins. It has become apparent that where there has been spray drift over the tiles there follows a noticeable increase in the amount of moss growth over the surface of the tiles; we also detect a degree of sulphide action causing a blackening on the surface, which is irreversible. We strongly advise that there should be no use of weed killers adjacent to tile pavements.

The mortar buffer zones around all outdoor pavements continue to show their value in that they prevent the incursion of grass roots into the pavement edges providing the grass is cut back to the outer edge of the mortar each year. The mortar zones should be maintained. There is always a degree of weed growth in the pavements caused by wind blown seed which should be removed, by hand, annually.

Visitors and vandalism (2001–04)

Visitors seem to have no compunction about walking on tile pavements; indeed they often seem to go out of their way to do so. Debris finding its way onto the pavements from the surrounding environment should be removed each year because it will be the cause of abrasion on the surface of the tiles when walked upon. Barriers across those pedestrian entrances which set down directly onto pavements are successful as a means of re-routing visitors; there is evidently less foot traffic on those pavements.

Gathering dust and debris does not cause damage to tiles in itself, provided they are not walked on, and overcleaning may do more harm than good to fragile surfaces. However, it can look unsightly and give an air of neglect. Droppings from birds and bats, however, do cause damage due to the acid and nitrate content in the droppings which will penetrate into the clay body giving rise to chemical change.

General assessment all locations, March 2001 to March 2004

Conclusions

Tile pavements situated out of doors benefit without exception from continuous annual maintenance. The visual presentation of the tiles is much improved and the rate of deterioration is slowed. Winter covers put in place annually are vital to the longevity of tiles in-situ out of doors, as they prevent frost damage and slow the growth rate of moss and weeds, all of which have been shown to cause the greatest amount of damage to outdoor sited tiles. The condition of the pavements would deteriorate rapidly if the maintenance regime ceases.

The use of a balanced pH detergent in the washing water of outdoor tiles has deterred the growth of silver/green lichen which tends to reappear when the detergent is absent from the washing water. The use of weed killers on tile surfaces encourages moss growth.

All pavements should be inspected annually to safeguard the option to intervene in potentially damaging situations. Our overall assessment concludes that the conservation programme as it stands strikes a good balance between conservation and visitor perception of a well-kept site.

Persian Water Rug fountain, San Diego, California, USA

One of the most subtle and too often overlooked tile fountains in San Diego's Balboa Park is the 'Persian Water Rug'. It is located at the isolated end of a small garden between the Casa de Balboa and the House of Hospitality on the El Prado, the southern terminus of the axis which ends on the north with the botanical building.

The garden between the buildings slopes down from the connecting arcade on the Prado, with the fountain centred on a low wall at its end. It provided a focal point of colour to catch the eye, framed against the lush background foliage of the earlier 1915 Exposition plantings. The combination of its subtle hues and water sparkling over its serrated surface, along with its location away from the bustle of the Prado, provided an area of quiet retreat for the Exposition visitors in 1935. Definitely, after dark, a more spectacular scene would have captured the eye. Concealed indirect lighting caused the surface to shimmer and glow, and the graceful urns on either side were softly lighted from below. The trees in the canyon behind were also highlighted by concealed soft hue floodlights set flush with the ground.

As relatively 'simple' as the fountain appears, a few tiles with water running down its face, the true artistry is the result of a combination of carefully designed and executed factors. The scale of the work in relation to its location was large enough to catch the eye from the Prado, yet it maintained human proportions when viewed close up. The colours and patterns of the tiles are striking; and the plain low wall on which the fountain is placed integrated it into the adjacent dense background foliage. In other words this was a well thought out artistic 'gem' and being off the beaten path is what has preserved it over the last 70 years.

The Persian Water Rug was conceived by nationally known architect Richard S Requa, AIA, of San Diego, the Supervisor of Architecture and Landscaping for the 1935 Exposition. The fountain's pedigree can be traced to ancient Persian gardens and palaces. The style is called 'chadar', meaning 'shawl'. Requa's 1935 photograph of it appears on page 141 of his book *Inside Lights on the Building of San Diego's Exposition: 1935*. However, only a brief mention is made of its location on page 100.

Requa's architectural philosophy centred on the Mediterranean style which dominated the 1920s in California. He made two extensive trips to Spain and the Mediterranean in the mid-1920s, publishing a lavish portfolio of photographs of architectural detail, gardens and fountains after the 1926 trip and a bound volume upon his return in 1928; both are collectors pieces today.

Overall the tile installation is 74 inches wide and 44 inches tall, with a 60 inch wide face panel and a 74 inch × 17 inch basin at the base.

The blue tile edging extends 30 inches past the basin on both sides of the base of the urn platforms. The top and face panel are 6 inch × 6 inch tiles by Gladding, McBean & Co., Pattern TA-18. The pattern is surrounded by a solid border of almost iridescent cobalt blue 6 inch × 6 inch tiles and a band of 6 inch × $1\frac{3}{4}$ inch tiles in gold.

I first assumed the border was from the D&M Tile Company, Los Angeles, based on a letter dated 10 April 1935, and Requa's reply on 11 April. However, with the opening of the Exposition only a few weeks away, I believe that Requa opted for a standard decorative panel from Gladding, McBean, rather than a custom design from D&M. The source of the solid colour border tile is certain as one of the fragments has the following markings on the back: T7S AET CO (American Encaustic Tiling Company).

Two light wells on either side illuminated the glazed urns, originally from Gladding, McBean. A row of waterproof lights in the basin illuminated the face of the tiles. A small perforated copper pipe across the top provided a gentle flow of water that rippled across the top and face of the tile fountain. The unique corrugated surface resulting from setting each row of face tiles with the top edge extending 1/2 inch out beyond the row above provides a pleasant rippling sound.

In 1995 the fountain's fate was uncertain. The adjacent House of Hospitality, also designed by Requa for the 1935 Exposition, was due to be dismantled and reconstructed with its 1935 configuration and details. The tiles of the Persian Water Rug were in basically good condition, but its location was in the path of all the major equipment needed for the contractor's work. Various proposals were suggested: place the fountain in a museum, replace it with a 'copy' in fibreglass or new tiles; remove it intact to storage; restore and reinstall the original. Thankfully the latter prevailed although the basin was destroyed in the process.

In November of 1995 the wall on both sides of the main panel and the concrete sidewalk around the basin were cut. Pipes were inserted through holes drilled on either side of the panel. Supported by a crane an attempt to rock it loose failed, and the basin separated from the back. The damage to the basin tiles was too extensive for repair, but it was kept to serve as a pattern for its replacement.

Sidewalk tiles, Joliet, Illinois

Around the turn of the twentieth century, in cities and towns across America and Canada, lettered tiles spelling out street names were often laid in sidewalks at intersections. Some of the most charming tiles were made by the dust-pressed method and were referred to as encaustic. An unfired porcelain tile would be stamped with a steel die under 20 to 30 tons of pressure, forming an impression in the shape of a letter. Nearly dry (hence 'dust'), unfired porcelain of a contrasting colour would be pressed into the impression. The tile face would be scraped smooth, and the tile would then be fired. This bonded the letter image permanently into the tile body and made the tile rock hard and impervious to moisture. These encaustic tiles were tough, but they were expensive and difficult to make.

Many of the tiles still found on American and Canadian street corners were made by the American Encaustic Tiling Company of Zanesville, Ohio, in a style called 'Alhambra'. The 'Alhambra' style consisted of a pearly white background and precise, royal blue Roman letters, each with a dark grey double outline. Each tile contained one letter, and street names were spelled out one letter at a time. Many of these tiles survive to this day, some 80 to 90 years later, despite tough sidewalk duty through season changes, freeze–thaw cycles, rollerskates, skateboards and countless other abuses. Despite their toughness, the number of these charming old street name tiles is dwindling (Figure 7.21). All those winters take their toll, and so does occasional need to upgrade streets and curbs. Joliet, Illinois, lost several intersections with old tiles last summer when a new storm sewer and new curbs were installed in one of its historic districts. Local residents who are members of the district's Cathedral Area Preservation Area, with help from members of a second area group, the Upper Bluff Society, began looking for replacement tiles to purchase.

Easier said than done. The American Encaustic Tiling Company, taken over some 60 years ago by what is now American Olean, long

Figure 7.21
Sidewalk tiles before replacement.

ago abandoned the machinery; and the skills to make encaustic tiles were lost. The 'Old House Journal' Restoration Directory contacted some 40 tile makers listed in their pages. They found to their dismay that very few still stocked tiles with letters on them, and none in the distinctive Alhambra style. A handful of manufacturers were willing to try to make the tiles as a custom order. Few tile makers, however, were confident their products would stand up to being laid face up on a horizontal sidewalk surface, totally exposed to summer's sun, winter's ice and snow, and the abuse and wear of pedestrian traffic, as well as the old Alhambras did.

Some other cities have tried to find replacements for their old Alhambras too – Kansas City, Missouri; Corpus Christi, Texas; and Victoria, British Colombia, among others. Their suppliers tried ceramic glazes and modified encaustic technology, but durability problems, high production costs and limited city budgets prevented fully satisfactory results.

Although the old dust-pressed encaustic machinery and methods have almost completely disappeared, new technology has been developed that can match the appearance of the old Alhambras. Using an abrasive waterjet saw and CAD/CAM computer technology, a tiny stream of water under extremely high pressure can precisely cut and etch hard porcelain as if it were cookie dough. A letter is simultaneously cut out of a white and blue tile. By reducing the water pressure, a second line is etched into the surface to form the double line appearance of the originals. The blue letter is then inserted into the identically shaped white tile, much like a puzzle piece, and epoxy grout is then used to secure it in place.

This combination of high technology and traditional design produces a tile with through-body colour, avoiding any danger of glaze wear, chipping or slickness. The tiles, properly cemented into the sidewalk, could be worn all the way through and still be readable. Joliet's Department of Public Works and Utilities (PW&U) learned of the neighbourhood's efforts to find a supplier of Alhambra reproductions. What happened next showed the co-operation between Joliet's various municipal departments and the growing sense of partnership between the city and its residents. Using the residents' work as a starting point, and with the support of the city's Historic Preservation Commission, PW&U selected Illahe Tileworks of Ashland, Oregon, to supply waterjet-cut tiles for a pilot project on six intersections in the historic district. The Joliet City Council allocated funds to pay for the tiles and their installation.

The new tiles, almost identical in appearance and texture to the original Alhambras, were installed in early August 1997 (Figure 7.22). They were designed slightly smaller than the originals in order to fit in reduced spaces resulting from federally mandated wheelchair ramps.

Figure 7.22
Grouting and removing protective
tape from new tiles after installation.

After seeing how the tiles fare through a Midwestern winter, the city
hopes to launch a programme to install them in other neighbourhoods
interested in having them once again grace their streets.

Joliet's Department of Public Works and Utilities would be pleased
to keep other communities informed of the success and failure of the
pilot project, to provide advice on installation and to share the details
of their follow-up programme.

Update

Lisa Dorithy reported in 2002 that the project has been a complete
success in terms of performance of the tiles under the duress of
temperature change and wear and tear, and that their programme
of replacement continues apace. However, there have been some
production difficulties and they are now on their third tile supplier,
the first two being unwilling to carry on production after the initial
order.

The current tile supplier is 'Tileworks', Porter Beach, Indiana. The
company undertaking the waterjet cutting is Midwest Waterjet and
Peter Sherf of that company is working to refine the process of cutting
in order to make it more affordable. He is researching the possibility
of bonding the brittle porcelain to other materials during the cutting
process in order to reduce the number of breakages which increase
the cost of production. Tight interior angles create the most stress with
only a one in three success rate in cutting Ws.

Conservation treatment report on three early 1960s tile panels from Sunderland Art Gallery for Tyne and Wear Museums

Introduction

The three tile panels were designed and executed by W. Hudspith, head of Sunderland College of Art, in 1963 and were located on an outer south facing wall of the 1960s extension to Sunderland Museum. Their design is related to modernism and their themes represent art, music and literature respectively. Each panel measured 1618 mm high by 2710 mm wide. The tiles measured 100 mm by 100 mm. The panels were set into shallow recesses beneath windows on the ground floor, the walls of the building were concrete block built and the tiles were fixed with a waterproof epoxy adhesive onto a hard cement mortar screed which covered the blocks.

The staff of the conservation unit at Tyne and Wear Museums had at first decided to cut each tile individually away from the wall on the basis that the panels gave off a hollow sound over a greater part of their surface when tapped with a rubber mallet. However, they began to encounter difficulties quite quickly because the layers of mortar and adhesive were exceptionally hard, had pushed in between the tiles into the joints, and in some areas were quite deep. Additionally the edges of the tiles were in danger of being damaged by the cutting process because the width of the grout joint varied considerably.

After careful deliberation they decided to change tack in their method and devised the support method for the panels as described below and proceeded to dismantle the wall behind the tile panels. The mortar screed had already become detached from the concrete block wall in many places, which accounted for the hollow ring and made dismantling the blocks relatively easy.

The panels were each cut into two parts to facilitate careful handling, they were lowered onto steel trolleys and taken to storage where they would await transportation to Jackfield Conservation Studio and continuing conservation treatment.

The panels had one unusual feature, as a result of the nature of the overall design each single tile bore no relationship to any of its neighbours in terms of colour or line, neither would it be possible to decide which way up was the correct way if a tile became dislocated from its original location. Although the panels had been photographed before commencement of works, we determined that it was essential that each tile be numbered and colour coded very carefully with a waterproof system, which would be robust enough to last through the complete process of mortar removal and cleaning without danger of loss, leading to possible confusion over the correct location of tiles. To fulfil these criteria we chose plastic electrical insulating tape cut into small squares and marked with 'biro' ink. The tape has the advantage of being waterproof with a good adhesive bond which nevertheless will peel off easily without tearing or leaving a residue of gum. It is also available in a number of different colours.

Conservation treatment

Panel 1 – Literature (Figure 7.23)
Panel 2 – Art (Figure 7.24)
Panel 3 – Music (Figure 7.25)

Figure 7.23
Literature.

Figure 7.24
Art.

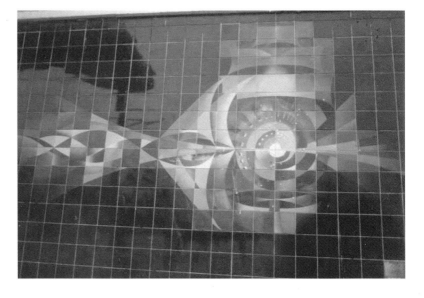

Figure 7.25
Music.

Condition

The condition of the tile panels on arrival was as described in the conservation report dated 19/2/2000. Each of the three panels was divided into two sections. Thirty-six tiles, which formed two rows of tiles in the centre of Panel No. 1, were packed separately into a box.

Each of the six sections was faced with a rigid timber frame made up of 2 inch × 2 inch timber glued with a thixotropic contact adhesive onto the ceramic face of the tiles. The timber battens were made rigid with plywood boards which were screwed to the frames. Between the timber battens and the tiles was a layer of thick cotton fabric which had also been glued to the face of the tiles with contact adhesive. The reverse of the tiles was coated with between 5 and 10 mm of white epoxy adhesive and approximately 20 mm of hard Portland cement mortar, though the depths of both materials varied considerably over the whole area of each panel. Each section was heavy to manoeuvre but had remained rigid and undamaged during transportation.

Treatment

It had previously been agreed with the Head of Conservation, Tyne and Wear Museums, that the combination of concrete and epoxy material on the reverse of the tiles was detrimental to their survival because:

- There was no flexibility in the mortar, it did not allow for either thermal movement or shifting of the building. Fracturing was already evident in two areas of the panels.

- These types of mortar and adhesive did not allow free movement of moisture and would eventually be the cause of frost damage to the face of the tiles.
- The panels had to be moved to allow for refurbishment of the building, making an ideal opportunity to replace the fixing method with a reversible flexible system which will allow for their easy removal to an indoor location in the future.

Our first concern was to divide each section into smaller sections so that they could be manoeuvred more easily thereby reducing the threat of accidental damage while handling. Each of the six sections was laid face down. Lines were drawn, corresponding with the grout lines exactly, onto the mortar dividing each panel into a further six sections which were identified by using a colour and number code (Figure 7.26).

We used a chasing saw fitted with a diamond blade to cut along the marked lines to a depth which reached to the reverse of the tile but no further. The depth of cut had to vary to correspond with the depth of the mortar.

We turned the sections over, unscrewed the plywood boards and cut through the cotton material with a sharp blade. We then cut the 2 × 2 bracing timbers in corresponding places to the mortar cuts on the reverse. We did this section by section.

As the timbers were cut through the grout between the tiles gave way, so dividing the tiles neatly into smaller sections. This was a difficult operation requiring great accuracy and forethought; it was very successful, resulting in damage to only six tiles out of a total number of 1296 over all three panels.

Figure 7.26
The reverse of the panels after cutting into small sections showing the Portland cement.

Figure 7.27
Sections of the panels face up showing the linen cloth and timber battens adhered with contact adhesive.

Figure 7.28
Removing the residue of adhesive with steam.

The 36 smaller sections were arranged face up on the bench in turn, according to their number/colour code, in order to remove the timber battens and cotton facing cloth, which was still adhered to the face of each section (Figure 7.27). We attempted to soften the adhesive using xylene as the recommended solvent. We found that although the glue softened readily it was still too viscous to remove cleanly and the volume of solvent required represented a health and safety hazard which would require the use of breather masks for all workshop personnel.

Our alternative method was to use non-pressurised steam directly onto the fabric. We found the fabric would then pull away from the tiles, with the use of extra pressure on the steam the battens also loosened. The remaining residue coating of adhesive on the tile face was also removed using steam combined with scraping by hand with plastic spatulas. The method was successful (Figure 7.28).

Each clean panel was then laid out and every tile carefully numbered. The numbering system had to be waterproof and easy to decipher. We colour coded the panels:

Red – Literature, Green – Music, Yellow – Art

We started the numbering from left to right in the bottom left-hand corner, making sure that each number was the correct way up. Numbering in this way facilitates the method of relaying (i.e. from the bottom left-hand corner). Each panel contained 432 tiles.

Using diamond bench cutting saws fitted with specialist jigs to hold the tiles in the correct position, we separated each tile from its neighbour by scoring on the reverse along the path of the grout joint. We then sliced the mortar from the reverse of each tile. The edges were cleaned by hand using a sharp blade, as we were anxious not to damage the edges of the tiles in any way.

It had previously been agreed that the panels should each be split into three sections for remounting. This would allow for much greater ease of manoeuvrability and therefore present less risk for the safety of the panels and handlers alike.

Mounting boards with backing frames were built as per the agreed specification, all parts being glued and screwed onto 1 inch thick marine ash plywood (Figure 5.37).

We refixed all tiles using BAL flexible adhesive. This is a 1:4 cement and sand mix with the addition of rubber granules which allows flexibility and breathability.

Additional treatment

Panel 1 – Literature
Two tiles among those packed separately in the box were broken (Nos 339–340). Two tiles were missing (Nos 204–205), these were replaced with painted copies of the original design.

Panel 3 – Music
Fifty-one tiles were damaged beyond restoration by grit blasting in an effort to remove graffiti at some time in the past, the glaze surface of the tiles was completely degraded. These were replaced with specially commissioned tiles which accurately matched the original glaze.

All panels had examples of tiles which were described as 'blanched' in the conservation report. These tiles were all examples which had initially been subject to inadequate firing and have weathered badly because of that reason. We coated them with microcrystalline wax tinted with black pigment in order to bring them to a condition, visually at least, in line with the original intention of the artist.

Reversing technique

To reverse the mounting system, place panels face down, mark the grout line grid. Use a depth gauged circular wood saw to separate each tile into single units.

Use a rough cut or reciprocating wood saw to cut down between the tile and the timber backing. Trim off excess mortar with a sharp blade.

Bibliography and references

Introduction

Ashurst, J. (1988) *Conservation of Building and Decorative Stone*. Butterworth-Heinemann, Oxford.

Buys, S. and Oakley, V. (1993) *Conservation and Restoration of Ceramics*. Butterworth-Heinemann, Oxford.

Fielden, B. (1992) *Conservation of Historic Buildings*. Butterworth-Heinemann, Oxford.

Sharpe, K. (2003) Obit. Hugh Trevor-Roper, Lord Dacre. *History Today*, Vol. 53(4).

Warren, J. (1999) *Conservation of Brick*. Butterworth-Heinemann, Oxford.

Chapter 1

Beaulah, K. (1987) *Church Tiles of the Nineteenth Century*. Shire Publications.

Curl, Prof. J.S. (1999) *Dictionary of Architecture*. Oxford University Press.

Eames, E.S. (1992) *English Tilers*. British Museum Press, London.

Jervis, S. (1984) *Dictionary of Design and Designers*. Penguin Books.

Jonker, M. and Tichelaar, P.J. (1992) *Willem van der Kloet*. Privately published.

Minton's Enamelled Tiles Catalogue c.1885 Reprinted (1996) Richard Dennis Publications.

Palmer, N. (2000) *Warwick Castle, Guy's Tower*. Warwick County Council Museum Field Services.

Riley, N. (1987) *Tile Art*. Apple Press, Herts.

Sims, M. (2003) The Encaustic Tile in America. *Journal of Tile Heritage of America*, Vol. 7, No. 1.

Acknowledgments:
The St Stephens Restoration and Preservation Trust

Chapter 2

Eames, E.S. (1980) *Catalogue of Medieval Tile*. B.M. Publications, London.

Furnival, W.J. (1904) *Leadless and Decorative Tiles, Faience and Mosaic*. Published privately.

Haberley, L. (1937) *Medieval Paving Tiles*. Oxford.

Hall, D., tilemaker (2002) Dorset UK, unpublished.

Harcourt, J. (2000) Medieval Floor Tiles of Cleeve Abbey. *Journal of British Archaeological Society*.

Palmer, N. (2000) *Warwick Castle, Guy's Tower*. Warwick County Council Museum Field Services.

Ray, A. *English Delftware Tiles*. Faber & Faber.

Tichelaar, P.J. (2002) *Royal Tichelaar*. Makkum, The Netherlands.

van der Werf, J. (2002) Conservation and Restoration of Tin Glazes Tiles. *Glazed Expressions*, No. 44.

van Lemmen, H. (1986) *Delftware Tiles*. Shire Publications.

van Lemmen, H. (1991) *Fired Earth*. Richard Dennis Publications.

Acknowledgements and thanks:
Chris Cox, Michelle Cox, Diana Hall, Pieter Jan Tichelaar, Faith Graham

Chapter 3

Furnival, W.J. (1904) *Leadless and Decorative Tiles, Faience and Mosaic*. Published privately.

Maw & Co. (1850) Company catalogue, courtesy Ironbridge Gorge Museum Trust.

Poster and Sherlock (1987) Denny Abbey, The Nun's Refectory. *Cambridge Antiquarian Soc.*, Vol. LXXVI.

Riley, N. (1987) *Tile Art*. Apple Press, Herts.

Skelton, A. (1998) The Carshalton Water Tower. *Journal of the Tiles and Architectural Soc.*, Vol. 7.

Technical Advice Notes 1. (1998) Preparation and Use of Lime Mortar. Historic Scotland Best Practice Guide for Hydraulic Lime Mortar. Forsight Lime Research Second Draft (2002) Bristol University.

Chapter 4

Adam, R. (2003) Heritage Authentincity Monument. *Context*, No. 79, IHBC.
News Bulletin of the Tile Heritage Foundation, *Flash Point*, Vols 1 to 11.

Acknowledgements and thanks:
Joseph Taylor. President and Co-Founder of the Tile Heritage Foundation.
Jonathon Taylor. MSc IHBC. Director, Cathedral Communications Ltd.

Chapter 5

Ashurst, J. and Ashurst, N. (1988) *Practical Building Conservation. Vol. 2. Brick, Terracotta and Earth*. English Heritage Technical Handbook.

Buys, S. and Oakley, V. (1993) *The Conservation and Restoration of Ceramics.* Butterworth-Heinemann Ltd.

Faulding and Thomas (2000) Ceramic Tiles in Historic Buildings: Examination, Recording and Treatment. *Journal of Architectural Conservation,* Vol. 6, No. 1.

Fidler, J. (1982) The Conservation of Architectural Terracotta and Faience. *ASCHB Transactions,* Vol. 6.

Fidler, J. (1996) Fragile Remains. *Transcript English Heritage Symposium,* September 1994, James and James.

Fielden, Sir B.M. (1982) *Conservation of Historic Buildings.* Butterworths.

Horie, C.V. (1987) *Materials for Conservation.* Butterworth-Heinemann Ltd.

Jackfield Conservation Studio, Ironbridge, UK. Case Studies and Reports (1990–2003) unpublished.

Koob, S. (1986) The Use of Paraloid B72 as an Adhesive, *Studies in Conservation 31,* Freer Gallery, Smithsonian Institute, Washington DC.

Lins, A. (1984) *Technical Notes, Dutch Tiles.* Philadelphia Museum of Art Exhibition Catalogue.

Warren, J. (1999) *Conservation of Brick.* Butterworth-Heinemann.

Chapter 7

Acknowledgments and thanks:
Osgoode Hall
Jill Taylor, Taylor Hazell Architects, Toronto
Michael Kay, Decorative Tile Works, Ironbridge

House of Commons
Chris Blanchett, Buckland Books, Little Hampton, West Sussex

Medieval tile pavements
Dr Sara Lunt, Senior Curator English Heritage
Lynne Bevan, Birmingham University Archeology Unit

References:
Yates, Davison, M. (1996) *Architectural Ceramics.* James & James.

Persian Water Rug fountain, San Diego, California, USA
Jackson, Parker H. (1999) *Flash Point,* Vol. 12, Nos 3 & 4.

Sidewalk tiles, Joliet, Illinois
Dorithy, L. (1998) *Flash Point,* Vol. 11, Nos 1 & 2.

Conservation treatment report on three early 1960s tile panels from Sunderland Art Gallery for Tyne and Wear Museums
Acknowledgments:
Jon Old, Head of Conservation, Tyne and Wear Museums, Newcastle on Tyne.

Appendix

Useful addresses

Conservation:
The Jackfield Conservation Studio, Jackfield Tile Museum, Ironbridge, Telford, TF8 7LJ, UK
Tile Heritage Foundation, PO Box 1850, Healdsburg, CA 95448, USA.
Institute of Historic Building Conservation. 3 Stafford Road, Tunbridge Wells, Kent. TN2 4QZ. UK
United Kingdom Institute for Conservation, 702 The Chandlery, 50 Westminster Bridge Road, London SE1 7QY UK
The Building Conservation Directory, Cathedral Communications Ltd ,High Street Tisbury Wiltshire UK SP3 6HA

Manufacturers:
Craven Dunnill Jackfield Ltd. Jackfield Tile Museum, Ironbridge, Telford, TF8 7LJ, UK
Diana Hall, Anne's Cottage, Wimbourne St Giles, Dorset, BH21 5NG, UK
Koninklijke Tichelaar Makkum, Post bus 11, 8754 ZN Makkum, Netherlands
BAL, Norcross Adhesives Ltd, Longton Road, Trentham, Stke-on-Trent, ST4 8JB
St Astier Limes, Setra Marketing Ltd, 16 Cavendish Drive, Claygate, Surrey KT10 0QE, UK
Stonehealth, JOS Cleaning, Bowers Court, Broadwell, Dursley, Gloucestershire, GL11 4JE, UK
Fein Industrial Power Tools UK Ltd, 4 Badby Park, Heartlands Business Park, Daventry, Northants NN11 5YT, UK

Specialist tile bookseller:
Buckland Books, Holly Tree House, 18 Woodland Road, Littlehampton, West Sussex, BN17 5PP.

Index